Women Educators

Women Educators

Employees of Schools in Western Countries

Edited by PATRICIA A. SCHMUCK

State University of New York Press

Published by
State University of New York Press, Albany

© 1987 State University of New York

For information, address State University of New York
Press, State University Plaza, Albany, N.Y., 12246

Library of Congress Cataloging in Publication Data

Women educators

  Includes index.
    1. Women teachers—Cross-cultural studies.
2. Women educators—Cross-cultural studies.
I. Schmuck, Patricia A.
LB2837.W66   1987   371.1′088042   86-14532
ISBN 0-88706-442-6
ISBN 0-88706-443-4 (pbk.)

10 9 8 7 6 5 4 3 2 1

Contents

Preface

Many of the chapters in this book were prepared for a symposium at the Second International Interdisciplinary Congress on Women held in the Netherlands in April 1984. This was the first international symposium about women's employment in schools. Although international conferences had been held and books with a cross-cultural perspective had been written about women in the labor market and educational opportunities for girls and women, no international meeting or book had previously been devoted specifically to the subject of women as employees of schools. The little attention that has been paid to women's contributions to the educational realm is indeed surprising, considering the fact that teaching has been one of the few professional fields open to Western women in the last century.

This international perspective should enrich and broaden our understanding of the roles that women play in the educational system; it should also reveal themes and issues that transcend cultural and national boundaries. Despite differences in histories, school organizational structures, educational roles, hiring practices, seniority systems, preparatory programs, and educational opportunities, certain common patterns emerge. For example, woman's role as an educational professional is usually related to the existing educational opportunity for girls. In most countries, woman's entrance into the modern systems of education occurred during the industrialization period, when there was a need to create common schools for all students, including girls.

Another common pattern is that the social ideology concerning women's place in the educational realm has changed over the years.

In all countries, at some time, women have been excluded from the teaching profession; teaching was not considered their proper place. This ideology changed, however, to the view that teaching was a proper role for women. In most countries, married women were also at some time excluded from the profession because it was seen as detracting from their primary role as wife and mother (Sysiharju points to Finland as an exception). Yet now teaching is seen as an ideal profession; the working hours and summer vacations allow women simultaneously to contribute to the profession and to fulfill their family obligations. These historical changes are discussed in the chapters by Schmuck (United States), van Essen (the Netherlands), Brehmer (West Germany), and Moeller (Denmark).

Women's presence as educators is also related to labor market trends. In times of war or affluence, women are more highly represented in education. Conversely, their rate of participation in education decreases when there is a large supply of men available for the educational market. Women's representation in education is also related to the availability of other professional roles. Today, in the United States, with opportunities available in other fields, fewer women are seeking careers in education than previously.

Sex-segregated employment patterns are related to sex-segregated educational systems. In schools for girls only, women appear in a variety of roles: as teachers of various subjects, as teachers of elementary and secondary schools, and as educational managers. In coeducational systems, however, women appear in more restricted roles: they are primarily teachers of young children, their number decreases at the secondary level, and they are segregated into certain subject matter areas. This pattern is demonstrated most vividly in countries that have had sex-segregated schools well into the twentieth century; see the chapters by Sysiharju (Finland) and Sampson (Australia).

Sex-segregated patterns also emerge in professional associations such as teacher's unions. Whereas women have been active participants and even founders of teacher's unions, they tend not to be in management or governing positions. Bystydzienski (United States and England); Moeller (Denmark), Sampson (Australia), and Sysiharju (Finland) all address this issue.

In all educational systems, managers and administrators are drawn from the ranks of teachers. Yet despite the greater proportion of women in those ranks, women are disproportionately underrepresented in educational governance in all coeducational systems and are a minority of the principals and district officers. All the chapters in Part I—Sysiharju (Finland), Sampson (Australia), Fenwick (New Zealand), and Schmuck (United States)—illustrate this phenomenon.

In all countries women's contributions to education have been ignored; educational historians have not recounted the efforts of women teachers, who have often founded schools or professional associations. Women have been virtually excluded as subjects of study in educational history. Gribskov's account of Adelaide Pollock and van Essen's revival of Alberdina Woldendorp, both written from original source material, illustrate the difficulty of finding "lost" women in educational history and of restoring them a place in history.

Indeed, the story of the woman educator may well be the story of all the social and psychological problems regarding gender in the middle-class Western world. This woman is educated, she is usually married, she usually has children, she performs an important social service, she is discriminated against, she works for pay, she is part of a bureaucracy where most of the leadership is male, and she is respected for her work and simultaneously injured by her stereotypes.

This volume is a saga of persistence and frustration. During 1980–81 I had the opportunity to live in Leuven, Belgium, where I tried to extend my studies of women in educational leadership to the European context. I was curious about the similarities and differences in women's roles as educators and began a search for cross-cultural studies on this subject. Although I found many such studies on educational access for girls and women, there was nothing about women as educational employees. I began searching for descriptive data about the proportion of women in the educational work force and what roles women occupied. This was no small feat. However, I had experienced similar problems in gathering such data for the United States and was not totally unprepared. In the United States, for instance, the national sources for educational statistics have not always reported employment by sex, and the categories of role descriptors do not remain constant over time. The data are elusive and often incomplete. My frustration was amplified when I tried to trace similar records for other Western countries. Neither the European Council of Ministers nor the Organization of Economic Cooperation and Development (OECD) could supply the information I requested. Yet I knew such data existed; I had seen Eileen Bryne's excellent summary about educational opportunities for the Council of European Ministers (1978) and her book, *Women in Education* (1979), in England. I could only suppose that the data could be uncovered if one knew whom to ask and where to look. Through a network of contacts, I finally found individuals in different countries to uncover what data they could and to write about women's role as educators. Upon my return to the United States, I tried unsuccessfully for two years to raise funds to support an international meeting of all the contributors. Time and time again I was told that this effort did not meet funding priorities. So the symposium participants, on their own, agreed to take the opportunity provided by the Second International Interdisciplinary Congress on Women to meet in the Netherlands. The articles in this book were therefore prepared without funding support. Had funds been available, the analyses and comparisons could have been more extensive than they are.

I hope this volume will generate interest and support for studying women's place in education. Educational institutions play an important role in all Western countries, and we have too long ignored the influence of gender on the educational work force.

Patricia A. Schmuck

Introduction

PATRICIA ANNE SCHMUCK

Although women professionals have predominated in numbers, if not authority, in all formal educational systems of the Western world, their contributions have received scant attention in the history, sociology, or philosophy of education. The study of teaching and educational administration has been carried out without consideration for the concept of gender. Women as active participants in the profession have been ignored.

This book pays attention to the roles taken and the tasks performed by women as teachers, administrators, and members of professional associations in eight different Western countries. It includes historical portraits, sociological investigations, enthographic studies, and data-based descriptions of schools as sex-segregated systems. And, in 1987, it is the first book to do so.

That is not to say there has been no work elucidating the relationship between gender and education. To the contrary, in the last decade and a half, several texts have illuminated such a relationship. Disturbed by the injustice of inequality in educational settings, many researchers and scholars have questioned the connections between the formal educational system and the blatant and subtle consequences of gender segregation, gender expectations, and gender outcomes. Some hallmark texts in the United States include Frazer and Sadker, *Sexism in School and Society* (1973); Pottker and Fischel, *Sex Bias in Schools* (1975); Guttentag and Bray, *Undoing Sex Stereotypes: Research and Resources for Educators* (1976); Stock, *Better Than Rubies* (1978); Stockard et al., *Sex Equity in Education* (1980); Sadker and Sadker, *Handbook for Sex Equity in Schools* (1981); Kelly and Elliot, *Women's Education in the Third World: Comparative Perspectives*

1

(1982); Fenema and Ayer, *Women and Education* (1984); and Klein, *Handbook for Achieving Sex Equity Through Education* (1985). And from England there are a variety of texts: Deem, *Women and Schooling* (1978); Byrne, *Women and Education* (1978); Spender, *Learning to Lose: Sexism in Education* (1980); Walker and Barton, *Gender, Class and Education* (1983); and Acker et al., *Women and Education: World Yearbook of Education 1984*. Brock-Utne in Norway (1982), Rijs in the Netherlands (1980), and Brehmer in West Germany (1980) attest to the attention devoted to gender and education in other countries. But although some of these books have included chapters on the role of women as school employees, by and large most studies have been on sex differentials in student learning, access, and outcomes.

There have also been a few books focusing on women in the profession of education; some examples are Gross and Trask, *The Sex Factor in School Management* (1976); Biklen and Brannigan, *Women and Educational Leadership* (1980); Schmuck, Charters, and Carlson, *Educational Policy and Management: Sex Differentials* (1981); and Ortiz, *Career Patterns in Education* (1982). But although these books have focused on women in education, they have concentrated on the roles and positions from which women are absent—primarily in school management and administration. They have investigated an arena where women are underrepresented but have not focused on the roles and tasks performed by the large majority of women in schools.

In reviewing this corpus of scholarship about gender and education developed over the last decade and a half, I am struck by the advances and changes in our thinking. Polemical treatises have given way to more dispassionate, data-based descriptions of differential treatment and access, and a focus on teaching and administrative strategies to implement sex equitable practices in schools has led to assessments of research and implementation strategies. Most of this effort has been prompted by the ideological commitment to gender equality in schools; scholars and activists have wanted to change the existing systems to offer equality of opportunity and outcomes. Legislation has been put in place, advocates for sex equity have drawn heavily upon the research generated over the decade. In the 1970s, at least in the United States, there was a clear alliance between researchers of gender and activists. This push for equality has led to some observable changes in some schools; we have learned that incremental change is possible. We have also learned how immutable, ingrained, and complex is the relationship between gender and schooling. Perhaps we have learned that it is not possible, nor likely, that in a mere decade we can redress the cultural norms, the psychological orientations, and the school policies and practices which result in sex differentials in opportunities or outcomes for students and employees.

The drive for equity in education has been accompanied by developing scholarship about gender as a legitimate variable for study, and this inquiry has led scholars in a variety of disciplines to raise critical questions about existing knowledge and to begin a process of redefinition. New questions and new notions of significance illuminating women's tradition, history, and culture have emerged. The work of Gerda Lerner in history (1979), Jean Baker Miller in psychology (1984), and Jesse Bernard in sociology (1973), to name only a few, is illustrative of this new scholarship. This work is often referred to as "feminist scholarship" or "the new scholarship on women." By paying attention to women as subjects and objects of study, scholars have found that the extant theories are no longer adequate. For instance, Gerda Lerner (1979) says, with regard to history, that "to document the experience of women would mean documenting all of history. They have always been of it, in it and making it (p. 160)." she means, of course, that to include the thoughts and experiences of women within the traditional domain would be to transform the discipline—history could no longer be confined to the public and productive sectors of society. If we include women, who have been part of the private and reproductive sector, we would change the content and methods of traditional history.

The study of the educational profession, albeit not a discipline in itself, also reveals this development thought. When educational researchers studied issues of sex equity in schools—for students or employees—we began to ask new questions, to form new strategies for investigating the process of schooling, and to develop new systems for critical analysis. Some of the more recent texts, such as Walker and Barton (1983), Acker (1984), Fenema and Ayer (1984), and Klein (1985), address the transformation of knowledge and provide new paths for study. In educational history we can see the process of such a redefinition; Hoffman (1982) and Kaufman (1984) have brought to life the travails and struggles of women teachers—some of those early and forgotten pioneers who were a part of the "feminization" of teaching but who have not been discussed in the textbooks on the history of formal education. The questions facing women students in public schools and institutions of higher education in the United States, for instance, have not received much attention since Woody's classic book, *Women's Education in the United States*, first published in 1929. Maxine Greene, a philosopher of education, shows how the consciousness about gender can lead to a redefinition of the study of education. She argues that women's education in the United States has been based primarily on distinctions of "irrelevant differences," and she calls for a redefinition of education, one which calls for demystifying and enlarging conversations about "the kind of subordination imposed on women and the kind of subordination imposed on schoolchildren." This kind of inquiry can perhaps "transform both men's and women's common world (1984, p. 36)."

In this chapter I will review the development of thinking about women in education as it has appeared in the literature over the last decade and a half. I lay out a framework of five stages of thinking, which are illustrated by the different chapters in this book. The five stages are sequential but not chronological. At any time we see thinking or research that is representative of any one of the states of development. I have adopted liberally from the work of Tetreault (1985), McIntosh (1983), and Schuster and Van Dyne (1984), who have explicated stage-level thinking as applied to integrating knowledge about women in the college curriculum.

Stage 1. *Exclusionary or Androcentric Thinking.* Women and issues of gender are not addressed. Generalizations about men are thought to hold true for women; men are the objects and subjects of study. The thoughts, experiences, and behaviors of women are not considered. This stage represents the primary body of literature on the profession of education in the last half century until about 1970.

Stage 2. *Compensatory Thinking.* Issues of gender are addressed only so far as women's achievements equal men's achievements; in educational history there is the search for the "lost" woman, or current studies on the profession include an emphasis on the "exceptional" contemporary woman. The purpose is to find female counterparts to male success.

Stage 3. *Woman as Deficient: Psychological Thinking.* Issues of gender are addressed to point out the differences in the psychology of men and women that result in social inequality. Females are seen as exceptions to the male norm.

Stage 4. *Women as Oppressed: System Thinking.* Gender is seen as the variable by which existing organizational practices discriminate against women. The focus is on the institutional processes and practices which treat women differently from men.

Stage 5. *The New Scholarship.* The variable of gender, as it applies to both men and women, becomes a primary area of concentration. Research is modified to include women as well as men as the objects and subjects of study. This scholarship is corrective: it provides alternative points of view and transforms existing knowledge.

Stage 1: Exclusionary Thinking

Exclusionary thinking represents an androcentric bias. It assumes that the experiences, thoughts, and expressions of one group of people—men—reflect the thoughts, experiences, and expressions of all human beings, including women. This stage might be called "genderless thinking" or what Peggy McIntosh refers to as "womanless" thinking (1983, p. 2). The model of the male is the model for humanity. Thus, educational history, philosophy, policy, research, and even school texts reveal the presence of men and the absence of women. Exclusion occurs in two ways: woman is omitted from discussions, and the concept of gender is ignored and the woman educator is cast within the general cultural stereotypes.

The work I cite in this section is corrective scholarship; the authors point out how the existing theory or research exhibits an androcentric bias. They show how females are excluded as subjects in educational research and how women's contributions to education are not preserved in writing. The chapters by van Essen and Brehmer give examples of this exclusionary thinking. Van Essen presents original historical research of women educators from the Netherlands in the nineteenth century who have not been included in texts or research, and Brehmer traces West Germany's educational history back to the fourteenth century. Both have focused on the work performed by women in education in their respective countries.

Several authors have pointed out androcentric thinking in education. Burstyn's analysis of American educational history texts (1983) and Martin's analysis of Western educational philosophy (1982) point out that females are excluded as subjects and objects of study from the standard texts and anthologies in education. In social science research, which is used heavily by educational researchers and practioners, men are the objects and subjects of study. Shakeshaft and Nowell (1984), who describe several leadership studies influencing our views and practices about educational leadership, make the following statement: "Studying male behavior is not in and of itself at issue here. What is at issue is the practice of studying male behavior and then assuming that the results are appropriate for understanding all behavior" (p. 188). They report findings on five important leadership theories in the educational literature and show that women are excluded as subjects of these theories; when they are included, they provide deviations from the extant theories. Thus women, when they are included as subjects, remain eclipsed from the conceptualization of leadership.

We need not draw only from examples of past research and practice to illustrate exclusionary thinking; recent examples of androcentric bias are also available. For instance, in the United States there is currently a strong reform movement in education; a plethora of books and commissioned reports calls for school improvement. Perhaps the most famous of these reports, *The Nation at Risk*, published in 1983 and authored by a prestigious panel of educators appointed by the President of the United States, has no reference to gender. Although different student attributes are mentioned—social class, race handicappedness, and ethnicity—there is no reference to boy students and girl students. This report, as well as others authored by prominent educators calling for reform, simply ignores the concept of gender as relevant for improving schools, despite the last decade of research and action on sex equity in education (Tetreault and Schmuck, 1985).

The second way that women and girls are excluded from educational thinking is by the use of cultural biases to explain away certain gender-related differences. Gender roles are seen as causative rather than problematic. Instead of asking, *why* is this a woman's role or *why* is this a man's role, sex differences are explained by socially constructed gender-based roles. Assumptions about woman's different motivations, life plans, and aspirations are not only heard on policy boards or in the public media, but also in scholarly books and journals about educators. In a corrective vein, Sandra Acker says, "When writers do consider women teachers, they frequently resort to commonsense and unsubstantiated assumptions about their deficiencies" (1983, p. 124). The image of spinster teacher or the married woman who has only a halfhearted interest in teaching has not only prevailed in the public eye; it has also prevailed in the literature about educators. Books which illustrate a cultural bias include Lortie, *School Teacher* (1975) Lieberman, *Education as a Profession* (1956), Wolcott, *The Man in the Principal's Office*(1975), and Etzioni, *The Semi-Professions and Their Organization*(1969); they all raise the subject of females and "explain" gender-related differences in the work force by cultural reasons. They do not explore the concept of gender as a manipulable variable but rather as a cultural given, thereby perpetuating the stereotype of the woman educator.

Examples of omission of culturally biased thinking are not confined to educational studies; examples permeate the social sciences. The classic Hawthorne Studies (Roethlisberger and Dickson, 1966) obstensibly taught us about the human dynamics of the workplace: about power relationships between bosses and workers. A focus on gender, however, would have included the fact that bosses were men and workers were women. Acker and Van Houton (1974), in reviewing this work, suggest that if gender had been included as a variable, we would have a different view of power relationships in organizational settings. Power is not only imbued in the legitimate authority of the boss, but is also carried in the male role. In another example, Horner

(1975) questions the psychological studies on achievement motivation because all the samples were based on men; she includes women in the subject pool and thereby creates some new ideas about achievement. Gilligan (1982) addresses the stages of human moral development which were supposedly unvarying and universal. She points out that the data look different when females are included as subjects, and she goes on the revise the theory on human moral development. These are but a few examples of research that have been critized because females have been omitted from the subject pool or because the researchers have treated gender as culturally given rather than problematic.

Stage 2: Compensatory Thinking

In 1985 the United States Congress sanctioned National Women's History Week. The United States also celebrates Black History Month. These are special times for celebrating the successes and notable achievements of women and blacks in our country; we must compensate for these excluded from our thinking and from our history. Black studies courses, ethnic studies courses, and women's studies have become a part of many of our colleges and universities and were born out of such a compensatory motive. It was recognized that women and minorities had been excluded from the traditional curriculum, and so a special curriculum was added. Little did we know that these courses would lead to major criticisms about the existing methods and content of study. Howe has documented the exponential rise of women's studies courses and programs since the 1970s and traced their attempts to transform the traditional college curriculum (1979).

At this stage of thinking, there is a consciousness that women are missing. In education we have tried to find the lost women in our history or to focus on those contemporary women who have rivaled men. Many of the chapters in this book exhibit this kind of thinking; they chronicle women who have been ignored in their respective countries or present data on sex-segregated employment patterns. Gribskov writes about the forgotten Adelaide Pollock, who was a school principal in Seattle and the founder of a woman's professional educational association; Sysiharju, Schmuck, Fenwick, and Sampson present data on the extent of sex segregation in school employment in their respective countries and women's absence from managerial and administrative roles. These examples of compensatory scholarship draw our attention to women who have been an exception among women educators and who have paralleled the accomplishments of men, or they point out the absence of women in stereotypically male-defined roles. "However, males are still perceived as the norm . . . . and theories continue to be developed which are derived from and standarized on . . . . males. There is no consciousness that the existence of women as a group is an anomaly which calls for a broader definition of knowledge"(Tetreault, 1985, p. 367).

In the United States most studies on educational employment have drawn our attention to those few women who have achieved positions in the male-dominated role of school administrator. The focus of research in the 1970s was on the careers and lives of those "exceptional" women who rose through the teaching ranks to become school administrators. This focus is well illustrated by a look at the concentration of doctoral dissertations completed in the 1970s about women in educational administration. Doctoral dissertations are often a good gauge of the contemporary issues in a field, and the 1970s marked a watershed for women doctoral students in this field (Stockard, 1980). One hundred fourteen doctoral dissertations were completed about women in educational administration during 1973–79, whereas previously no work had focused on women in these roles. (Schmuck, 1980; Shakeshaft, 1981). Most of these dissertations were written by women. Although women administrators remain the exception rather than the norm among women educators and administrators, there has been a search for those women who have occupied roles primarily held by men. Indeed, we know more about those few women who are principals and superintendents than we know about the majority of women who populate the ranks of teacher.

Perhaps it is natural that researchers who pay attention to women in education (primarily women researchers) focus their attention on the same roles that have already had a great deal of attention (held primarily by men). Perhaps, however, it reveals a more important fact, what Jesse Bernard (1973) refers to as the "machismo factor" in research. We are guided by our current paradigms—the underlying assumptions about the way we construct the world. The research which focuses on women in educational administration makes the same fundamental assumptions about the relative importance of different educational roles as other research. School administrators are seen as more important than teachers. Thus although compensatory models of thinking have enriched our lives, broadened our understanding about what women have contributed to educational systems, and clarified the particular problems which face women seeking careers in male-dominated roles such thinking has not changed the view of the educational world. Women are included, but only within the traditional modes of inquiry. The topics and the structure of the inquiry remain unquestioned and unchallenged. One cannot "just add women and stir." The inclusion of women within the domain of inquiry must change the nature of the inquiry.

Stage 3: Women as Deficient—Psychological Thinking

In the 1960s and 1970s in the United States, the focus of research and action, in education, as well as in other fields, attempted to explain gender inequality in the society and the workplace by focusing on the psychological differences between men and women. These studies concentrated primarily on the differences in the socialization of boys and girls and described the differences between men and women in life responsibilities, career orientations, and life ambitions. Socially constructed gender roles were seen as causative to the differing psychological aspirations of men and women. Women are deficient because they have been socialized differently than men. This focus on the individual has emerged from the general literature on social change as well as from those studying women's issues. Daniel Katz (1983) points out that social psychologists generally have been too preoccupied with individual causation, which has meant that individuals are held responsible for their own problems. Katz says, "the remedy had been to change the defect or weakness in the individual."

The studies comparing women and men educators show psychological differences in personal and career motivations, family responsibilities, life plans, and plans for mobility (Adkison, 1981; Havens, 1980). In this volume, Sampson and Fenwick support, with good evidence, the differences in womens' and mens' career mobility within the educational hierarchy in Australia and New Zealand. They have used the typical socialization model of inquiry; they have conducted their research on teachers and have tried to ferret out why women—who are the majority of teachers—are the minority of managers and administrators.

The findings from studies on teacher socialization have been put to use. Workshops, conferences, and books are available to help women teachers improve their perceived deficiencies for upward mobility in the educational hierarchy. There are volumes written—in education and in business—to help women "succeed" (Smith, Kalvelage, and Schmuck, 1980). In the United States there are established professional groups, such as Northwest Women in Educational Administration and the Northeast Coalition of Educational Leaders, which help women prepare for leadership positions and support those few women who manage to aspire "upwards." The minority of women who achieve in a male-dominated system have special issues of self identity and unique needs (Marshall, 1985).

The problem with this approach is that it reinforces the male definition of the "appropriate" motivations and ambitions for advancement in education. Women are "blamed" for not have the prerequisite motivations or ambitions. Thus the model for success remains male. We have taken these findings on differences and have tried to eliminate the differences; we have tried to help women fit the male model and have not considered that cultural roles regarding women remain different from those of men. We have a considerable body of literature on what deters women from seeking certain roles in education, but we do not have a comparable body of literature on what attracts and keeps women where they are—primarily in classroom teaching. The prevailing assumption in this view is that women are teachers because they do not have the psychological motivation or prerequisite skills to become administrators. By focusing on inequality, we focus on those roles where women are *not*. Perhaps we need to ask the question in a different way: what are the factors which attract and retain classroom teachers, the majority of whom are women?

Stage 4: Women as Oppressed—System Thinking

At this stage in our thinking, we look more to the sociological approach to change. We turn away from the psychology of teachers and instead look at those institutional structures which discriminate—blatantly or subtly—and perpetuate inequality in the workplace. In education, most of the research has focused on the career mobility of men and women teachers and has pointed to the organizational constraints to women's mobility, such as differential grooming and recruitment of male teachers, sex biased preparatory programs and materials, the mentoring and sponsorhship of young male professionals by the older established males in the field, the lack of female role models, different opportunities for males and females to exhibit leadership behaviors, male domination on screening and selection committees and unfair hiring practices. These are among the institutional barriers that discriminate, formally or informally, against women in the profession of education (Ortiz and Marshall, forthcoming). In this volume, Fenwick and Sampson indicate the barriers to women's upward mobility by pointing out factors in the system which oppress women. Bystydzienski and Moeller explore this theme with teachers unions in Great Britain, the United States, and Denmark.

This is a reform strategy which calls for incremental structural changes in the existing arrangements of educational institutions. As Katz points out, "These changes can be consistent with the nature of the system and can make it more of what it theoretically is supposed to be" (1983, p. 27). The educational system ostensibly should offer equal opportunities for male and female teachers, and most of the policies and laws banning sex discrimination have been aimed at making the system operate more equitably. Affirmative action, procedures outlined for fair hiring practices, published policies about nondiscrimination, and the establishment of grievance procedures are all examples of institutional practices that are aimed at breaking down the barriers of discrimination in education.

Despite these attempts, the fact remains that the educational hierarchy is basically unaltered, and sex-segregated patterns of employment continue. Schools, as institutions, are complex and difficult to change. There are some who say that they may be impervious to change. The substantial literature on school change indicates that role expectations, norms, established patterns of behavior, communication patterns, power relationships, and individual values all play an important part in changing school practices (Schmuck and Runkel, 1985). The problem is compounded when we add the cultural imperatives and emotional overtones of gender roles. In one study, which outlines several attempts to change school practices to provide more sexually equitable treatment, the authors conclude that we have "limited knowledge of how to actually institutionalize sex equity in schools" and that "we do not know what general strategies or elements will sustain sex equity." (Schmuck et al., 1985). Incremental structural changes are difficult to effect and even more difficult to accurately measure.

The second problem to this approoch is that it remains dualistic in its orientation. It dichotomizes male and female experiences and focuses on issues of inequality, primarily on females as oppressed victims. Human experience is conceptualized in dualistic categories; males and females are compared, and the focus is on women's oppression because women have not achieved the accomplishments of men. As in the earlier stages, therefore, this approach does not concentrate our attention on women and what they are doing.

Stage 5: The New Scholarship

Margrit Eichler offers a useful definition of feminist research. According to her, it fulfills three functions: it is critical of existing social structures and ways of perceiving them, it serves as a corrective mechanism by providing an alternative viewpoint and data to substantiate it, and it starts to lay the groundwork for the transformation of knowledge (1980, p. 9). These three elements—criticism, alternative viewpoints, and transformation—are cyclical; each leads to the other. Knowledge is seen as mutable, something that will not pass the test of time.

The new scholarship criticises androcentrism and calls for the inclusion of women as objects of study. Women must become the center of inquiry, what Schuster and Van Dyne call "women studied on their own terms" (1984). In education, we need to focus on what women do as professionals in schools. Biklen's chapter on women elementary-school teachers accomplishes that task in this volume. Enders-Dragasser, looks at women in a broader context—on the unpaid work of mothers in the formally established homework policies of schools in West Germany. Reynolds, investigates the context and meaning of some specific policies regarding married women teachers. By including women as objects and subjects of study, we can begin to see how institutions are 'genderized'. We begin to question the obvious, such as in the following example by Apple: "The fact that schools have tended to be largely organized around male leadership and female teachers is simply that, a social fact, unless one realizes that this means that educational authority relationships have been formally patriarchal. Like the home and the office, male dominance is there; but teachers—like wives and mothers and clerical workers—have carved out spheres of power and control in their long struggle to gain some autonomy" (1983,p. 613). By questioning the meaning of the obvious fact of patriarchy, we bring new perspectives to the inquiry of the education profession.

Conclusion

Educational institutions are unique in the social fabric; they have different purposes, outcomes, clients, and procedures from other social organizations. They are among the small number of organizations with a majority of women in the professional ranks (indeed, teaching is referred to as a "feminized profession") and with roughly an even representation of males and females as clients. Schools are perhaps the most integrated organizations by sex within all Western cultures and perhaps, simultaneously, the most genderized. Issues of learning, of professionals' task roles, of reward structures (for students as well as employees), of the exercise of power and authority (within the classroom as well as within the school or district organization), of role distributions, and of individual motivation and aspiration all involve gender as a variable. We cannot fully comprehend the dynamics of school organizations, classrooms, or the people who inhabit them unless we consider this concept. In many of the disciplines, there is now a call for a consideration of gender as an important variable for study. In education, we too should be calling for new paradigms and new methods of inquiry which include a full consideration of gender as a relevant concept for studying the clients of schooling and the professionals who perform the tasks of educating.

References

Acker, Joan, and Donald Van Houton (1974). "Differential Recruitment and Control: The Sex Structure of Organizations." *Administrative Science Quarterly* 19, pp. 152–162.

Acker, Sandra (1933). "Women and Teaching: A Semi-Detached Sociology of a Semi-Profession." *Gender, Class and Education*, ed. Steven Walker and Len Barton. London: Falmer Press.

Acker, Sandra, et al., eds. (1984). *Women and Education: World Yearbook of Education, 1984*. London: Kogan Page.

Adkison, Judy (1981). "Women in School Administration: A Review of the Research." *Review of Educational Research* 51, no. 3, (Fall), pp. 311–343.

Apple, Michael (1983). "Work, Gender and Teaching." *Teachers College Record* 84, no. 3 (Spring), pp. 611–628.

Bernard, Jesse (1973). "My Four Revolutions: An Autobiographical History of the American Sociology Association." In *Changing Women in a Changing Society*, ed. Chicago: University of Chicago Press.

Biklen, Sari Knopp and Marilyn Brannigan. (1980) *Women and Educational Leadership*, Lexington, Mass., Lexington Press.

Brehmer, Ilse (1982). *Sexism in der Schule*. Weinheim: Basel.

Brock-utne, Birgit, *Sexism and Education*, Tidskrift for Forening for Pedagogist Forskning, Lund, Sweden. 1982.

Burstyn, Joan (1983). "Women in the History of Education." Paper presented at the annual meeting of the American Educational Research Association, Montreal.

Byrne, Eileen (1978). *Women and Education.* London: Tavistock Publications.

Deem, Rosemary (1978). *Women and Schooling.* London: Routledge and Kegan Paul.

Eichler, Margrit (1980). *The Double Standard: A Feminist Critique of Feminist Social Science.* New York: St. Martin's Press.

Etzioni, Amitai (1969). *The Semi-Professions and Their Organization.* New York: The Free Press.

Fenema, Elizabeth, and M. Jane Ayer, eds. (1984). *Women and Education,* Berkeley: McCutchan.

Frazier, Nancy, and Myra Sadker (1973). (Editors) *Sexism in School and Society.* New York: Harper and Row.

Gilligan, Carol (1982). *A Different Voice.* Cambridge, Mass.: Harvard University Press.

Greene, Maxine (1984). "The Impact of Irrelevance: Women in the History of American Education." In Fenema and Ayer, *Women and Education.*

Gross, Neil and Ann Trask (1976). *The Sex Factor in the Management Schools,* New York: John Wiley and Sons

Guttentag, Marcia, and Helen Bray (1976). *Undoing Sex Stereotypes: Research and Resources for Educators.* New York: McGraw-Hill.

Havens, Elizabeth (1980) "Women in Educational Administration, The Principalship." National Institute of Education, Washington, D.C.

Hoffman, Nancy (1982). *Women's True Profession.* Westbury, N.Y.: Feminist Press.

Horner, Matina (1972). "Toward an Understanding of Achievement-Related Conflicts in Women." *Journal of Social Issues* 25, no. 2, v. 28, pp. 157–176.

Howe, Florence (1979). "The First Decade of Women's Studies." *Harvard Educational Review* 49, pp. 413–421.

Huber, Joan (1973). *Changing Women in a Changing Society,* University of Chicago Press.

Katz, Daniel (1983). "Factors Affecting Social Change: A Social Psychological Perspective." *Journal of Social Issues* 39, no. 4, pp. 25–44.

Kaufman, Paulie (1984). *Women Teachers on the Frontier*. New Haven: Yale University Press.

Kelly, Gail, and Carolyn M. Elliot (1982). *Women's Education in the Third World: Comparative Perspectives*. Albany, N.Y.: State University of New York Press.

Klein, Susan, ed. (1985). *Handbook for Achieving Sex Equity Through Education*. Baltimore, Md.: Johns Hopkins University Press.

Lerner, Gerda (1979). *The Majority Finds Its Past*. New York: Oxford University Press.

Lieberman, M. ed. (1956) *Education as a Profession*. Englewood Cliffs, N.J.: Prentice-Hall.

Lortie, Daniel (1975). *School Teacher*. Chicago: University of Chicago Press.

Marshall, Catherine (1985). The Stigmatized Woman: The Profesional Woman in a Male-Typed Career." Unpublished paper.

McIntosh, Peggy (1983). "Stages of Curricular Revision." Claremont College Conference on Women' Studies, Claremont California, February.

Martin, Jane Roland (1982). "Excluding Women from the Educational Realm." *Harvard Educational Review* 52, n. 2., pp. 133–148.

Miller, Jean Baker (1976, 1984). *Toward a New Psychology of Women*. Boston: Beacon Press.

Ortiz, Flora, and Catherine Marshall "Women in Educational Administration." In *Handbook of Research on Educational Administration*, forthcoming. Baltimore: Johns Hopkins Press.

Pottker, Janice and Andrew Fischel, eds. (1977) *Sex Bias in the Schools*. New Jersey Fairleigh Dickinson University Press.

Roethlisberger, F.J., and William J. Dickson (1966). *Management and the Worker*. Cambridge, Mass.: Harvard University Press.

Sadker, Myra, and David Sadker (1982). (Editor) *Handbook for Sex Equity in Schools*. New York: Longman.

Schmuck, Patricia, et al. (1985). "Administrative Strategies for Institutionalizing Sex Equity in Education and the Role of Government." In *Achieving Sex Equity Through Education*, ed. Susan Klein. Baltimore, Md.: Johns Hopkins University Press.

Schmuck, Patricia, W.W. Charters Jr. and Richard Carlson, eds. (1981). *Educational Policy and Management: Sex Differentials* New York: Academic Press.

Schmuck, Patricia (1980). *Sex Equity in Educational Leadership: the Oregon Story*. Newton Mass.: Education Development Corporation.

Schmuck, Richard, and Philip J. Runkel (1985). *Third Handbook of Organized Development in Schools*. Palo Alto, Ca.: Mayfield Press.

Schuster, Marilyn, and Susan Van Dyne (1984). "Placing Women in the Liberal Arts: Stages of Curriculum Transformation." *Harvard Educational Review* 34, no. 4, pp. 443-457.

Shakeshaft, Charole (1981). "Women in Educational Administration: A Descriptive Analysis of Dissertation Research and Paradigm for Future Research." In *Educational Policy and Management: Sex Differentials*, ed. Schmuck, Charters, Carlson, New York: Academic Press.

Shakeshaft, Charole, and Irene Nowell (1984). "Research on Theories, Concepts and Models of Organizational Behavior: The Influence of Gender." *Issues in Education* 2, n. 3 (Winter), pp. 186-203.

Smith, Mary Ann, Joan Kalvelage, and Patricia Schmuck (1980). *Sex Equity in Educational Leadership: Women Getting Together and Getting Ahead*. Newton, Massachusetts: Education Development Corporation.

Smock, Audrey (1981). *Women's Education in Developing Countries*. New York: Praeger Press.

Spender, Dale, and E. Sarah, eds. (1980). *Learning to Lose: Sexism in Education*. London: The Women's Press.

Stock, Phyllis (1978). *Better Than Rubies*. New York: G. P. Putnam's Sons.

Stockard, Jean (1980). *Sex Equity in Educational Leadership. An Analysis of a Planned Social Change Project*. Newton, Massachusetts: Educational Development Corporation.

Stockard, Jean, et al. (1980). *Sex Equity in Education*. New York: Academic Press.

Tetreault, Mary Kay (1985). "Feminist Phase Theory: An Experience-Derived Evaluation Model." *Journal of Higher Education* 56, no. 4 (Summer), pp. 364-384.

Tetreault, Mary Kay, and Patricia Schmuck (1985). "Equity, Educational Reform and Gender." *Issues in Education* 3, n. 1 (Summer), pp 45–67.

Walker, Steven, and Len Barton (1983). (Editors). *Gender, Class and Education.* London. Falmer Press.

Wolcott, Harry (1975). *The Man in the Principal's Office.* New York: Holt, Rinehart, and Winston.

Woody, Thomas (1974). *Women's Education in the United States.* New York: Octagon Books.

Part I

Women as Educators In Some Western Countries

P art I is a description of women's place as employees of schools in four countries—Finland, Australia, New Zealand, and the United States. They each have different cultural and national histories and arrangements for schooling. Despite these national differences, there are striking similarities concerning women's historic and current role in schooling. For instance, there is a similar story from each country about when women entered the teaching ranks. In each case that development was prompted by a commitment to an educational system that would reach all citizens and a commitment to educate girls. There is also a similar story told about the debate on whether women should be educated and their struggle to enter institutions of higher education. In all these countries, women's entrance into teaching did not come easily; the social ideology concerning women's place in the public sphere underwent scrutiny until finally the woman teacher became an acceptable social reality. The ban on married women existed in all the English-speaking countries and was not abolished until the mid-twentieth century. And of course, women's place in the sex-segregated system of schools appears similar in all these countries; women are most represented as teachers at the elementary level, less represented at the high school level, and uniformly absent in positions of management and governance.

It is also striking to note that in all these countries the role of women in education changed at about the same time. For instance, higher education became available to women in the United States when Oberlin opened its doors to women for the first time in 1848. In Finland, the first teacher-training college was opened in Jyvaskyla for both men and women in 1863, and the women of New Zealand were granted rights for higher education in 1871. The appearance of women as teachers in the late 1800s in both the United States and Finland following a strong feminist drive in both countries which focused on educational opportunities for women.

It is also noteworthy that despite differences in school operations in these countries, the outcome for women's placement in schools is similar. It is an interesting phenomenon, for instance, that the sex segregation of school employees reads the same regardless of the structure of schooling and career paths for educators whether it is the lock-step career system of promotion and seniority in New Zealand and Australia which have a strong centralized authority, or the loose, informal, and relatively autonomous system of hiring at the local level in the United States. Gender appears to be the relevant category that transcends differences in school structure and operations.

Certainly the constant issue appearing in all these chapters is the connection between women's function in the home and women's teaching. Even though the argument that women's place was only in the home was laid to rest in the last century, women's dual role as homemaker and teacher remains fundamental to explanations for sex segregation, as does the relationship between the sphere of domesticity and women's active role in the education of young children, where women are most represented in all countries.

It is also interesting to read the different authors' explanations for women's absence in positions of governance in the educational hierarchy. Issues of institutional discrimination (blatant and subtle) and issues of differences in women's and men's career aspirations (sometimes referred to as the "blame-the-victim" approach) are the most common frameworks offered, especially by Sampson (Australia) and Fenwick (New Zealand). Undoubtedly these variables do operate; nevertheless, such analyses are fundamentally limited (see introduction). It is perhaps our built-in gender bias which has led us to compare women to men and to presume that the traditional career path that has worked so well for men should also be the model that should work for everyone. The strength of these chapters, I believe, is in their rich descriptions of the system of schooling and women's place in that system. They show us *how* sex segregation operates in various countries. They do not, however, provide us with adequate and alternative frameworks for understanding *why* such systems have been created and perpetuated.

Chapter 1

Women School Employees In Finland

ANNA-LIISA SYSIHARJU

T he development and present situation of women as educators in any country is intertwined with many other general developments and social forces. This analysis of women as educators in Finland will be described in the light of the country's historical development. Detailed references to the sources are only included in the Finnish version of this paper because most are accessible only in Finnish. The sources readily available for foreigners are the official series *Statistical Yearbook of Finland* and *Official Statistics of Finland*, and the new Statistical Survey No. 72, *Position of Women 1984*, all published by the Central Statistical Office of Finland.

The Early Centuries to 1800

For six centuries, beginning with the twelfth, the main part of today's Finland formed the eastern part of the kingdom of Sweden and participated in its educational development. As early as 1640, a university was founded in Finland in the city of Turku; it was later moved to the new capital, Helsinki.

As a consequence of the Reformation, the Lutheran State Church was the only church allowed in all of Sweden. It administered all educational matters, for the rank and file as well as for the Latin schools for the clergy and civil servants. Reading and learning the catechism by heart was considered a prerequisite for Holy Communion and for legal marriage, for women as well as for men. This was controlled and registered in the books by the parish parsons at yearly catechetical meetings in the villages. It seems that women often had better records than men, and in the villages they could be appointed to teach not only their own children but also others to read.

The latin schools—at that time only for boys—were assigned new statutes in 1724, but because of the recent long Nordic war, these schools were mainly replicas of the old system dating from 1693. Swedish schools remained the same up to the nineteenth century. For the acquirement of French etiquette and manners for the girls of rank in the Swedish cities, some private pensions existed, often led by widows. A discussion of schools for girls, however, had hardly begun.

In the eighteenth century, as a result of the harsh defeat of Sweden in the above-mentioned Nordic War, the eastern Wiborg Province of Finland (preserving its separate character) was transferred to the rule of the Russian Empire. This event produced some unexpected results for Finnish girls. The Empress Catherine the Great, born a German princess, in the spirit of Enlightenment initiated many educational reforms, some of them specifically concerning girls. In 1788 there was founded—not only in St. Petersburg, but also in Wiborg—a separate *Demoisselen-Classe* for girls in connection the Germal-language *Hauptschule* functioning there. The *Aufseherin* or *Klassendame* for that class, Christine Trinite (1788-95), appears to have been the first Finnish woman educator employed by the government.

The *Demoisellen-Classe* was not merely a passing caprice of an autocratic sovereign, but rapidly drew into a separate, highly appreciated *Tochter-Schjule* and before 1811 was followed by the foundation of seven other *Tochter-Schule* for the bourgeoisie in the towns of the Wiborg Province. Administratively they were not subordinated to any church, but to the German-language University of Dorpat (Tartu) in Estonia. Locally each *Tochter-Schule* was led by a female 'first teacher', usually a women from a highly educated family. The majority of the other teachers were male and came from the neighboring boys' schools.

1800–60: A Grand Duchy

The long-debated reform of the Latin schools in Sweden led to the new school statutes of 1807, which subsequently were enforced there, but never in Finland. In 1808–09 a severe war between Sweden and Russia erupted, as a result the whole of Finland was transferred from Swedish rule to the Russian Empire in 1809. This transference, however, was carred out, according to the wishes of the Emperor

Alexander I, by declaring Finland an autonomous grand duchy, giving it the status of a nation among nations, and preserving for it the Swedish legislation, the Lutheran church, and the use of the Swedish language as the language of administration and education. In 1811 even the Wiborg Province, the so-called Old Finland, was unified with the new Grand Duchy of Finland.

For education this change meant that Finland inherited both the already outdated Swedish Latin school system and the enlightened ideas already applied in the Wiborg Province, including the eight girls' schools. After several school commission arguments, the 1724 statutes still in force in Finland were replaced with new ones in 1843. These were the first statutes in Scandinavia that recognized, in principle, the need for state girls schools. In practice, however, there were no new schools developed. Only the five existing girls schools, designated for daughters of the higher ranks, and conducted in Swedish (the official language) operated. In these girls' schools two to four female teachers were always responsible for education and discipline, as well as for teaching art, needlework (twenty-four weekly lessons) and foreign languages. They also had to be present at the theoretical lessons given by the male teachers of the school.

Although the competence of the female teachers could not as yet be based on university studies of specific teacher training, and although they were not obliged, when appointed, to make the formal oath of allegiance required of their male colleagues, the female principals of the state girls' schools had real authority, even over the men.

In addition to the official girls' schools, several small private schools existed in the Finnish cities and towns. The founders and teachers were usually female if the schools were either for small children of both sexes (the entering age for boys' as well as girls' schools was about eleven years) or were private girls' schools. Among these early independent women educators was Sara Wacklin (1790–1846). She directed both children's and girls' schools for thirty-seven years, both in the northern town of Oulu and in the capital Helsinki, and during the academic year of 1835–36 she studied in Paris, obtaining the competence of a French *institutrice*. In her last years she wrote an interesting book of memoirs from northern Finland.

The Lutheran State Church continued to be in charge of the educational administration of the country. Through its bishops' councils and the inspecting clergymen sent out by them, the church also continued to have the responsibility for the literacy and religious education of the ordinary Finnish-speaking rural population—in other words, the vast majority of the Finnish people. But a discussion and even some experimentation concerning the need for a broader and deeper elementary education for all was already going on. This discussion was coupled with the ever louder demands for the right to use Finnish, the national language of the people, in administration and in secondary and higher education. In 1858 it was declared that doctoral dissertations written in Finnish would be accepted at the university, and in that same year the first Finnish-language secondary school aimed at preparing students for the university was founded (though it was only for boys). The nation, its women by no means excluded, began to awake to a self-consciousness. At the same time, it was taking its first fumbling steps on the road to economic change, industrialization, and a marketing economy.

1860–90: Three Stormy Decade of Rapid Change

The succession to the throne of Alexander II, which brought with it liberal policies, meant the starting point for many far-reaching reforms already long awaited. One of them was the declaration in 1863 that after twenty years, in 1883, the Finnish language should have the same official status in Finland's administration as the Swedish language. This declaration, of course, had many educational implications.

The 1860s saw the beginning of the movement toward making general elementary education compulsory by law. In 1863 the first state teacher-training college for elementary schools was founded in Jyvaskyla, and from the beginning it was a dual college, with one course of study for men and one for women. In principle, both had the same program except for handicrafts, but in practice there were many restrictions aimed at maintaining the moral standards. Nevertheless, this was the first possibility for women to obtain, as educators, a formal competence equal to men.

A state-owned 'normal school' for boys was founded as part of the formal and systematic training of university students (all still male) for teaching in secondary schools. Only a few years later, in 1868, the female principal of the Swedish state girls' school in Helsinki founded a private continuation class for alumni planning to be teachers at the girls' schools. The national awakening of women was mirrored in the founding in 1864 and 1869 of the first two Finnish-language girls' schools. Both were private, and the latter was located in Helsinki.

It is certainly no accident that almost simultaneously, in 1864, unmarried women twenty five years of age were declared legally and economically independent. (Married women were still for a long time under the guardianship of their spouses.) It is interesting to note that when, in 1873, the seven first alumni classes (1867–73) of the college were studied, the majority of the 96 men (ninety percent) as well as of the 92 women (seventy-nine percent) were employed in elementary schools, and that only 9 of the women had married and therefore left teaching. For these "first," teaching was truly a calling and a road to independence.

In 1866 the first statutes concerning the rural elementary schools also came into effect. They provided for boys and girls being taught separately and for four years of courses. Preparatory teaching was still considered the duty of the home or the church. The church was developing small ambulatory schools for that purpose—mainly with women as teachers. Only elementary schools in cities and towns, often considered "the poor schools," were to contain two preparatory grades as well as the four ordinary grades. This difference may explain the fact revealed in the first elementary-school statistics, presented for the school year 1873–74, that 71 percent of the 150 teachers employed by the cities and towns were female, while only 39 percent of the 234 teachers employed by the rural communities were female. In all, of the 384 teachers employed in the elementary schools, 52 percent were female.

The time was now ripe for transferring the administration of the rapidly enlarging educational system from the church to the state. A National Board of General Education was founded in 1870, and in 1872 the new statutes prepared by it were enacted for the secondary schools. The girls' schools were now acknowledged and enlarged in many ways, and formal restrictions on the social background of their pupils disappeared—though girls still were not prepared for university or working life. However, at the very same time, in 1870, the first Finnish woman, through private studies and an application to the emperor "for an exemption because of her sex," had obtained permission to study at the university.

Some interesting facts can be extracted from the first official report of the new National Board of General Education. In the school year 1874–75, fifty-seven state secondary schools existed in Finland, forty-nine of which were boys' schools (partly lower-level, partly upper-level) and eight were girls' schools. Even in the boys' schools, 41 percent had a female teacher, usually for art, and 10 percent of the school councils appointed for the boys' schools had a female member. At the eight state girls' schools, 49 percent of the teachers were women, all the principals were female, and in each of their councils one, two, or three of the four to give members were female.

The decade of the 1880s saw the continued advancement of both the Finnish language and of women. The number of Finnish secondary-school pupils had already outgrown that of Swedish pupils (the percentage of the Swedish-speaking population being around 14 percent during the period in question). And the demands for an opportunity for women to participate in higher secondary studies directly leading to the university were growing stronger and stronger. At the university the first female physician had taken her degree in 1878, and the first woman had taken a master's degree in 1882. Thus, when the government was unwilling to change the character of the girls' schools, private coeducational schools leading to university studies were founded, the first Swedish one in 1883 and the first Finnish one, with a woman principal, in 1886. The university itself had already been willing to accept female students on an equal basis, but up to 1901 the Russian emperor continued to require from each of them an individual application of "exemption based on sex."

It is no accident that during these years, in 1884, the first emancipatory woman's organization, Suomen Naidyhdistys, was founded. A remarkable number of its first membership were women teachers.

As for the girls' schools, as early as 1881 a private Finnish 'continuation college' which prepared teachers for Finnish girls' schools, had been founded to accommodate the rapidly growing number of private Finnish girls' schools. The government finally had to act, and in 1885 new statutes were adopted specifically for the girls' schools. The study courses were modernized and increased to five years starting from the age of eleven, and the first five Finnish private girls' schools were taken over by the state. Similarly, the state now took responsibility for the education of teachers for the girls' schools, taking over both the Finnish and the Swedish private three-year continuation colleges. But the competence of the female teachers graduating from these institutions was not sufficient for teaching outside the girls' schools, nor for direct access to the university. Even at the girls' school, the salary for a female teacher was lower than for her male counterpart, the principal always had to be a woman. The road towards equality now led, more and more, away from the girls' schools towards the rapidly multiplying coeducational schools and university studies. However, it should also be mentioned that during these very same decades many special teacher-training colleges were founded that gave women competence in teaching handicrafts, needlework, home economics, gymnastics, etc., in different kinds of schools.

Elementary schooling was still voluntary and was only slowly increasing because of the reluctance of the local municipalities, which were economically responsible for the founding of schools. In 1881 new directions were given according to which boys and girls could be taught together so long as each sex obtained its appropriate instruction in handicrafts. In practice this meant a differentiation between male and female elementary-school teachers and a quota system in teaching training that seems to have had after effects up to the present day. These effects can also be traced to the fact that in this early period it was considered natural for inspectors and principals of larger elementary schools to be male.

1890–1917: Slower and More Difficult Progress

These last decades as a Russian grand duchy were difficult for Finland. The empire adopted a russification program, and counteracting reforms followed. General political disquietude, revolutionary activity, and finally World War I and the Russian Revolution also occurred at this time. However, these years also brought great progress. As a consequence of the first empirewide general strike in 1905, a new legislation was accepted enacting a total reform of the Finnish parliament and giving a general franchise to all Finnish citizens, women as well as men. As the first women in Europe to hold political office, nineteen Finnish women, many of them educators, assembled in 1907 to the first democratic diet, which comprised two-hundred members.

But the repeated proposals of this parliament for compulsory elementary education for all Finnish citizens were never accepted by the emperor. Nevertheless, elementary school began to be accepted more and more by the people themselves. Around 1900 there were about 28,500 pupils in the city and town elementary schools which were taught by 864 teachers, 73 percent of whom were female (largely because of the existence of the lowest preparatory grades in the cities); on the other hand, in the rural elementary schools there were about 76,500 pupils taught by 2,022 teachers, 49 percent of whom were female. Thus, in total, there were 2,886 teachers, 56 percent of whom were employed by the municipally administered elementary schools in Finland.

Even though only some (since 1906, even some of the girls' schools) of the secondary schools included upper grades leading to the university level, the number of women studying at the university had in 1901 reached 385, or 16 percent of the student body. In that very year these women gained equal rights with men and were no longer obliged to get an "exemption because of sex." In 1915 as much as a third of the student body at the university was female. With more and more women taking university degrees, women also increasingly began to avail themselves of the same opportunities as male graduates for obtaining full competence to teach at secondary schools by studying and practising at the boys' normal schools. In 1909 as many as twenty women were practicing there.

In 1906 the difference between the salaries of men and women holding the same position in state secondary schools was abolished. However, not until 1906 were women generally given equal rights with men in appointments to teaching positions. Until then, women, even in this case, had to apply for an "exemption because of sex." On the other hand, it must be stressed that Finland has never had any kind of formal order requiring female teachers to leave their position in the event of marriage. (In Sweden such an order was given as late as 1905.) Whether or not informal pressure may have been exerted is another matter. In any case, the statistics for the school year 1910–11 report that 46 percent of all the 1,957 secondary-school teachers employed were women. The principal of a coeducational school could be either a man or a woman, and quite often schools had both.

1918–69: The First Fifty Years of Finnish Independence

After the close of World War I and the Russian Revolution, Finland succeeded, at the end of 1917, in declaring itself a sovereign state and in obtaining a general foreign acknowledgement of this independence. Nevertheless, the nation had still to wage a tragic civil war in 1918, the wounds of which have been slowly healing.

Now heading towards independent development, the country had 3.2 million inhabitants in 1920, with 70 percent of its economically active population occupied in agriculture and forestry and only 16 percent of its total population living in urban municipalities. Forty yhears later, in 1960, the total population was 4.5 million, 38 percent of which were living in urban municipalities, while the percentage of the economically active population occupied by agriculture and forestry had decreased by one-half, to 36 percent. Meanwhile, between 1939 and 1944 Finland had two difficult wars with its eastern neighbor. The many changes that lay ahead could not possible have been imagined.

For women, some of the obvious remaining legislative inequalities were corrected during the first decade. Women achieved full municipal franchise in 1917, after 1919, a married woman could take up a profession or business without formally presenting the consent of her spouse. Beginning in 1926, women had equal rights with men to be appointed to any public office (with some exceptions in the military or police sectors), and in 1929 a new marriage law was finally enacted, the leading principle of which was the independence and equality of the spouses.

Legislation introducing a compulsory, municipally administered but state-supervised elementary education was enacted in 1921. Now children had to attend school at age seven, and the two lowest grades were usually taught by female teachers. Male teachers were found in the four upper grades, either in single-sex classes of boys or in mixed classes in which the women teachers taught girls handicrafts and gymnastics. But the upper grades in larger schools, women could also in the upper grades have their own single-sex classes for girls. Teachers were similarly divided in the continuation classes of the elementary school, and the length of these courses grew during the half-century from short courses to two-year courses. Thus the final length of the compulsory elementary school was eight years, or up to the age of fifteen. But, as we shall see, more and more children were leaving the elementary school after the first four grades, at the age of eleven, to apply for the right to study at the rapidly growing parallel system of secondary schools

At first the elementary-school system and its teaching force grew—though without much change in the proportion of male to female teachers. In 1920 there were 6,800 elementary-school teachers, 59 percent of which were female; in 1967 the number was 25,000 and again 59 percent were female. This similarity, however, hides the many changes in this teacher force, perhaps the most important being the rise in educational level. The early training colleges for elementary-school teachers only required completion of the elementary school proper (though especially the female applicants often had more education), and, with four to six years of study, these colleges did not quite reach the level of an upper secondary school (foreign languages in particular were totally absent). From 1934 on, however, there also existed one teacher-training college with a two-year course requiring completion of the upper secondary school. And as the "baby boom" after World War II produced an immediate need for more elementary-school teachers a speedy solution was the creation of a few other temporary training colleges similarly requiring upper-secondary-school education. Thus already in the 1950s and 1960s more than half the new elementary-school teachers had this higher educational background.

As mentioned earlier, despite the apparent equality of male and female elementary-school teachers, some differentiation seemed to persist. During the first year of independence, therefore, women teachers formed their own association with a program to abolish the old sex difference in salary—though this goal was not attained until in the 1950s. Administrative posts for elementary schools were still considered a privilege and an appropriate form of advancement for male teachers. The first female school inspector for elementary schools was appointed as late as in 1965.

As for the secondary-school system, the last sex differences in teacher education were rapidly disappearing. In 1922 the old continuation colleges for women were discontinued. When the old normal school for boys could no longer on its own satisfy the need for training the increased numbers of secondary-school teachers, the leading upper secondary girl's school in Helsinki was in 1934 made into a second normal school. However, practicing university graduates were required to teach one term in each of the two institutions. Since after the war even the secondary schools were rapidly swelling, five new state normal schools, now all of them coeducational, were created between 1955 and 1961.

In principle there was not much change in the Finnish system of secondary schools during the first fifty years of the country's independence, although many school commissions were debating problems and although the content of the study courses naturally developed with the times. Secondary schools generally received their pupils from among applicants who were eleven years of age and who had completed the first four grades of elementary school. Then followed five years (in the case of the girls' schools, six years) of study to complete the lower-secondary-level course. After this the pupil (about sixteen years of age), with a certificate of graduation, could either leave for vocational studies or working life or could continue at the upper secondary (gymnasium) level for three years, and work toward a matriculation examination for university competence.

Since there was not much structural change, the increase in numbers and the development in the directions already perceptible before independence were even more conspicuous. In 1930–31 there were 232 secondary schools, with about 50,000 pupils and about a third of the schools were located in rural municipalities. Twenty years later, in 1950–51, the number of schools was 338, with about 95,000 pupils and with 42 percent of the schools in rural municipalities. Only sixteen years after that, in 1966–67, there were 614 secondary schools with 182,000 pupils and nearly as many schools located in rural as in urban municipalities. The state schools continued to be in the minority (around 25–30 percent) and the private schools in the majority (about 60 percent), the only new feature being the municipal lower secondary schools, the proportion of which grew from 5 percent in 1950 to 17 percent in 1967. The proportion of coeducational schools was around 80 percent at the end of the period, the few remaining single-sex schools being in most cases old, venerable, state schools.

All these numbers clearly show that the Finnish secondary school during the first fifty years of independence had developed from a school for a selected, privileged minority to a general education system for the whole nation; in the 1960s, in fact, about half of each birth group were transferring from the elementary to the secondary school at the age of eleven. However, this fact also meant that the continued maintenance of a parallel school system was creating increasingly greater problems for the society.

The explosive growth of the secondary-school system was naturally accompanied by a corresponding growth in the teaching force. Table 1 shows the statistics concerning this developed and the participation of women in it.

Table 1. Female Teachers in Secondary Schools, Finland, 1920–67

School year	Number of teachers	% women
1920–21	2,480	48.1
1930–31	3,243	51.5
1940–41	3,285	53.5
1947–48	4,880	56.8
1955–56	6,863	59.9
1960–61	10,450	57.2
1966–67	14,838	58.7

Source: Statistical Yearbook of Finland, 1948 and 1967.

Almost from the beginning of Finland's independence, women have been in the majority among secondary-school teachers, and their proportion increased until it reached about 60 percent in the years just before the great school reorganization. There have been discussions concerning what the consequences of a large female majority among educators might be, especially for the development of male pupils. However, no sex quota system similar to that used in elementary-school teacher training has been used to select candidates for teaching in secondary schools. In fact, such a system has hardly been discussed.

It must be emphasized that all the secondary-school teachers in Finland have always been subject teachers; that is, they teach one to three closely related subjects to many different classes and grades in the school—in contrast to elementary-school teachers, who usually have their own class of pupils (in small schools, a combination of several grades) to whom they taught almost all subjects. But in the secondary schools sex segregation was apparent; women taught certain subjects and men others. This subject matter segregation appears in the proportions of men and women studying different subjects at the university.

1970–87: Reorganization of Finnish Education

The beginning of this chapter described the great economic and social changes that occurred in Finland during the first half-century of its independence. This remote, northern country of small farmers had within one lifetime taken great steps on the road towards industrialization and urbanization, thus effecting a transformation which had begun much earlier in many other European countries and had taken one to two centuries. After 1960, this transformation accelerated even more. In 1960, 38 percent of the nation's 4.5 million inhabitants were living in urban municipalities, while in 1980 as many as 60 percent of the 4.8 million inhabitants were in cities. In 1960, 36 percent of the economically active population were still occupied in agriculture and forestry, and in 1980, in only twenty years, this proportion had dropped to only 13 percent.

If we then add to these general conditions the facts concerning earlier schools described it is not difficult to see that a great change in the educational system had been long overdue. During the 1960s many commissions, cabinets, and parliaments had conferred on this subject. Finally, in 1968, one of the great decisive resolutions in the school question was passed by the Finnish parliament. Finland was to abandon the parallel school system, in existence for a century, as well as the state and private school connected with it, and to go over to a municipally administered but state supervised comprenhensive school that would be compulsory for nine years for all children between seven and sixteen years of age. In addition, both the upper secondary level leading to university studies, as well as the vocational education sector which was unevenly developed and divided into many parts, were to be reformed and made more coherent. These schools would together form the *middle level* of education, to follow the *basic level*. Finally, higher education, with its many new, more or less regional, universities, was to go through a radical reform of its study and examination structures, as well as of its administration. Teacher education was included in this reform. Programs of adult education were were around the corner.

The implementation of the new comprehensive, compulsory basic school (peruskoulu) was begun in 1970. Since then, the planning and realization of all the above-mentioned reforms, down to the smallest details, have continued. In reviewing the following statistical reports (tables 2–7), it must be kept in mind that in many cases they are describing systems and terms that cannot be directly compared to schools of earlier decades.

The teachers working in the new basic comprehensive school are now divided into two categories: classroom teachers and subject teachers. Classroom teachers work in grades one through six, which form the *lower level* of the comprehensive school. These teachers resemble the former elementary school teachers in that in principle they teach most subjects in one, their "own," class of pupils.(Subject teachers of foreign languages may participate already at this level.) One result of the reform in teacher education, however, is that even the teachers at this lower level are now educated at the universities and receive a degree comparable to that of the other teacher categories. Most of the classroom teachers described in table 2 are of course still products of the teacher training described earlier. From table 2 it can be seen that (until 1984) the proportion of women among classroom teachers was somewhat higher than among elementary-school teachers. Even after transferring the teacher training to the universities, the Ministry of Education has maintained the sex quota system for the training of classroom teachers and has kept it around 40 percent for men and 60 percent for women. The applicants in 1983, 24 percent were men and 76 percent were women, obviously the competition has been somewhat easier for men: 15.5 percent of the male applicants and 8.5 percent of the female applicants were accepted, the men with somewhat lower points.

The difference between the subject teachers of the comprehensive schools described in table 2 and the subject teachers of the senior secondary schools described in table 3 is somewhat theoretical. The statistics indicate the formal appointment of the teacher, and in principle the teachers of the senior secondary schools must have a higher academic competence in their subjects. But in practice many senior secondary schools are cooperating closely with the upper level of some comprehensive schools, so that the same teacher may have lessons in both schools provided he or she has the appropriate competence.

Table 2. Female Teachers and Principals in Basic Comprehensive schools, Finland, 1980–83

Category	Number of teachers		% women	
Lower level	80–81	83–84	80–81	83–84
Classroom teachers	16,749	17,063	62.5	62.1
Principals	395	429	4.3	5.8
Total	19,545	19,954	62.5	62.0
Upper level (subjects)				
Finnish/Swedish (vernacular)	634	645	89.0	88.4
Swedish/Finnish (not vernacular)	353	347	84.4	84.7
English	394	373	92.4	92.2
English and Swedish/ Finnish	928	1,026	83.9	86.5
Swedish/Finnish and German	210	224	89.5	90.2
Finnish/Swedish and History	455	473	77.8	79.9
History and social Science	305	307	64.3	65.1
Religion	117	117	79.5	77.8
Mathematics, physics and chemistry	2,066	2,229	47.0	49.8
Geography and Natural History	749	778	69.0	69.4
Music	213	271	53.0	44.3
Physical education	802	784	55.6	55.1
Art	344	352	68.0	66.5
Home economics	848	813	99.4	98.6
Textile work	511	480	99.6	99.8
Technical work	709	682	0.4	0.7
Commercial subjects	134	131	49.3	55.0
Study guidance	611	662	41.2	44.0
Principals	579	591	18.5	19.5
Total	12,294	12,558	61.5	62.4
Special education				
Auxiliary teaching	681	689	51.8	52.4
Observation classes	365	428	17.3	17.8
Speech disorders	181	179	80.1	84.4
Reading/writing handicaps	571	603	69.5	70.3

Table 2. Female Teachers and Principals in Basic Comprehensive schools, Finland, 1980–83 (Cont'd)

Category	Number of teachers		% women	
Principals	120	119	20.8	19.3
Total	2,400	2,738	51.9	52.2
Total	34,267	35,285	61.2	61.3

Source: Data registers of the National Board of General Education.

Note: Some of the less important, smallest categories have been excluded.

Table 3. Female Teachers and Principals in Senior Secondary Schools, Finland, 1980–83

	Number of teachers		% women	
Category	80–81	83–84	80–81	83–84
Subject teachers				
Finnish/Swedish (vernacular)	519	532	79.0	79.7
Swedish/Finnish (not vernacular)	466	492	76.8	75.0
English	643	662	80.7	81.6
German	449	451	81.5	82.7
French	87	93	81.6	84.9
Russian	53	60	77.4	81.7
Latin	23	24	56.5	54.2
History and social science	380	387	44.2	41.9
Religion	353	361	77.3	77.3
Psychology/philosophy	14	18	85.7	88.9
Mathematics	704	759	33.5	33.7
Physics	126	137	22.2	23.4
Chemistry	39	43	56.4	60.5
Biology	252	274	52.0	49.6
Geography	46	49	65.2	63.3
Music	14	19	50.0	47.4
Physical education	194	204	57.2	55.9
Art	69	77	84.1	85.7
All evening	271	303	63.8	64.4
Principals, day	443	452	14.7	14.8
Principals, evening	40	43	15.0	20.9
Senior secondary schools total	5,148	5,401	60.1	60.0

Source: Data registers of the National Board of General Education

In comparing the subject teachers in tables 2 and 3, it can easily be observed that the sex ratios for the different subjects vary in a familiar way: more women are teaching languages, home economics, and textile work than are teaching mathematics, physics, and chemistry. The only categories with very few women are technical work and observation classes, the latter usually being classes with a large majority of boys with severe behavioral problems. On the other hand, the overall proportion of female teachers is around 60 percent for all these levels of general education, and the percentage for the senior secondary schools is only slightly lower than for the upper level of the comprehensive schools. (It must be added that the proportion of female students in higher education now is also slightly above 50 percent.)

The proportions for the female principals recorded in tables 2 and 3 show a somewhat different picture: females are in a clear minority everywhere. This minority is clearest at the lower level of the comprehensive schools (where the traditions from the elementary school probably weigh heavily). The figures are somewhat lower for the senior secondary schools than for the upper level of the comprehensive school and special education, where the difference between the last two is rather small. But the general trend seems to be towards slowly rising female proportions. Moreover, there have been so many recent administrative changes in the duties, position, and election of principals that it is difficult to predict what the future development will be.

Table 4 presents statistics for teachers in vocational education over a somewhat longer period. The general trend here shows somewhat rising proportions of women, while the typical differences remain among different kinds of vocational education. Here the field is still in a reorganization phase—problems regarding the education of teachers are by no means solved—so that it is difficult to predict future trends. Unfortunately, figures for principals are not available at this time.

In this connection it might also be interesting to look at the position of female teachers in some teachers' trade unions. Table 5 can well be compared with tables 2, 3, and 4. Table 5 shows that Finnish teachers are generally well organized, that union memberships reach and may even exceed the official number of appointments (members unemployed, retired, or on leave for study, sickness, or motherhood are some most obvious explanations for the difference), and that the percentages of women members also reach and may even exceed those for appointments. Second, it is easy to observe that the percen-

Table 4. Female Teachers at Institutions of Vocational Education, Finland, 1974-82

Type of institution	Number of Teachers		% women	
	Autumn 1974	Autumn 1982	Autumn 1974	Autumn 1982
Agriculture	527	790	27.0	31.3
Forestry	235	871	3.8	19.8
Technical training	1,741	1,756	10.1	12.8
Vocational schools*				
State central	529	639	35.7	35.8
Municipal associations	1,974	2,740	31.1	33.2
Municipal	971	1,206	33.0	35.4
Industry	641	504	7.3	8.3
Handicapped	189	212	30.7	30.7
Seafaring	151	197	32.4	28.9
Commerce	1,671	1,894	59.0	64.4
Commerce special	156	163	30.8	39.3
Nursing	591	991	98.8	96.7
Cosmetology	37	33	83.8	87.9
Home economics	428	776	92.5	88.9
Hotels and restaurants	130	260	56.2	59.2
Short courses for reschooling	889	1,622	37.9	28.4
Teacher training	138	53	72.5	50.9
Vocational education total	11,637	15,668	37.8	41.6

Source: Data register of the National Board of Vocational Education
Note: Some small or changing categories have been excluded.
*These are schools operated at different levels of governance.

tages of women are generally lower at the higher, more "important" decision levels of the organizations—a phenomenon well known from all other fields in society and probably as well known internationally. However, it is interesting to note how deep this drop is in the large Teachers' Trade Union (representing) comprehensive-school and senior secondary-school teachers) as compared with some other unions with much lower proportions of women in their membership. The difference in size between the unions in question is, however, so great that many factors play a role. In any case, all these percentages stand up to international comparison rather well.

Table 6 gives some information, concerning women employed at higher levels in educational administration, although the information on municipalities is based on a restricted survey and the important in-

Table 5. Women in Teacher Trade Unions, Finland, 1982

Union and position	% women
Teachers' Trade Union in Finland	
Membership ($N=42{,}612$)	65.3
Participants in general union meeting	37.9
Members in union central council	35.5
Members in executive committee	23.5
Association of Commercial School Teachers	
Membership ($N=1{,}752$)	65.9
Participants in general union meeting	61.3
Members in union central council	50.0
Members in executive committee	37.5
Vocational School Teachers Union	
Membership ($N=6{,}854$)	46.5
Participants in general union meeting	36.8
Members in union central council	42.5
Members in executive committee	25.0
Association of Teachers at Technical Institutes	
Membership ($N=1{,}068$)	15.4
Participants in general union meeting	21.6
Members in union central council	9.3
Members in executive committee	25.0
Association of Workers' Institute Principals and Teachers	
Membership ($N=556$)	57.2
Participants in general union meeting	50.0
Members in union central council	
Members in executive committee	33.3

Source: Position of Women 1984, Statistical Survey No. 72, Central Statistical Office of Finland, 1984.

termedial level of educational administration in the provinces (N:12) is lacking. In any case, the table shows that there are quite a few women at the important municipal level immediately above the schools, especially considering the proportion of women in the schools proper. On the level of the state central administration, the usual hierarchical pyramid with men on the top is confirmed. However, it must be added that during the last ten to twenty years more of a balance has been achieved.

Table 6. Women in Municipal and State Educational Administration, Finland 1980, 1982, and 1983

Administrative position	Number	% women
Municipalities (total number 464 in 1980)		
Director of educational system	319	6.6
Secretry of educational system	20	45.0
Director of instruction	28	39.3
National Board of General Education (1982)		
Leading posts (director of department,		
head of bureau, and higher posts)	26	15.4
Others in responsible positions	44	40.1
Referendaries, etc.	78	69.2
Office personnel	86	97.7
Service personnel	11	54.5
Total	245	67.8
National Board of Vocational Education (1983)		
Leading posts (not defined)	23	30.4
Referendaries, etc. (not defined)	95	46.3
Others (not defined)	143	90.2
Total	261	69.0
Ministry of Education (1980)		
Leading posts (head of bureau, director		
of department, and higher posts)	22	9.1
Others in responsible positions	43	18.6
Referendaries, etc.	50	60.0
Office personnel	92	98.9
Service personnel	17	35.3
Total	224	61.2

Sources: Surveys by working groups for equality in administration.

Finally, table 7 gives some statistics on the participation of women in political decision making and planning. Of course, there is still a long way to go towards equality; women are everywhere in a minority, even though they form a majority of the voters. Even here many steps forward have recently been taken; however, it must also be admitted that education does not show the lowest percentages, probably because there exists in society a feeling that "education is a woman's place."

Table 7. Women's Participation in Political Decision Making and Planning, Finland, 1980, 1982, and 1983

Position	Number of Positions	% women
Parliament and government level		
Members of parliament elected in 1983	200	31.0
Cabinet members sitting since 1983	17	17.6
Ministers of education (and culture)	2	50.0
Members of all state committees (1983)	5,661	10.7
Chairs of state committees	551	4.7
Secretaries of state committees	—	27.8
Members of committees appointed by the ministry of education	1,337	19.4
Chairs of these committees	139	10.8
Secretaries of these committees	—	40.3
Municipality level		
Municipal councillors elected in 1980	12,777	22.2
Members of municipal governments (sample survey in 1982)	—	11.3
Alternate members of municipal governments (sample survey in 1982)	—	20.8
Chairs of municipal governments	—	2.8
Vice chairs of municipal governments	—	8.4
Members of municipal boards (sample survey 1982)	—	22.3
Chairs of municipal boards (sample survey 1982)	2,020	11.8
Members of municipal boards of education	—	35.1
Chairs of municipal boards of education	105	14.3

Sources: Position of Women 1984, Statistical Survey No. 72, Central Statistical Office

Sources: for Equality between Men and Women, Prime Minister's Office, 1983.

It must also be strongly stressed that behind all these many different observations is the general fact that Finnish women have always been hard working. They work outside the home (transferring directly from the fields of small farms to factories and offices) as well as in the home; therefore, they form an integral part of the total society. According to the statistical survey *Position of Women,* in 1984 women formed 47.7 percent of the total labor force in Finland. These

1,173 million women formed 71.6 percent of all women between fifteen and sixty-four years of age, and that among them 69.9 percent were married, 49.7 percent had children under eighteen years of age, and 22.3 percent had children under seven years of age. Of all the 339,000 women having children under seven years of age, 77.3 percent belonged to the labor force. Thus, according to the 1979 use of time study made by the Central Statistical office of Finland, in the adult population the average so-called total work time, which includes gainful employment, education, and domestic work, was clearly higher for women (33 percent) than for men (31 percent). Transformed into weekly hours, this fact means five hours more work and less free time per week for women. Although specific statistics for teachers cannot be presented, these factors certainly operate similarly for them and thus form one of the explanations for the inequalities observed above.

Chapter 2

Teacher Careers and Promotion in Australia

SHIRLEY N. SAMPSON

O ne consequence of the isolation of colonial administrations and the nature of the constitution of the Commonwealth of Australia is that education at all levels in Australia is the responsibility of one federal and eight state (or territorial) governments. Changes in tax distribution during World II made education more centralized and the national government more fiscally powerful—in fact the only authority funding educational innovation. In the 1980s this situation means that the states are responsible for the provision of free primary and secondary schooling and the Commonwealth funds universities and colleges (which are also free) as well as initiatives such as (the improvement of laboratories and libraries) and equity programs in schools.

In Australia, about three-quarters of all school students attend publicly owned and administered government schools, and the allocation of 188,000 staff members in 7,500 schools in urban and remote rural areas requires vast expenditures through centralized bureaucracies. The Commonwealth is the only one of nine Australian Parliaments to have a woman as minister of Education (from 1983) and is the only educational organization to be headed by a woman from 1984. Eight of the nine educational bureaucracies are further divided into regional administrations, and at present there is only one regional director who is a woman. By contrast, women constitute 61 percent of school staff members in Australia, 71 percent of the primary teachers, and 49 percent of the secondary teachers. Only when the smallest primary schools are included do women constitute one-quarter of all primary principals. In secondary schools they constitute 6 percent to 13 percent of the principals.

The Commonwealth Affirmative Action legislation projected for 1986 required major employers of women to formulate and periodically report on long-term plans for action towards equality within their own organizations. Although penalties are not currently proposed for noncompliance with this legislation, these plans likely to improve conditions for women teachers working within politically sensitive state government systems, some of which have already established high-level executive committees in anticipation of the new legislation.

Within the nongovernment school sector, which represents less than one-quarter of all students and employed staff, there is no single organization of career structure. Each school is governed by its own council (or local system in Catholic schools) using income derived from student fees and, to an increasing extent, government (especially commonwealth) contributions. Despite legislation for affirmative action or equal opportunity, no government in Australia has ever sought to make those who spend the tax dollar on education accountable in terms of such equity objectives. Thus the situation in nongovernment schools closely resembles that in free government systems, with no women at the top. Single-sex schools have male principals if they are for boys, and either male or female principals if they are for girls. Recent changes from religious to lay principals have markedly reduced the number of women principals in girls' and coeducational schools at primary and secondary levels in Catholoic systems. The absence of women in senior decision-making levels in state education departments and nongovernment schools supports the Organization for Economic Cooperation and Development (OECD) finding that Australia has the most sex-segregated work force of all countries with that organization (OECD,1977). In common with other public servants, men and women teachers between 1958 and 1972 were accorded equal pay in state and federal systems. Despite this mandate, sex biases remain. A recent survey of graduate earnings five years after graduation from six universities found that among those who had become teachers, male average annual income was already 3 percent higher than that of females, and this difference increased with length of service (Sydney University Graduate Employment Survey, 1985).

Until the late 1950s it was mandatory in all systems for women teachers to resign from the permanent staff upon marriage, thereby losing entitlements to promotion and superannuation. Positions such as principal of single-sex schools were designated for that sex only, and women could only be in charge of infant departments. Since the 1970s such sex differences in conditions of employment have been virtually eliminated in the majority of states. Nevertheless, benefits such as maternity leave are still limited. Paternity leave is available only in three systems, and child care is provided only rarely, after school hours.

A major problem in the improvement of teachers working conditions in Australia is related to geographic and demographic realities. More than 80 percent of the 15.5 million population lives in seven capital cities on the seacoast and in a small number of larger inland towns. Nevertheless, government systems, which provide the bulk of schooling, must also staff schools in remote mining towns and scattered agricultural areas. A system of rewards giving promotion on the basis of length and type of service, which was caused by the necessity to staff less desirable locations, has led to a promotion system based on rigid seniority regulations. This system has seriously disadvantaged women in all states. Ambitious teachers must teach for several years in remote areas to qualify for later promotion. Thus, women, whose husbands' work is more likely to be located near the center of population on the coast, would need to live away from their families, and many are not prepared to do this. Several states have tried to introduce more equity by basing promotion on merit. Predictably, this attempt has aroused incredible hostility from those who have "been to the country" hoping to gain from it. In 1985, wives of primary principals met in a Western Australian country town to voice their protest at the introduction of merit promotion (*Sunday Times*, 1985), which they saw as delaying their husband's promotion to a more desirable coastal location. At the same time, however, a South Australian system has designated half of all positions becoming vacant in any year as appointments to which seniority regulations do not apply. This system is in its third year and working well, and has also resulted in a small increase in the appointment of women principals.

Finally, a major handicap to the promotion of women in Australian school systems has been the lack of support or activity from teachers' unions. Until 1979, only New South Wales had a full-time staff appointment concerned with equity. Action since that time has been only halfhearted because the majority of union officials continue to be male. Membership in a union has never been compulsory for teachers, but it is a common path to political prominence in Australia, and it is only recently that younger women have begun to use it in that way. Union support for greater equity for women has increased markedly since 1980.

From this brief outline of the Australian school systems, in which so many women are employees, it might be expected that once barriers to equity were removed and government affirmative action and teacher union policies became more supportive that a great many more women would apply for promotion positions as they are advertised at the school, regional, and state or Commonwealth level. This has not been happening, however, and in recent years departmental officials have frequently used this fact to suggest that women themselves are to blame for their position at or close to the bottom of all educational hierarchies.

The Australian Teacher Career Study

In order to better understand the reasons for woman's position in education, I undertook an investigation of the situation in 1984. Questionnaires were sent to a 3 percent sample of members of the Australian Teachers' Federation, and a 55 percent response rate was achieved without a follow-up. There were 2,380 responses to a twelve-page questionnaire, and 61 percent of the responses were from women teachers. Their distribution is representative of the eight government school systems according to age and present position of respondents.

Whereas 45 percent of the male respondents in this study had applied for promotion within their system in the last five years, only 24 percent of women had done so. To some extent, the assertion by male leaders that women were not seeking promotion was thus supported; however, 37 percent of the women, compared with 48 percent of the men, had applied for promotion to positions advertised within their present school. Although such internal appointments would provide valuable administrative experience, however, it is the nature of Australian systems that appointments (such as level of subject coordinators) are not permanent and do not confer a more senior position in the hierarchy of any departmental work force.

In this study, a minority of respondents rejected the idea of promotion altogether (9 percent), but among those who expected to reach a higher level in the future, women aspired less than men. Forty-two percent of the women expected to remain as class teachers, compared with 15 percent of the men. Thirty-two percent of the women and 31 percent of the men intended to become senior mistress or master, but 44 percent of the men and only 17 percent of the women sought principalships or work as a central or regional office administrator.

Responses reported here show that a much small proportion of women than men are seeking promotion of any kind, and reasons were sought to explain this difference. Following the findings of a previous study (ILEA, 1984), respondents were asked to describe the importance to them of a number of reasons commonly given for seeking or not seeking promotion.

Reasons for Seeking Promotion

On matters related to their professional lives, men and women showed somewhat similar levels of motivation. The challenge of more responsibility, the opportunity to influence the system, and the organization of schools or the curriculum were important or very important to over 60 percent of all female and male respondents, and the difference in responses of each sex was small and not significant.

A slightly greater proportion of the females (44 percent) and 39 percent (n.s.) of the males were interested in promotion because they were dissatisfied with their present position, while 52 percent of the females and 49 percent of the males (n.s.;$p = .001$) were interested with their present position.* Much more important was resistance by women to leaving the classroom: 63 percent (compared to only 46 percent of the men) said that an important reason for *not* applying for promotion was that they would have less teaching time with pupils. Thus, although more than half of all women seek responsibility or a change in their present position, they do not want to lose touch with their pupils. This finding could well explain some of women's reluctance to apply for promotion compared to men, for whom pupil contact was not such an important factor.

The Issue of Financial Reward

Salary is a more important influence for men than for women, both as a reason for applying for promotion of the men (71 percent and 62 percent of the women) and for not applying (60 percent of the men and 48 percent of the women names "lack of financial incentive" as important or very important) Sex differences were significant for all responses but were most significant those indications that an increase in salary was a very important reason for seeking promotion (31 percent of the men and 21 percent of the women $p < .001$). Despite these findings, it is obvious that a majority of women teachers are in-

---

*All statistical tests of significance used in this chapter are chi-squared tests. N.S. = not significant.

terested in salary as a reason for promotion (62 percent); therefore, this factor does not explain the fact that they are not applying as often as men.

Family-related Reasons for Not Seeking Promotion

Much greater differences between men's and women's motivation towards promotion emerged when family-related factors were considered. Although more men had children living in the same household (62 percent of the men but only 38 percent of the women), women were much more likely to be solely responsible for a child for more than four hours a day (65 percent of the women who had children living in the household, compared with 28 percent of the men). Moreover, although 62 percent of the women had no children living in the household, women teachers across all age groups did much more housework of various kinds than men (88 percent of the women and 65 percent of the men performed three or more tasks for themselves as well as for others).

In line with these family responsibilities, women, far more than men, named as reasons for not seeking promotion that they felt unable to cope with the extra demands and responsibilities (37 percent of the women and 20 percent of the men; $p < .0001$), that they were reluctant to devote the necessary time to extra responsibilities (56 percent of the women and 39 percent of the men; $p < .0001$), and that they perceived a conflict between after-school commitments and domestic responsibilities (65 percent of the women and 52 percent of the men;). Clearly these factors illustrate a most important reason why many women do not seek promotion. Both employer and employee will need to consider more flexible administrative arrangements if women are to increase their decision-making role within education system.

Women's family ties have also been used to explain their reluctance to apply widely for more senior positions and may help explain why more women are applying for positions within schools than for promotion generally. Certainly women more often than men give their partner's career as an important reason for their unwillingness to seek promotion (54 percent of the women and 40 percent of the men; $p < .001$); however, when asked whether their own career was less, equally, or more important to the household than their partner's 61 percent of the women replied that their own career was equally or more important (these responses were given by 67 percent of the men). In addition, 38 percent of the women (though 55 percent of the men) replied that they would be prepared to take a job which necessitated moving and a change of job for their partner.

From findings such as these it can hardly be alleged that large numbers of women are not taking their careers seriously; moreover, lack of mobility is no long quite such an influential factor. Men's careers, too, are not influenced by that of their partner, since 40 percent of the male respondents named their partner's career as equally important and 45 percent replied that they would not take an appointment which meant a change of job for their spouse.

These data also help explain a rather unexpected finding indicating men's reduced mobility. This was the evidence from this questionnaire that, of the men who had applied for promotion in the last five years, 89 percent had applied for less that five positions (compared with 95 percent of the women). It is still true that a greater proportion of men were more mobile than women, for 11.6 percent of the men had apjplied for twenty or more positions within five years (compared to only 2 percent of the women). Nevertheless, a large number of men now appear to be less than completely mobile. Current sex differences in mobility cannot explain the present position of women relative to men in educational hierarchies, though they may explain past patterns of mobility.

In the light of these findings on the influence of family factors on promotion, it is obvious that more women are affected by these responsibilities than men. In the past, this issue has been dismissed by educational authorities as the individual's responsibility; however, it is not for women along to face unpalatable choices between work and family tasks. If society as a whole is convinced that women, who are over two-thirds of all teachers, have a wealth of commitment and experience to contribute to the effective organization of schooling, it behooves administrators themselves to critically examine the male advantage derived from present forms of organizations (or lack of it, as in the case of child-care provision, job sharing, etc.). Also to be examined are the assumptions about men's lack of involvement with their own families.

The Issue of Women's Experience and Qualifications

Finally, among the reasons given by individual men and women for not applying for promotion were two which were highly significant or widely supported. The first related to the perception of a lack of experience, a reason advanced for not seeking promotion by 45 percent of the women compared to only 28 percent of the men ($p < .0001$).

To investigate whether it is a fact that women teachers lack experience more than men, questions were asked concerning sex differences in initial and further qualifications, in-service involvement, early experiences in organizations or administrative tasks as beginning teachers, familiarity with a range of leadership tasks, and perceptions of support or lack of it from significant others, including those at home and in the schools system.

Second, was the issue of qualifications. Women were not initially less qualified than men to enter teacher; in fact, many more women than men had three years or more of training (73.5 percent of the women and 64 percent of the men; $p < .01$). In addition, 32 percent of the women and 33 percent of the men had degrees or degrees with diplomas at the start of their teaching careers.

It was in improving their qualifications that men secured some advantage. Not only had they increased their initial qualifications more (62 percent of the men and 53 percent of the women; $p < .01$), they had done so at a more advanced level. Seventeen percent of the men gaining qualifications after entry to teaching obtained a second or higher degree, in contrast to only 10 percent of the women, and this was a highly significant difference ($p < .0001$).

It cannot be argued that paper credentials automatically improve the quality of teaching or administrative capacity or practice, but the possession of further qualifications does indicate an effort to continue learning and to update skills, and it remains a significant factor in any promotion system based on merit. However, data from this study show that over helf of all female teachers have added further qualifications since entering the service; therefore, many more women could apply for promotion equally with men.

IN-SERVICE ACTIVITIES. Specific information was sought about the types of in-service training activities in which teachers has been involved. Men undertook more of this retraining (80 percent of the men compared with 70 percent of the women) and were significantly more likely to have had two days or more of such activity in administrative tasks (alone or in combination with other activities) such as running a department, training for senior management, or timetabling (33 percent of the men compared with 18 percent of the women; $p < .0001$). Women were more involved that men in curriculum or counseling and student-related activities, but these differences were not as significant. Predictably, perhaps, in view of common stereotypes, men were significantly more involved with in-service computer activities than women (31 percent of the men compared with only 22 percent of the women; $p < .01$). See table 1.

An overview of in-service participation as an indicator of training or preparation for promotion into administrative levels of the educational system reveals one further reason that women might not apply for promotion as often as men: they appear to undertake less training

Table 1. Male and Female Participation in In-Service Activities, Australia, 1984

Type of activity	% participation Females	Males
	Present participation in any activity	
Administration	17.8	33.1
Counseling, student-related	35.5	30.5
Computers	22.1	30.7
Curriculum	79.3	74.4
Other	0.46	0.26
	Participation in last 5 years (76%)	
	73.8	80.1

Note: 1,817 respondents (1,073 females and 744 males) had undertaken 2 or more days of in-service training in the last 5 years; however, many had been involved in more than one type of activity and thus the totals exceed 100%.

for administrative posts, perhaps because the people who are trained in administration in-service activities have already been appointed as administrators of one kind or another. It may also be that women do not choose to undertake such activities, that they do not receive notice of them, or that they are not often encouraged to attend. This research did not provide evidence which would enable a more definitive analysis to be undertaken: however, some indication of past departmental practices in encouraging women into administration can be gauged from the following section on sex differences in tasks allocated to beginning teachers.

APPRENTICESHIP EXPERIENCES. Teachers were asked whether they had ever been allocated organizational or administrative tasks of any kind in their first five years of teaching. Only 57 percent of the women replied in the affirmative, compared with 73 percent of men ($p < .0001$). When the nature of these tasks was examined, clear differences in apprenticeship experiences were revealed. It was found that these women teachers, far more often than the men, had been allocated work to do with children or teaching and the library. This research revealed that of all the respondents, 61 percent of the male teachers had organizational or administrative tasks in their first five years of teaching, compared with only 45 percent of the female teachers. It is clear that an important factor in women teachers' reluctance to apply for promotion could be, first, lack of early apprenticeship in organizational or administrative tasks and, second, the resulting legitimation of stereotyped perceptions concerning appropriate roles for women and men in schools. This process continued long after the first years of teaching, as other evidence showed.

As every teacher is aware, there are multitudes of tasks within schools which are often shared among staff members. Even though many teachers have senior appointments entitling them to perform leadership tasks, assistant-level staff are asked to carry out these duties from time to time. Experiences of this kind were listed in this study, and teachers were asked whether they had ever carried out such duties and whether the task has been by choice or by allocation.

It is apparent from the findings presented in table 2 that women have had fewer opportunities than men to try themselves at any of these everyday organizational activities. Those who had performed such tasks had also been allocated their duties by others within the school less often than men.

Table 2. Male and Female Apprenticeship in School Administrative Tasks, Australia, 1984

| | Apprenticeship experience | | | |
| | Female (%) | | Male (%) | |
Task	Yes[a] (N = 1,234)	Task allocated	Yes[a] (N = 829)	Task allocated
Organizing major school activities (sports, open days, parents' nights)	61.1	19.9	78.2	22.8
Arranging student camps or travel	59.2	9.7	81.7	15.3
Leading school in-service activities	37.6	12.3	60.9	15.9
Leading committees on				
Course curriculum	31.8	11.8	58.0	17.7
Student discipline	20.1	7.2	40.9	15.6
Counseling	20.7	5.6	34.9	10.3
Drawing up timetables	29.8	13.8	50.5	21.0
Running a school assembly	51.2	30.7	69.5	31.8

a. Teachers were asked the following question: "Have you ever taken major responsibility for any of the following tasks in schools in which you have taught? If *yes*, was it by choice or allocation?"

b. p = <.0001 in all cases.

The results reported here support earlier evidence that young women teachers are not asked to perform administrative tasks as often as young men, and that women are often stereotyped by both men and women as not being "administrative material." Therefore, it must be accepted that when 45 percent of the women gave "lack of experience" as a reason for not applying for promotion, they may have been correct. When the proportion of women who have had the opportunity to try themselves at administrative tasks is examined, it is clear that individual women do not often have the experience of seeing other women do well as such tasks, nor to try such tasks themselves and to develop their own sense of competence by *doing*.

SENSE OF COMPETENCE. For a majority of both women and men teachers, the feeling that they could do a senior job better than others was an important or very important reason for applying for promotions (53 percent of the women and 60 percent of the men; n.s.). Differences by sex were significant only among those who saw this as a very important motivation (16 percent of the women and 22 percent of the men; $p < .01$).

A related finding occurred in response to a question asking whether respondents felt they were excellent, good as the general run; not particularly good, or didn't know how to rate themselves on performance of administrative tasks in schools. Twenty-five percent of the males rated themselves as excellent compared with 18 percent of the females.

These exercises in self-assessment in comparison with others reveal commonly found sex-based differences in estimation and, however, in view of the evidence given above concerning actual experiences allowed to them, women's actual sense of competence must be seen as not far below that of men.

PERCEPTIONS OF ENCOURAGEMENT. Throughout their lives, women do not receive the kind of social messages that men do encouraging them to aspire to the top, in particular to manage or controll other people, or that it is appropriate for them to be leaders of men. Many images relating to outstanding women are negative or threatening.

Respondents were asked whether certain officers with whom they had contact in schools had ever invited or encouraged them to apply for promotion. Sex differences here were highly significant. Inspectors, superintendents, or other departmental officers had encouraged 36 percent of the men to apply for promotion and only 21 percent of the women. Principals, who must be more personally familiar with women teachers' competence, did encourage females rather more often than their departmental superiors, but even so, men got this message more frequently than women. Forty-two percent of the women reported the encourgement of their head or principal, but so did 50 percent of the men.

Equal proportions of females and males reported that their immediate superiors had invited or encouraged them to apply for promotion, but men reported more often than women that their spouse had do so (42 percent of the men and 35 percent of the women). In addition, 98 percent of the men compared with 90 percent of the women believed they had support of males on the staff in performing school organizational tasks. Thus the social perception that leadership or decision making in administration was appropriate for males was confirmed by significant others for men teachers. The question of perceptions of discouragement for either sex was not asked. However, it is clear from these responses that men teachers receive personal affirmation to apply for promotion more often than do their female counterparts.

It is not surprising that, as reported in an earlier section, men teachers gave "superior competence" as a reason for wanting to do a more senior job. They are more often encouraged to believe that they *can* do it. In the view of this reasearcher, the really surprising finding, in the light of the lower incidence of encouragement to women, is that so many women—over half of all women respondencts (53 percent)—believed that they could do a senior job better than others.

Perceptions of Discrimination

Respondents were asked whether they thought women were discriminated against in promotion, either explicitly or implicitly, in the system in which they worked, and to give reasons for their response. Fifty-four percent of the women and 24 percent of the men replied in the affirmative, and of those who gave either response (n = 2,286), 62 percent wrote reasons in support of their reply (889 women and 526 men). Of those who believed that women suffered discrimination, there was surprising agreement among both men and women on the major causes. Reasons most often advanced were that women were not perceived as having administrative potential (30 percent of the women and 30 percent of the men), perceived as having administrative potential that men ran the schools (37 percent of the women and 29 percent of the men), and that males were prejudiced against females (36 percent of the women and 25 percent of the men). That women had a break in service for child bearing and rearing (11 percent of the women and 16 percent of the men) and had to look after their husbands and families were the next most frequently cited reasons. Women (20 percent) and men (27 percent) still saw departmental regulations as discriminatory. In line with finding reported earlier, 21 percent of the women and 16 percent of the men suggested that women were not given the chance to get experience or were not encouraged to apply for promotion.

Most of the respondents who gave reasons why women were not discriminated against cited regulations as being far and equal (47 percent of the women and 45 percent of the men) or that the facts showed that there was no discrimination or that they themselves had never known of any (51 percent of the women and 40 percent of the men). A small group used women's family commitments or past discrimination as a reason, and a very small number cited male biological superiority.

Conclusions

This national study has drawn attention to sex-based differences in participation in government-funded teacher retraining programs and in self-selected further studies which have clearly given male teachers an advantage in seeking promotion. These inequalities must be rectified.

Discriminatory practices and perceptions that result in significantly lower experience in administrative tasks among junior women teachers than among men should be exposed and contested wherever equal opportunity legislation exists. Finally, arrangements which allow males as well as females after-school time commitments, must become more commonplace. Only then will large numbers of younger women be able to advance to more senior positions in Australian educational systems.

References

ILEA (Inner London Education Authority) (1984). *Women's Careers in Teaching: Survey of Teachers' Views.* Research and Statistics Report, January. London: Inner London Education Authority.

OECD (Organization for Economic Cooperation and Development) (1977). *Women in the Economy: Australia.* Paris: Organization for Economic Cooperation and Development.

Sunday Times (1985). "Principals' Wives Meet." Perth: Western Australian Newspapers Pty. Ltd., 14 April 1985.

Sydney University Graduate Employment Survey (1985). Sydney, Australia.

Chapter 3

New Zealand Women Teachers: Career and Promotion Prospects

PENNY FENWICK

This chapter is based on a study of women teachers' career patterns in the primary and secondary schools of New Zealand which are the core of the state education system. The major findings of the study are set within the context of women's history as teachers in New Zealand. The chapter concludes with some indications of trends in women's appointment to senior teaching positions and some predictions regarding the future of teaching as a career for women.

Primary Education

The primary service in New Zealand provides for the education of children from about five to thirteen years of age. In 1984 the total state primary-school population of 446,309 was spread among 2,326 primary schools which ranged in size from one-teacher rural schools with as few as nine pupils to large intermediate schools with more than 800 pupils and 30 teachers. These pupils were taught by some 18,307 state primary-school teachers, 66 percent of whom were women. The types of schools constituting the primary service were full primary schools (infants to form 2), contributing schools (infants to standard 4), and intermediate schools (forms 1 and 2).[1] Primary schools are administered by ten education boards, which are also responsible for the appointment of staff to those schools. A majority of education board members are elected community representatives.

For at least twenty years, a Teachers College Certificate has been a prerequisite for permanent appointment to the primary service. Gone are the days when a primary teacher was trained by a master teacher or by the apprenticeship method, that is by teaching alongside another, experienced teacher. Almost all applicants for teacher training are interviewed, and since 1959 there has been an understanding that at least one member of the interviewing panel will be a woman. Primary teacher training usually comprises a three-year course at a teachers' college, and an increasing number of primary trainees undertake concurrent university courses. After graduation a wide variety of in-service and refresher courses are available, as well as some opportunities for specialist university courses.

The career structure in the primary service consists of six basic positions: Year 1 teacher, Scale A teacher, Senior Teacher, Senior Teacher of Junior Classes (STJC), deputy principal, and principal. The allocation of these positions to a school is determined by its grade, which in turn is dependent on its roll size. Thus, while all schools have a principal, a certain size must be reached before deputy principal or STJC positions can be designated. The grading (and salary) of the three senior positions is determined by the size of the school.

On completion of a teachers' college course, a graduate receives the Teachers College Certificate and is placed in a year 1 position by the education board, and after a year's successful teaching is awarded a Trained Teachers Certificate, which makes her or him eligible to be appointed to a permanent (scale A) position. After five years of service in a scale A position, the teacher may apply for assessment by an inspector and use the assessment to win a senior teacher's position. After twelve years of certified service and a minimum of three years in a senior teacher's position, teachers can apply for reassessment and try to win a deputy principal or principal's position. Further advancement (for example, to principal of a large intermediate) is ususally by interview.

The primary service in New Zealand includes many small, rural schools. To ensure a supply of teachers for these schools, a country service bar used to operate within the primary promotion structure. A teacher had to spend between two and four years in such a school to be eligible to gain a senior teachers' position, although the bar was waived when the teacher reached the age of thirty. Although this bar was abolished in late 1980, it may well have had a detrimental effect on the careers of many women teachers, who were made ineligible for promotion by their immobility.

Unpaid maternity leave for a total of twelve months is available for women teachers, and their positions must be held for them while they take this leave.

Secondary Education

The state secondary service in New Zealand comprised 215,819 students in 315 schools taught by 12,574 teachers. The two major types of schools in the secondary service are coeducational and single-sex schools, which cater to pupils from form 3 to form 7. The service also includes forms 1 to 7 schools. While secondary schools are not as remotely located as some of the small rural primaries, in 1984 they did range from a mere 214 pupils and 10 teachers to about 2,000 pupils and 100 teachers.

Previously, many teachers entered the secondary service with university degrees or trade qualifications but with no formal teacher training. However, in recent years most teachers entering the service have completed a secondary teachers' college course. The secondary-teaching career structure consists of nine levels: assistant teacher (scales A and B), position of responsibility (PR) 1, PR2, PR3, PR4, senior master or mistress, deputy principal, and principal. As in the primary service, the number of senior positions in the school depends upon its size. Most secondary schools are headed by a senior administrative group made up of the principal, the deputy principal, and the senior master or mistress.

In 1973 the position designated "senior assistant mistress" in coeducational schools (always held by a woman, to ensure that there was a woman in the top three positions to deal with "girls' discipline and welfare") was abolished in favor of the unisex senior master or mistress position. This move was intended to open up all positions in the hierarchy to either women or men, but it was still the expectation (though not a regulation) that there would be at least one woman in the senior administrative group in a coeducational schools.

Upon graduation from a teachers' college, a teacher is classified in list A and holds that classification for a minimum of two years. Following satisfactory assessement, a teacher may apply for a list B (tenured) position, after three years in list B she or he can apply for a PR1 or PR2 position, and after five years in list B (or one year in a PR1 or PR2 position) she or he can apply for a PR3 or PR4 position. A senior master or mistress or deputy principal's position can be won after seven years in list B service. To apply for a principals's position, a teacher must have completed eleven years of list B service and hold either a deputy principal or senior master or mistress position.

Historical Perspective[2]

New Zealand's white settlers were predominantly from wage-earning British backgrounds, and it has been argued that "the absence of a strong middle class weakened the impact of the view that women should not be in occupations..."[3] The first schools established by the European missionaries taught both girls and boys. In 1877 education was made free, secular, and compulsory for all girls and boys seven to thirteen years of age. Schooling in general, and schooling for girls in particular, was thus much more widespread than in Britain at this time. Moreover, women were often the teachers in these early primary schools. The first Annual Report of the Minister of Education in 1878 reported that 41 percent of teachers were women. Secondary-school development in New Zealand was slower, and until the twentieth centery was largely confined to those who could afford the fees. Where it did exist, however, there is strong evidence that the curriculum for both sexes was very similar. There were close connections between the women who campaigned for women's suffrage and those who championed the cause of schooling (especially secondary schooling) for girls.

Upon its establishment in 1871, the first New Zealand university admitted women, and early graduates such as Kate Edgar and Helen Connon went on to become principals of girls' secondary schools. Both women combined their teaching careers with marriage and families.[4] From the late 1880s, however, "domestic science" was increasingly promoted as the proper learning for girls, first at the university level, then gradually in the secondary and primary-service curricula. Sex differentiation crept into other subjects of the curriculum and was responsible for a decline in girls' participation in mathematics and science.[5]

This sexism had its effect on the position of women teachers as well. In 1920 women constituted 40 percent of the principals of state secondary schools and nearly 50 percent of the principals of state primary schools. In 1984 the proportions were 15 percent and 14 percent, respectively. What is the explanation for this reversal of women's strength in the teaching services? The Teacher Career and Promotion Study was conducted to answer this question.

Background to the Teacher Career and Promotion Study

It was inevitable that the reawakened feminist movement of the late 1960s and early 1970s would focus attention on sexism in education. In New Zealand that sexism was very obvious: teaching, it was said, was "a good career for women," and classroom teachers, especially in the primary service, were predominantly women. Yet, decision-making positions in education were held predominantly by men.

Campaigns were waged against overt sex discrimination, and in 1975 court action overturned the ruling that married women teachers were ineligible for removal expenses when taking up a promotion position, thus removing one of the last formal discriminatory regulations. In the same year, however, an Education Amendment Act was passed to cope with an "oversupply" of primary service teachers. It decreed that all those who had not been employed as teachers for three years or more were required to undertake a three months' retraining course before they could regain a tenured position. Those affected were almost exclusively women who had broken their careers for family reasons.

A number of small-scale studies were undertaken which focused on the absence of women from decision-making positions in both services.[6] It was argued that this invisibility of women not only reflected a lack of opportunities for women teachers, but also affected the climate of schools and in particular the aspirations of young women passing through the school system.

Women in the secondary service also felt that the freeing of sex distinctions was working to their advantage. Two particular examples were cited. First, girls' schools had previously been a stronghold of women's educational influence, but men seemed to be increasingly taking over even the senior positions in these schools. The second concern related to the decision to abolish the senior assistant mistress position. Rather than opening up deputy principal and principal positions to women (as had been the intention), it seemed that this unisex position was providing yet another career slot for men, with the result that an increasing number of coeducational schools were without a woman in a senior decision-making position.

In November 1975 the Department of Education and a government advisory body, the Committee on Women, jointly sponsored a conference on women in education which gave consideration to women's career opportunities within teaching.[7] Conference participants were concerned that the prevailing explanation for women's absence from senior positions was that "women don't apply because they don't want to take responsibility." The small studies which had been undertaken indicated that the explanation was much more complex, and the conference recommended further research.

In January 1979 the Teacher Career and Promotion Study began. It was undertaken by the Department of Education in conjunction with the primary and secondary teachers' unions and the National

Advisory Committee on Women in Education.[8] After some background investigations of the research literature and available statistics, a four-phase study was completed. The phases were as follows:

1. Forty-eight case-study interviews with women and men primary and secondary teachers. These teachers were chosen to represent a wide range of positions, and their responses were used in part to frame the questionnaire for phase 4.

2. A statistical analysis of the position of women in primary teaching, including a study of the data on assessments and applications for senior positions.

3. A statistical analysis of the position of women in secondary teaching, including a study of data on applications for senior positions.

4. A national survey of a representative sample of 1,829 primary and secondary teachers (about 5 percent of the teaching force at that time). The design of the study was influenced by relevant overseas work, especially the work of Gross and Trask (1976) and the study by the National Union of Teachers in Britain (1980).[9] While the concerns were similar, the study was designed to meet the uniquely New Zealand circumstances.

Findings of the Teacher Career and Promotion Study[10]

The motivation and design of the study reflected a desire to test the validity of the traditional argument that women do not achieve senior positions because their first commitment is to home and family, not to their career. In response, the study's findings led to the conclusion that no one factor was responsible for the relative absence of women from decision-making positions in the primary and secondary services.

Career Patterns

Woman's and men's careers (for primary and secondary services separately) were placed alongside the model career path. It was shown that men's careers were more likely to match the model than women's, and that this was so to a greater extent in the primary than in the secondary service. In the primary service, women entered teaching at a younger age than men, were as well qualified at this stage but gained fewer qualifications later, and were considerably more likely to have an interruption in service (and a longer interruption), to make family-related rather than promotion-related moves, to be much less likely to apply for promotion, and to be less successful when they did.

Findings in the secondary service presented a modified version of the differences in the primary. The younger age at entry for women was confirmed, but in the secondary service women were more poorly qualified at entry but more likely to gain qualifications after entry. More secondary women than men had moved, and more women than men had had a break in service. While secondary women made even more family-related moves than primary women, both sexes in the secondary service made a higher number of personal moves than their primary counterparts. The sex differences in the rates of application for promotion were not as prominent in the secondary service, but frequent application was again a male pattern. When they did apply, however, secondary women had the highest success rate of all four sample groups.

The traditional argument that women are family oriented rather than career oriented appeared to be confirmed by these data. However, this conclusion was tested by removing from the analysis women who had had a service break for family reasons. When the remaining women, with at least five year's service, were compared with men with comparable service, substantially the same sex differences remained. Clearly, factors other than a break for child rearing alone were causing the disproportionately small number of women in senior positions.

Career Constraints

An assessment was made of the importance of family and personal constraints on teachers' careers and of whether these constraints affected women and men differently. Gender differences in the impact of regulations were also investigated.

Fewer women than men teachers in both services had children living at home, and fewer women than men had preschool children. Many men, but few women in senior positions, had children living at home. Women teachers in both services were considerably more likely than men teachers to be unhappy with the way responsibility for domestic tasks was allocated in their home. This was especially the case where the women felt they were responsible for all domestic chores (14 percent of the primary women and 18 percent of the secondary women). There was some indication that women from households with an equitable sharing of domestic tasks achieved senior positions more readily, but the allocation of these tasks appeared to have no impact on men's achievement. Women primary teachers identified fewer family and personal constraints on their careers than did primary men, while in the secondary service, the gender difference was reversed.

Another finding was that women expressed less concern than men about the regulations governing their careers and more often used informal sources of information (for instance, the principal or other teachers), while men relied on formal written sources.

Career Planning

Teachers were asked about the critical career decisions they had had to make, their future intentions about remaining in teaching, and the positions they aspired to hold. Women in both services seemed more settled in teaching in that they were less likely than men to have considered leaving and apply for other jobs.

However, women were much likely than men to say they would leave within ten years for family reasons. Only four men in the entire sample predicted that they would leave teaching within ten years for family reasons. All were in untenured positions. Women's aspiration level in the primary service was markedly lower than men's. Their most common aspiration was to be a principal. In the secondary service, women's aspiration level was again lower than men's, but not as markedly so. The more senior the position the teacher held, the more confident she or he was about her or his future in teaching.

Visibility

It is recognized that there are also "push" factors that affect promotion—in the case factors which promote teachers in the eyes of those with control over teachers' careers. They study sought to determine whether women or men teachers were more likely to be noticed by such people.

It had been suggested that involvement in the primary or secondary teachers' union was associated with career advancement. Fewer women than men in both services belonged to their union, and of those who did belong there was a marked tendency for men to be more heavily involved than women, especially in the primary service. Moreover, women were less likely than men to see involvement in the union as a means of career advancement.

In-service training courses are other places where teachers can be "noticed" by those responsible for promotions. Fewer women than men had been to the prestigious national residential courses, but equal numbers of both sexes had attended school-based and nonresidential courses.

As with other professions, individual teachers do not make career decisions alone. Almost all follow their career paths in an environment of encouragement or discouragement from colleagues, seniors, and partners. Fewer women than men in the primary service reported receiving encouragement to apply for promotion or gain additional qualifications; in the secondary service, the gender difference was the reverse. Women in senior positions in both services were more likely to have received encouragement than men in senior positions. In both services, neither sex was more likely to have been discouraged from applying for a position, but secondary women in senior positions reported much less discouragement than secondary women in general.

Sexism

It was recognized by participants at the 1975 conference which initiated the Teacher Career and Promotion Study that while steps could be taken to remove the obviously sex-discriminatory regulations, a social climate still existed in which more subtle forms of discrimination operated to keep women in lower positions. The question must be posed whether there remains a set of attitudes which make it difficult for those responsible for appointing teachers to senior positions to visualize a woman in the principal's position. Do they still see a male teacher as having a greater commitment to a teaching career than a female teacher? Do men and women teachers also find it hard to visualize women in senior positions?

Teachers were asked about their attitude to women in senior positions. Women were most likely to say they were "strongly in favor": this was the response of half of primary women and two-thirds of the secondary. Fewer than half the men in each service were in favor of women in senior positions, and the majority said they were "neutral." One in eight of the men in the study stated categorically that he would not be prepared to teach at a school with a woman principal.

In the primary service, women in senior positions were more favorably included to women holding such positions than primary women in general. In the secondary service, men in senior positions were more favorably included than men in general. Younger men in the primary service were more supportive of women holding senior positions, and in both services younger men and women were happier about teaching at a school with a woman principal.

Conclusions

The Teacher Career and Promotion Study explored many of the arguments commonly raised in answer to the question, "Why don't more women achieve senior positions in the teaching services?" Some of the study's findings appear to confirm the traditional arguments that women have a stronger commitment to their family than to their career, do not aspire to hold senior positions, and do not know about, or make themselves visible in, the promotion system. To focus on these findings, however, is to ignore other findings which lead to different conclusions. Most important are those regarding how women fare within the system of promotions. No teacher pursues a career in isolation—all are encouraged or discouraged by peers, relatives, and senior teachers and administrators. There is evidence from this study that the present system does not treat women as well as it treats men.

There is evidence, too, of sexism and prejudice towards women among teachers. While efforts have been made to remove all the sex-discriminatory regulations, it appears that some men, though very few women, are opposed to women holding senior positions. If encouragement and support are crucial to more women achieving senior positions, as the Teacher Career and Promotion Study has indicated they are, then it would appear that women are more likely to find that support among other women, and in the primary service at least, among younger men.

Developments Since the Study[11]

Information from the Teacher Career and Promotion Study was made widely available through the occasional papers released in the course of the research, presentation of the results in a large number of in-service courses for teachers, women and management seminars, and other similar forums. Presentations were also made to teams of inspectors and Department of Education officials. One outcome of the study was the establishment of several annual research exercises to monitor progress in the movement of women into senior teaching positions. Five years after the Teacher Career and Promotion Survey, it is appropriate to study the results of this activity as they are reflected in the statistics.

Number of Women in Senior Positions

Table 1 shows that in the primary service there has been some progress with the movement of women into senior positions. A steadily increasing proportion of principals are women—5 percent in 1979 and 14 percent in 1984. The increased number of women deputy principals is even more evident: 12 percent in 1979 and 31 percent in 1984. Put differently, in 1979 2 percent of women primary-service teachers were principals or deputy principals, while in 1984 7 percent held either of these positions. However, while this progress is important, it still remains true that men in the primary service are far more likely to hold decision-making positions than women, and in fact the proportion of men holding either principal or deputy principal positions increased during this time: from 44 percent in 1979 to 50 percent in 1984.

There is some evidence from table 1 that the numbers of women entering senior positions may have slowed over the last two years. An important complicating factor during the early 1980s was the integration of private schools into the state system. Many of these small religious schools are headed by women (usually Catholic sisters). An assessment of the influence of integration on these statistics would require a special research exercise. Obviously, continued monitoring of the statistics is essential.

Table 2 shows the distribution for the secondary service and a similar, though less marked, movement of women into senior positions. By 1984, 15 percent of principals were women, compared with 10 percent in 1978. For deputy principal positions the figures were 20 percent in 1984 and 14 percent in 1978. Not shown on the table is the slowly, but steadily, increasing proportions of women in the deputy principal role occupying PR3 (usually head of department) positions. However, women teachers' concerned with the fate of the senior master or mistress position is justified by these figures. The proportion of these positions held by women continues to decline—from 67 percent in 1978 to 60 percent in 1984, although 1984 figures show a slight increase over 1983. The effect of the decline in senior master or mistress positions held by women is to offset women's gain in principal and deputy principal positions, so that the proportion of senior administrative positions held by women showed virtually no change between 1978 (30 percent) and 1984 (31.4 percent).

Applications for Promotion

Obviously, increased numbers of women cannot be appointed to senior positions unless women increase their application rate. The Teacher Career and Promotion Study showed that women had a lower application rate than men, and women's application rates have

Table 1. Distribution of Women in Primary Teaching Service, New Zealand, 1979–84

	1979		1981		1982		1983		1984	
	# women	% women	# women	% women	# women	% women	# women	% women	# women	% women
Principal	101	4.7	171	7.9	230	10.2	284	12.2	317	13.7
Deputy principal	126	12.2	290	22.9	380	27.1	434	29.5	462	30.8
Senior teacher of junior classes	789	85.4	764	87.6	785	87.9	771	88.2	766	88.9
Senior teacher	1,105	53.1	1,238	56.2	1,264	56.9	1,281	58.3	1,222	57.8
Scale A teacher	7,826	78.2	7,923	80.1	7,806	80.7	8,079	81.3	7,974	81.2
Year 1 teacher	1,484	78.8	1,199	80.0	1,206	80.9	1,236	83.2	1,083	84.5
Total	11,431	63.2	11,585	64.8	11,671	65.1	12,085	66.1	11,824	66.2

1979: Data derived from the teachers' payroll on March 1.
1981: Data derived from the teachers' payroll on March 1.
1982: Data derived from the teachers' payroll on March 17.
1983: Data derived from the teachers' payroll on May 10.
1984: Data derived from the teachers' payroll on May 23.

Table 2. Distribution of Women in Secondary Teaching Service, New Zealand, 1978–84

	1978		1981		1982		1983		1984	
	# women	% women	# women	% women	# women	% women	# women	% women	# women	% women
Principal	26	10.2	32	11.2	36	11.9	43	13.7	50	15.3
Deputy principal	39	14.0	46	16.6	54	17.9	54	17.1	66	20.4
Senior master or mistress	181	66.8	175	62.7	182	61.7	175	58.5	187	59.6
PR4	23	11.8	22	11.6	24	12.8	23	12.2	24	13.0
PR3	83	11.6	103	13.8	113	14.6	121	15.7	128	15.9
PR2	420	24.0	430	24.9	487	26.1	499	26.2	548	26.8
PR1	239	35.4	300	37.8	329	37.3	348	37.9	388	38.9
Assistant teacher	3,023	45.9	3,272	47.4	3,339	47.1	3,345	47.4	3,479	48.2

1978: Data derived from E2/5 (secondary staffing) returns (1979 data unavailable).
1981: Data derived from teachers' payroll on March 1.
1982: Data derived from teachers' payroll on March 17.
1983: Data derived from teachers' payroll on May 10.
1984: Data derived from teachers' payroll on May 23.

been monitored since the study was undertaken. In both the primary and secondary services, there has been a decline in the number of positions advertised because of a decline in teacher turnover. The figures for the primary service shown in table 3 show a marked increase in women's application rate—from 20 percent of applicants in 1979 to 30 percent in 1983.[12] Again, there is some indication that the rate of increase may be tapering off.

Table 3. Women Applicants for Primary-Service Positions, New Zealand, 1979–83

Year	Number of women applicants	Number of total applicants	% women
1979	2,324	11,806	19.7
1980	2,930	10,925	26.8
1981	2,474	9,507	26.0
1982	3,433	11,454	30.0
1983	3,317	10,978	30.2

Source: Joy Vasbenter, Sex Differences in Applicants for and Appointees to Senior Primary Teaching Positions, 1983 (Department of Education, March, 1984).

As in all the years for which data are available, women in 1983 had a higher success rate than men, when success is calculated as the proportion of appointees to applicants for each sex. Twelve percent of the women but only 7 percent of the men were successful in applications for B positions. For C positions the proportions were 7 percent and 4 percent, respectively.

To assess whether there has been a decline in the sex stereotyping of positions, particular interest has been taken in the number of positions for which only women or only men applied. Such a decline appears to have occurred: in 1979, 24 percent of positions were applied for only by men and 18 percent by women. By 1983, these figures had declined to 11 percent and 9 percent respectively.

Analysis undertaken during the Teacher Career and Promotion Study showed that, for the 1978 figures, women in the secondary service were less likely to apply for positions than men, but more likely to be appointed when they did apply. Table 4 shows these figures and also those for a replication study undertaken in 1984 with 1983 data. Overall, in 1983 women constituted 30 percent of the applicants for senior positions, an increase from 20 percent in 1978. The proportion of appointees who were women increased from 30 percent in 1978 to

37 percent in 1983. Of the women who applied, 44 percent were successful, compared with 32 percent of the men who applied. However, the sex difference in success rates declined between 1978 and 1983.

Table 4. Women Applicants for Secondary-Service Positions, New Zealand, 1978 and 1983

Year	% applicants who were women	% appointees who were women	% success rate Women	Men
1978	19.5	30.0	54.2	30.6
1983	29.6	36.6	44.3	32.2

Source: Helen Norman, Sex Differences in Applicants for and Appointees to Senior Secondary Teaching Positions, 1983 (Department of Education, June, 1984).

Internal appointment (appointment of an applicant, who is already on the staff of the school in which the vacancy occurs) had always been a feature of the secondary service, and the proportion of appointments which were internal increased over the period under review: from 73 percent in 1978 to 81 percent in 1983. In both years, women were more likely than men to be appointed through an internal appointment.

Table 5 shows that women have increased their rate of application for all types of schools, including single-sex boys' schools. Sex differences in success rates were most obvious at single-sex schools, and even at boys' schools women's success rate was considerably above men's

Table 5. Women Applicants and Appointees by Type of Secondary School, New Zealand, 1978 and 1983

Type of School	% applicants who were women		% appointees who were women		% success rate (1983)	
	1978	1983	1978	1983	Women	Men
Coeducational	17.9	27.0	27.2	31.8	39.8	31.6
Single-sex boys	5.1	8.2	5.0	11.1	52.4	37.4
Single-sex girls	59.5	70.7	78.0	85.1	54.1	22.7

Source: Helen Norman. Sex Differences in Appointments for and Opportunities to Senior Secondary Teaching Positions, 1983. (Department of Education, June, 1984).

Predictions for the Future

The Teacher Career and Promotion Study suggested that rather than seek to refine the explanation for women's absence from senior teaching positions, methods of intervention in the problem should be tried and evaluated. Acceptance of this suggestion would mean, at the very least, the adoption of an affirmative action policy. Instead, the climate in which the slight increases in women's movement into senior teaching positions has occurred has, if anything, been discouraging to women.

Not long after the study was published, the National Advisory Committee on Women in Education was disbanded by the Minister of Education and the position of education officer for women within the Department of Education was abolished. The conservative economic and social climate of the early 1980s has been characterised by a backlash against women (especially married women) in paid employment. In such a climate, the increases in senior positions held by women teachers may be more remarkable than the figures would indicate.

However, the minimal movement during 1978-1983 suggests very strongly that much more than a laissez-faire approach is needed if women teachers are to have equality of opportunity. The Teacher Career and Promotion Study suggested intervention in "the problem." But has the problem been appropriately identified? Part of the reason for encouraging women to seek senior administrative positions in the teaching services is to provide opportunities for female (and at times feminist) perspectives to be brought to bear on educational decision making at the school, regional, and national levels. Should women (or for that matter, men) teachers have to achieve a senior position in the school hierarchy before they can have any influence over the educational administration and policy making? The hierarchical nature of the promotion system was not challenged by the Teacher Career and Promotion STudy. Perhaps women teachers in the future will take up that challenge.

Notes

1. Up to about age ten, children are enrolled in *standards*; after that they go to *forms*. They move from standard 4 to form 1.

2. A comprehensive history of women teachers in New Zealand has yet to be written. Very little statistical data are available, and there are minimal descriptive analyses. As with most of New Zealand's written history, the perspective in this section is inherently pekeha. The educational practices of

Maori people, the tangatawhenua of Aotearoa, and to some extent the importance of Maori women in the education of their people have been documented by the pakeha. A Maori perspective on Maori women teachers remains to be written.

3. W.B. Sutch, *Women with a Cause* (Wellington: Price Milburn, 1974), 71.

4. See Beryl Hughes, "Women and the Professions in New Zealand," pp. 118–138 in Phillida Bunkle and Beryl Hughes (eds.), *Women in New Zealand Society* (Sydney: George Allen and Unwin, 1980).

5. See Geraldine McDonald, "Education and the Movement Towards Equality," pp. 139–158 in Bunkle and Hughes, *Women in New Zealand Society*.

6. Florence Mayo, "How Far Can Women Go?" *NZPPTA Journal* (June, 1970), pp. 15–16; Leonore Webster, "Women as Teachers," *NZPPTA Journal* (May, 1975); Margaret Malcolm, "The Almost Invisible Woman," *Set 78*, number 2, item 12 (Wellington: New Zealand Council for Educational Research, 1978).

7. Department of Education, *Education and the Equality of the Sexes* Wellington: Government Printing Office, 1976).

8 A research advisory committee was established which included representatives of the Department of Education, the New Zealand Educational Institute (the primary teachers' union), the New Zealand Post-Primary Teachers Association (the secondary teachers' union), the National Advisory Committee on Women in Education, and the New Zealand Council for Educational Research. Judy Whitcombe and Penny Fenwick acted in turn as principal researchers for the project.

9. N. Gross and A.E. Trask, *The Sex Factor and the Management of Schools* (New York: Wiley, 1976); National Union of Teachers, *Promotion and the Woman Teacher* (NUT and Equal Oportunities Commission, Wellington, 1980).

10. The approval of the Department of Education for the use of data arising from the Teacher Career and Promotion Study is gratefully acknowledged. Interpretations and conclusions drawn from the data remain the responsibility of the author.

11. The assistance of Department of Education officers, in particular Mr. Bob Garden and Mr. Ron Ross, in obtaining up-to-date statistics is gratefully acknowledged.

Photo from the New York State Archives

Chapter 4

Women School Employees in the United States

PATRICIA A. SCHMUCK

In colonial America, before the United States was founded, the teaching of basic skills in reading, writing, and arithmetic was the task of women, and was carried out by wives and mothers at home or by women working with groups of youngsters in neighborhood dame schools. Some towns offered fees to successful teachers who would offer their services regularly to the youngest children. In 1682, for example, the town of Springfield, Massachusetts, contracted with "Goodwife Mirick to encourage her in the good work of training up the children, and teaching the children to read, and that she should have three pence a week for every child that she takes to perform this good work for " (Kerber, 1980, p. 3). Both girls and boys attended the same schools, but the next level of education, the grammar school, was intended primarily for boys, who were taught by a male schoolmaster. Although there were some isolated examples of women teaching grammar schools in colonial America, most formal contractual agreements were with men hired to teach boys seven years or older. At the time the United States was formally constituted in 1776, it was not considered appropriate nor desirable to hire women as teachers except for the very youngest children.

That attitude reversed itself completely when the industrialization of the eastern seaboard and the movement of pioneers westward created so many employment opportunities for men that schools could no longer attract enough males. Many new social forces were at work in the mid-nineteenth century: industrial employment with higher pay lured schoolmasters away from teaching, urban schools were growing rapidly with the press for "common schools", and there was an influx of both rural Americans and non-English-speaking immigrants into urban centers. All this created a need for literate English speakers in the schools. The only population that fit that social need was women; thus what was once inappropriate became socially desirable. School teaching became a good exercise for the young and unmarried female because it provided excellent training for the care of children, thus preparing her for her "natural" destiny of wife and mother. It was also cost efficient; women earned less than men. And it provided lifelong employment for the less fortunate woman who would not be chosen to be someone's wife.

Teacher-training institutions were established to fill this need, and all women's higher education was in these institutes. Mary Lyon in 1937, when laying out the plan for Mount Holyoke Female Seminary, claimed that its purpose was to "furnish a supply of female teachers." The call to teach, according to Lyon, as to all women. "Teaching is really the business of almost every useful woman. If there are any to whom this does not apply, they may be considered as exceptions to the general rule. Of course, no female is well educated who has not all the acquisitions necessary for a good teacher" (Goodsell, 1931, pp. 278–303). Many of these young women left the proper and secure teacher institutes in the East and traveled west to face the unknown challenges of the barely developed communities in the Midwest and the West. Paulie Kaufman's book, *Women Teachers on the Frontier*, (1984) vividly illustrates the difficulties faced by young women in responding to their calling as teachers. The shift in the sex composition of the teaching force is an interesting social phenomenon. What was once the province of men and inappropriate for women became, within only a few years, women's second-highest calling. Their first calling, of course, remained that of wife and mother.

The shift from the production of the agrarian society to the consumption of the industrial society changed the portrait of the educational world. Teaching was one of the few occupations, other than domestic service or work in the textile mills, open to women. By 1860 a majority of teachers were women. Indeed, since that time women have always outnumbered men as employees of schools. In 1870 women constituted 66 percent of all teachers; in 1900, 70 percent; and in 1920, 85 percent. In 1983 women returned to their earlier proportions: 67 percent (National Education Association, 1983). See table 1.

Of black teachers, about 50 percent were women in 1900 (Collier-Thomas, 1982). Black women, especially in the south, became a major force in the segregated educational system. Black men, like white men, were lured away from teaching by more lucrative employment opportunities.

Table 1. Male and Female Elementary and Secondary Teachers, in Public and Private Schools in United States, by Number and Placement, 1929–83

	Male teachers		Female teachers	
Year	Number	% of total	Number	% of total
1929–30[a]	154,983	16.3	795,178	83.7
1939–40	212,084	21.6	769,182	78.4
1949–50	221,635	21.2	823,590	78.8
1959–60	430,436	27.8	1,119,314	72.2
1969–70	1,140,860	40.6	1,669,243	59.4
1975–76	1,399,600	43.1	1,846,740	56.9
1979–80[b]	607,839	37.5	1,164,181	62.5
1982–83[c]	683, 162	31.9	1,455,410	68.1

a. *Source:* W.V. Grant and Leo J. Eiden, *Digest of Education Statistics* (Washington, D.C.: National Center for Educational Statistics, 1982), p. 11.

b. *Source:* Equal Employment Opportunities Commission, *Minorities and Women in Public Elementary and Secondary Schools.* Reduction in numbers is due to report on public schools only; private schools are not included.

c. *Source:* National Education Association, *Estimate of School Statistics* (Washington, D.C., National Education Association, 1982–83).

In 1938 the ranks of women teachers were so full that Frances Donovan, a journalist, captured the stereotype of the teacher in a delightful book, *The School Ma'am,* in which she described the life of a young unmarried woman who left her nuclear family to teach in rural communities. This young woman was hired by the local school board and usually lived with a local family, who undertook to ensure that their school teacher was the proper, upright, and moral person to direct their children's education.

In 1974 I interviewed Lucille Brunskill, a member of that early cohort of women teachers and typical of the school marms depicted by Donovan in the 1930s. Brunskill entered teaching as an unmarried female in the 1930s in a small town in Oregon. As if it had happened yesterday, she vividly recounted her first job. She was not allowed to smoke or drink and was granted only one free weekend a month. She taught students, reported to the school board, kept the budget, and maintained the building. She stayed in education and retired as one of the highest-ranking females in the largest school district in Oregon. Upon her retirement, like other members of her cohort, she was replaced by a man.

In the 1940s another dramatic shift in ideology occurred. Married women were finally permitted to teach school. Because men were serving in the armed forces during World War II, married women who had been teachers were called back into educational service. Thus again, an accepted notion was laid to rest. The idea that teaching was best for the young, unmarried woman was replaced by another idea—that for married women, teaching was an especially suitable profession. The long summer months and the daytime teaching hours permitted women to successfully integrate both family and professional commitments. And many of these women became school administrators and their retirement saw no new cohort of women to replace them. Most of the women who had returned to teaching during World War II remained and advanced in their profession. But when they retired, they were replaced by men.

Elementary School Teachers:The Changing Sex Composition

Shifts in the sex composition of teachers are most clearly visible in elementary schools. What was once women's place—as far back as the dame schools in early America—has been increasingly populated by men since their return from service in World War II. In 1929 men were 10 percent of all teachers in elementary schools, and by 1981 they were up to 17 percent. (table 2). These figures, however, do not fully account for the male presence in the elementary schools. When one includes other nonsupervisory personnel, the proportion of men has risen from 21 percent in 1949 to 33 percent in 1974. (table 3). And male principals of elementary schools have increased from 59 percent in 1949 to 87 percent in 1983 (Pharis, 1975, p. 5; NEA, 1983, p. 29). Whereas women elementary teachers by and large remain elementary teachers, men in elementary classrooms move on to other positions. In this analysis of the American schoolteacher, Lortie, a sociologist of education, describes teaching for men as but one step in a sequence of career moves; for women, teaching is a job with little or no advancement. (1975).

Table 2. Male Elementary Teachers in Public Schools, United States, 1929–81

Year	Total number of teachers	% male
1929–30	640,957	10.5
1939–40	575,200	11.7
1949–50	589,578	9.0
1959–60	833,772	14.1
1969–70	1,126,467	15.6
1973–74	1,175,980	16.7
1980–81	1,186,000	16.9

Sources: For 1929–74: W.V. Grant and C.G. Lind, *Digest of Education Statistics (Washington, D.C.: National Center for Education Statistics, 1979), p. 11.* For 1980–81: W.V. Grant and Leo J. Eiden, Digest of Education Statistics* (Washington, .C.: National Center for Education Statistics, 1982), p. 52.

Note: Figures for the Years before 1959–60 do not include Alaska and Hawaii.

Table 3. Male Teachers, Librarians, and Other Nonsupervisory Instructional Staff in Elementary Schools, United States, 1969–74

Year	% male
1869– 70	38.7
1879– 80	42.8
1889– 90	34.5
1899–1900[a]	29.9
1909– 10	21.1
1919– 20	14.1
1929– 30	16.6
1939– 40	22.2
1949– 50	21.3
1959– 60	29.0[b]
1969– 70	32.4[b]
1973– 74[c]	33.5[b]

Source: W.V. Grant and C.G. Lind, *Digest of Education Statistics (Washington, D.C.: National Center for Education Statistics, 1979), p. 38.*

a. *Most schools in the United States prior to 1900 were elementary buildings.*

b. *Estimated by the National Center for Education Statistics.*

c. *The 1980–81 Digest of Education Statistics* does not give comparable information about male staff in elementary schools, thus information is not available beyond 1974.

Active efforts to encourage men to enter elementary teaching have been successful. Indeed, some analyses have been written to show the destructive consequences of the "all-female world" of the elementary school. Perhaps the most flagrant example of this point of view is Patricia Sexton's charge that schools are emasculating our boys and that the woman teacher is to blame (1973). This antiwoman voice was joined by a chorus of voices, such as the American Association of Elementary, Kindergarten and Nursery Educators, who unanimously resolved and believed "that . . . . children, especially those brought up without a father in the home, need a male image" and strongly urged "the recruitment of more male teachers in elementary classrooms" (Ellenburg, 1975; Shakeshaft, 1982).

The effort to bring more men into elementary teaching has been successful. And as more men enter elementary classrooms, the inducement for other men to enter the field increases. Males today do not acquire the negative stigma of doing "womens' work" by teaching younger children. As one male put it: "It's more acceptable for a man to go into education. They now can make more salary and there is a professionalism about the field. Men in schools, especially elementary schools, just don't bathe in lavendar water any more". (Schmuck, 1975, p. 90).

Secondary-School Teachers: An Internally Sex-Segregated System

In 1982-83 proportion of men and women at the secondary level of teaching in the United States was about equal; there were 51 percent males and 49 percent females in secondary education. The proportion of male teachers has increased over the years; in 1929 it was about 35 percent. (table 4).

Men who teach, however, are more often in secondary education, whereas women who teach are more often in elementary education. In 1982–83, 71 percent of all male teachers were in secondary schools and 67 percent of all female teachers were in elementary schools. Why do men who enter teaching most often enter secondary schools? The stereotype of women's work as caring for young children undoubtedly drives some men to work with older students. As in all Western countries, as one goes up the age-graded hierarchy of schooling, the proportion of men increases. Secondary teachers also have a subject matter specialty—they teach math or science or English. The specialization of subject matter is clearly sex segregated. Males

Table 4. Male and Female Teachers in U.S. Public High Schools, 1929-1

Year	Number of teachers	% male	% female
1929-30	213,306	34.9	65.1
1939-40	300,277	42.2	57.8
1949-50	324,093	43.8	56.2
1959-60	521,186	52.8	47.2
1969-70	896,786	53.5	46.5
1973-74	979,468	53.6	46.4
1980-81	997,500	51.1	48.9

Source: Adapted from W.V. Grant and C.G. Lind, *Digest of Education Statistics* (Washington, D.C.: National Center for Education Statistics 1979), p. 11.

Source: W.V. Grant and Leo J. Eiden, *Digest of Education Statistics*, (Washington, D.C.: National Center for Educational Statistics, 1982), p. 52.

predominate as teachers in science and math, classes, which also have a predominance of male students. In the vocational areas in the comprehensive high schools, men teahers predominate in areas which are also dominated by males in the occupational world. The sex segregation of secondary-school teachers is shown in table 6.

Table 5. Subjects Taught by Male and Female Teachers in Public Secondary Schools, United States, 1971

Subject	% male	% female
Home economics	0.0	100.0
Foreign language	26.5	73.5
Business education	33.3	66.7
English	35.4	64.6
Health and physical education	45.8	54.2
Art	46.1	53.9
Music	70.4	29.6
Social studies	76.8	23.2
Science	85.3	14.7
Industrial arts	95.4	4.6
Agriculture	100.0	0.0

Source: Adapted from National Education Association, *Status of the American Public School Teacher*, 1970-71, Research Report 1972-R3 (Washington, D.C.: National Education Association), p. 29. Differentiation by sex in subject matter taught is not available in the *Status of the American Public School Teacher, 1980-81*. Nor is such information available in other national data sources.

Wages are another reason for the differences between schools. Although pay differential between elementary and secondary schools is small, there are extra opportunities for increased pay in secondary schools that do not exist in elementary schools. The National Education Association (1983) gives the average salary for elementary teachers as $20,042 and for secondary teachers as $21,000. Coaching, department chair, or other quasi-administrative assignments earn extra pay, and these positions are most often held by men. The earning of men and women in education show salary differentials. Although women teachers can no longer be paid less than men teachers, there remain differences in the earnings of men and women. In 1961 the average salary was $5,568 for men and $5,120 for women. In 1981 (during the inflationary economy) the average salary was $18,473 for men and $16,558 for women. Whereas males increased their earning power by 178 percent, women increased it by only 172 percent (Bartholemew and Gardener, 1982, p. 80). In 1961 female teachers earned 92 percent of what male teachers earned; in 1978 this discrepency was increased to earning only 85 percent of what men earned (Butler, 1979).

So, although there appears to be an equitable division of males and females at the secondary level, further analysis shows inequity in the subjects taught, which in turn is directly related to inequities in the labor force.

Women as Administrators

Although women predominate as teachers in United States public schools, they are a distinct minority in administrative positions. In 1981–82 women constituted only 25 percent of all positions (Jones and Montenegro, 1981).

There are approximately 16,000 school districts in the United States. The United States Constitution leaves the education of its citizens up to the states; each state has a department of education which authorizes and certifies the local school districts. Although each district must abide by certain federal and state standards, there is a long history and a strong sentiment for local control of schools. Each local school district is relatively autonomous in determining the school curriculum and hiring its own personnel. It is governed by a local school board of elected officials, and each school district (except for the very small ones) has a superintendent who is responsible to the school board. Each school building has a principal, and often there are vice-principals in larger buildings, especially in the secondary schools. Thus one superintendent, several school principals and vice-principals, and teachers constitute the usual organizational structure of a district. Larger districts have additional staff personnel, usually located in the central office of a district; these may be associate superintendents, directors, or coordinators of services such as personnel, budget, curriculum, special education, and community relations. Districts vary considerably as to how these staff positions are organized.

The local autonomy of school districts has clear implications for the hiring of administrators. Although one must have state credentials to become an administrator, each school district writes its own job descriptions and hires its own personnel. There is considerable variation from district to district. Pay also varies; there are usually no statewide salary scales. An individual applies for a position within a district, and there is a great deal of mobility—especially for administrators—from one school district to another.

Many administrative positions are open every year, and each spring there is a flurry of job seeking, application, and hiring. For instance, in Oregon, which has about 300 different local school districts, 300 different administrative positions were open in 120 different districts in 1977–78. There were about 1,000 applications for these 300 positions (it should be noted that many people apply to more than one district, so these applications do not equal numbers of persons applying). Of those 1,000 applications, 19 percent were by women. Of those hired, 78 percent were men, who most often filled the positions of district superintendent and building principal. The 22 percent women hired most often became staff people providing coordinating and directing activities. The proportions of men and women hired that year in Oregon were generally the same as elsewhere across the country (Schmuck and Wyant, 1981). Table 7 shows the distribution of males and females in all administrative positions for the past decade in the United States.

Table 6. Male and Female Public School Administrators, United States, 1972–82

Position	1972–73[a]		1976–77[b]		1981–82[c]	
	% male	% female	% male	% female	% male	% female
Superintendents and assistant superintendents	96.1	3.9	94.6	5.4	96.2	3.8

Table 6. Male and Female Public School Administrators, United States, 1972–82 (Cont'd)

Position	1972–73[a]		1976–77[b]		1981–82[c]	
	% male	% female	% male	% female	% male	% female
Principals	92.2	7.8	87.1	12.9[d]	84.0	16.0
Other administrators supervisors, directors)	35.0	65.0	45.4	54.6[e]	Not Available	

Note: These data are from four different sources, and categories of administrators change in each data collection. There are no data available from national data collection sources on sex of administrators in the 1980s.

a. *Source:* Adapted from National Education Association Research Division, *26th Biennial Salary and Staff Survey of Public School Professional Personnel, 1972–73* (Washington, D.C., 1973), pp. 9–10.

b. *Source:* Adapted from B. Foster and J. Carpenter, *Statistics of Public Elementary and Secondary Day Schools* Washington, D.C.: Department of Health, Education and Welfare, 1976), p. 20.

c. *Source:* Adapted from Effie Jones and Xenia Montenegro, *Recent Trends in the Representation of Women and Minorities in School Administration and Problems in Documentation* Arlington, Va.: American Association of School Administrators, 1982), pp. 4, 9, 12.

d. Includes principals and assistant principals.

e. *Source:* Adapted from Equal Employment Opportunity Commission, *Elementary-Secondry Staff Information (EEO-5) Annual Surveys* (1976), unpublished; reported in Elizabeth Havens, "Women in Educational Administration: The Principalship" (Washington, D.C.: National Institute of Education, Contract 400-79-0698, 1980), p. 2.

In the following sections I will describe the incidence of women in the different categories of administrative jobs relating to education. As these sections will show, women have never been represented highly in any administrative positions except that of the elementary-school principal and staff positions that do not entail supervisory responsibility over adult professionals.

Elementary-School Principals

The proportion of women elementary-school principals has changed significantly during this century. In 1928, when most school buildings in the United States were small elementary schools, about

55 percent of all elementary school principals were women (Haven, 1980). In 1926 women so dominated the ranks of the elementary principalship that the editors of *School Life*, a publication of the U.S. Bureau of Education (a forerunner to the Department of Education), published an article entitled "The Woman Principal: A Fixture in American Public Schools." She did not turn out to be a fixture, however. That percentage has decreased yearly to the 1978 figure of 18 percent (Pharus and Zakariya, 1979). (table 7). In 1977 the same United States bureau published an article entitled "No Room At the Top" chronicling the obstacles faced by women who wanted to be elementary principals (Clement, et al., 1977). In 1985, with the mementum of the women's movement and active attempts to encourage women to enter administration, it was estimated that women were returning to their former role: in this year 23 percent of elementary principals were women. (Council, 1982, p. 2).

Table 7. Female Elementary Principals Public Schools, United States, 1928–78

Year	% female
1928	55
1948	41
1958	38
1968	22
1971	21
1973	20
1978	18

Source: William L. Pharis and Sally Banks Zakariya, *The Elementary School Principalship in 1978: A Research Study* (Arlington, Va.: National Association of Elementary School Principals, 1979), p. 5.

These national trends are mirrored in the example of the Los Angeles, California, Public Schools, one of the largest school districts in the country. In 1908 this district had 84 schools, and more than half had female principals; presumably, most of these were elementary schools. By 1974 only 31 percent of the district's 591 principals were women, and by 1976 the figure remained at about 30 percent (Barnes, 1976; LosAngeles, 1976–77).

The decrease in numbers of female elementary-school principals is attributed to several different causes: the increase in men in elementary teaching after World War II, when the GI Bill gave financial aid to veterans returing to college: the consolidation of many small school districts into one larger district (and women who were the heads of small rural schools were replaced by men, who were put in charge of larger buildings); the increased certifications requirements for administrative positions, which necessitated a return to graduate school; and the increasing sexual stereotypes in most organizations, including education, that management was a "man's job."

Comparisons between men and women elementary-school principals show some stark differences; in 1973-74 pay for women with similar years of experience and educational level was $800 to $3,000 less than for men (Havens, 1980).

Secondary-School Principals

Women have never been highly represented as principals of schools with older students. The best estimate for 1920 is about 8 percent of secondary-school principals were women; in 1965 about 10 percent of high school principals were women, and in 1977 that figure was reduced to 7 percent. These figures, however, include both public and private schools, and many of these women were principals in private—and often sex-segregated—religious schools (Byrne, Hines, and McCleary, 1978). Most female high school principals earn considerably less than their male counterparts, and private religious schools often pay less than public schools. In 1978, 70 percent of women high school principals earned less that $20,000, while only 25 percent of the men earned less than that. Fifteen percent of the women and 18 percent of the men high school principals earned over $28,000 (National Association for Secondary Principals, 1978; reported in Havens, 1980, p. 9.)

District Superintendents

In 1922 there were 31 female district superintendents among approximately 1,000,000 local school districts—less than 1 percent of the total. A decade later the number had increased, but there were still 25 states in which no woman served as a district superintendent (Tyack and Hansot, 1982, p. 188). The few existing women superintendents were concentrated in the poorest paid and least prestigious positions in small, rural communities. The same situation existed in 1977 when Paddock (1981) sent a questionnaire to all woman superintendents in the United States and found 93 female superintendents in the approximately 16,000 school districts—still less than 1 percent. In 1982 there were 241 female superintendents—1.8 percent of the total (Jones and Montenegro, 1982).

County and State Superintendents

A county (or province) system of education exists in many states wherein the county often provides services to many school districts within its jurisdiction. Historically, in the 1920s and 30s the county system was more powerful than it is today, school districts were very small and the county superintendent engaged in school inspections and provided services. Women were quite active in this role in the 1920s and 1930s; in fact, county superintendent was a targeted role for women during the earlier movement in the United States. In 1922 Edith Lathrop of the United States Office of Education advised women to enter these positions and noted that the number of female county superintendents rose from 276 in 1900 to 857 in 1922. Most of these women were concentrated in the West and placed where county superintendents were elected rather than appointed (Tyack and Hansot, 1982, p. 187). In many states this was an elected position, and women were successful in gaining elective office despite not being granted universal suffrage nationally until 1920. Women could vote in school elections in twenty-four states. By 1926 women were about 25 percent of county superintendents; in other words, they were gaining in elective office wherever women could vote in school elections (Tyack and Hansot, 1982; Gribskov, 1980). It seems that when women are part of the system that elects representatives, there is a greater likelihood of a woman being chosen that when all the decisionmakers are men. This fact is also borne out for state superintendents. (each state has a state superintendent). In 1983 there were 5 female state superintendents—1 percent. Again, there seems to be a relationship between whether the position is elected or appointed; women are more often state superintendents when the position is an elected position (Bailey, 1984).

Staff Positions

Large school districts have many staff positions that require district coordination or provide support services for district personnel and students. Women who are administrators are most likely to be in these staff positions; furthermore, they are more likely to be in staff positions that deal directly with students. Staff positions which entail supervision of adults are usually held by men (Ortiz, 1982; Schmuck, 1975).

School Board Members

Each local school district has a school board which determines school policy and is active in the hiring of the district superintendent.

Board officials constitute the revered system of "local control of schools." Although the power of the school board to set policy has eroded considerably with the advent of large, complex, organizational systems, board members remain the official policymakers of each local school district. In 1926 and 1956 women constituted about 10 percent of school board members; by 1983 their representation was at 37 percent. Women's representation on school boards has always been higher in urban rather than rural districts (National School Boards Association, 1978, 1983). Although the influence of womens' voices on school boards early in this century has been documented (Kerber, 1980), the nineteenth century emphasis on education as a technical skill resulted in male domination. This patriarchal view was best represented by Ellwood Cubberly, one of the first leaders of educational administration and a writer on the topic. He said, in 1916, that those who did NOT make good school board members were "inexperienced young men, unsuccessful men, old men who have retired from business, politicians, saloon-keepers, uneducated or ignorant men, men in minor business positions, and women." (Cubberly, 1916)

Today a primary task of school boards is to hire superintendents; they bear some responsibility for the hiring of primarily male and white superintendents. School boards naturally want to hire the "best" person for the job, one in whom they have confidence and trust. It is not surprising that predominately white and male boards tend to entrust this sacred responsibility to someone like themselves—a white male.

The Federal Structure of Educational Systems
Local Control

While the United States educational system is decentralized and organized into local school districts, the federal administration includes a Department of Education headed by a Secretary of Education (similar to a minister of education). The department has no power to dictate, instruct, certify or establish educational requirements. However, the department does have power to set national policy and to influence the sentiments regarding education. This power has increased in the past decades because most local schools receive some federal funds that require that certain mandates (especially with regard to equal educational opportunities) are followed. The Department of Education has two main branches: the Office of Education (which regulates federal mandates and hears complaints) and the Institute for Innovation in Education (which grants monies for educational research and dissemination). Women's representation in these federal agencies is skewed; whereas women constitute the majority of workers, most of the senior positions are filled by men. In the highest civil service rankings, women constituted only 15 percent of the positions (Steiger and Szanton, 1977).

Sex Equity Policy and Action in the United States

No person in the United States shall, on the basis of sex, be excluded from participation in, be denied the benefits of, or be subjected to discrimination under any education program or activity receiving Federal financial assistance.

So reads Title IX of the Education Amendment of 1972. The accompanying regulations are very specific and cover most aspects of schooling. This amendment mandates sex equality under the law and is the most significant piece of legislation for women in education that has ever been formulated by the United States Congress. While the interpretation and implementation of the law undergoes alterations during different presidential administrations, it remains an important mandate disallowing discrimination in our nation's schools. Organizational arrangements were also authorized to implement the mandate. For instance, the Womens's Educational Equity Act Program authorizes funding for model programs to achieve sex equity in education and published over one-hundred programs through the Education Development Center. Sex desegregation centers provide regional technical assistance to local school districts to implement sex equity. Each state department of education is required to appoint a coordinator to ensure that equal educational opportunity is provided. Each local school district is also required to appoint a Title IX representative to ensure equality of opportunity. Thus the mandate is from the United States Congress, but the strength of its implementation differs from district to district (Schmuck, et al., 1985). Some school districts have worked hard to enforce the spirit as well as the intent of the law; other school districts perfunctorily perform the work necessary to ensure that they are in compliance with the law.

Private funding agencies have also supported research and action to implement sex equity in schools; The Ford Foundation supported Project Aware under the auspices of the American Association of School Administrators to actively encourage more women to enter positions of leadership in the public schools. It must be noted, however, that the zenith of public action on sex inequities in our nation's schools appears to have been reached. Public policy regarding sex equity in the United States is being seriously eroded by the administration, the courts, and Congress. Even the public sentiment of educators is shifting away from considerations of gender equality in schools. Tetreault and Schmuck, after completing an analysis of selected educational reform reports and books written in the 1980s concluded: "The reform books and commissioned reports selected for our analysis clearly indicate the past decade of legislation, new scholarship on women, research and action for sex equity in schools has gone unheeded. Gender is not a relevant category in the analysis of excellence in schools . . . . even Title IX is ignored, 1985, p. 63."

Equality of opportunity marked the era of educational reforms in the 1960s and 1970s in the United States. In the 1980s there is a new public sentiment which puts in jeopardy many of the gains made in the last decade. But despite the current erosion of interest, issues of equity, gains have been made which cannot be overturned. Foremost among these gains are the new conceptual frameworks for building theories and research about women and education.

The Excluded Majority and the New Scholarship

Women have been active participants in United States public schools for over one hundred years; they have been the majority of teachers since 1860. They have created schools, they have taught students, and they have exercised positions of leadership. They have been valuable contributors to our educational system. Indeed, the historical pattern of paying women less than men has contributed a hidden subsidy to the field of education. And since education used to be one of the few professions open to women, the educational profession gained the best and the brightest of our nation's women.

It is indeed surprising that these facts have been largely ignored by educational scholars. Joan Burstyn, an educational historian, describes two major texts in American educational history written by men (1983). There is no mention of women in either of the texts. Where were the women? While it is true that women's contributions to educational scholarship or leadership do not parallel the contributions of men in our educational history, the fact remains that education was one of the few professional fields open to women in a restricted and confining social system. And women did participate in education in the United States. Jane Roland Martin, in her analysis of a philosophy of education text recounting thee centuries of educational thought, points out that no women are mentioned. Martin aptly titled her artcle "Excluding Women from the Educational Realm;; (1982). The exclusion of women from a field in which they have been active participants has distorted history, created false illusions about women's role in schools, and has been conceptually faulty. Education has not been the exclusive province of men.

There is a resurgence of books and articles devoted to restoring women to their proper place in American educational history. Educational classes such as Thomas Woody's *A History of Women's Education in the United States*, and Willystine Goodsell's *Pioneers of Women's Education in the United States* (1931) have been reprinted. Buried and long forgotten women—the exceptional as well as the ordinary—are being unearthed and remembered; Polly Kaufeman (1984), Nancy Hoffman (1982), Linda Kerber (1980), Gerda Lerner (1979), Tyack and Hansot (1982), Keith Melder (1977), and Eleanor Flexner (1959) are among those restoring women to their rightful place in American educational history. And in educational research attention is now being paid to the role of gender in educational employment. Sari Knoop Biklen (1984); Sara Lawrence Lightfoot (1983); Sara Freedman, Jackson, and Boles (1983); Michael Apple (1983); Charole Shakeshaft (1984); Patti Lather (1984); and Flora Ortiz and Catherine Marshall (forthcoming) are among a growing number of researchers who are studying the roles of women in education or the influences of gender in educational institutions.

Educators in the United States have never held high social status; the devalued role of education is inextricably intertwined with the devalued status of women in the society at large. Indeed, the positive social value of a profession is inversely related to the number of women in the field. This concept has been documented time and time again. Perhaps it was best said in 1949 by Margaret Mead, who was among the first to point out that males are granted higher social status than females. Whatever activities men do are more highly valued than activities women do. If men decide to cook, hunt, weave, dress dolls, or collect hummingbird wings, these will be the valued social activities. Perhaps, finally, we are recognizing the formal and informal impact of gender-related issues on our educational institutions. But it is not the first time such a connection has been made. One of our early advocates of women's equality in education was Susan B. Anthony. She is now revered for her outspokenness and insightful critiques of education. In 1853, she "hit the nail on the head" when she directly attached the low esteem given to women in American society and in education. She attended a meeting of educators (only men were allowed to belong) and listened with rising anger as the men debated for three days the reasons that teachers lacked the respect accorded doctors, lawyers, and ministers. Finally she asked to speak. The men argued for half an hour about whether to grant her the exceptional permission for a woman to speak in public. Finally, they reluctantly granted her permission. She said:

> It seems to me, gentlemen, that none of you quite comprehend the cause of disrespect of which you complain. Do you not see that so long as society says a woman is incompetent to be a lawyer, minister, or doctor, but has ample ability to be a teacher, that every man of you who chooses that profession tacitly acknowledges that he has no more brains than a woman? . . . . Would you exalt your profession, exalt those who labor with you. (Quoted in Tyack and Hansot, 1982, pp. 64-65)

There remains concern about the respect given our nation's teachers and the future of our American educational institutions. Education has been labeled the "imperiled" profession (Duke, 1984; Freedman, Jackson, and Boles, 1984). Our social history reveals persistently equivocal attitudes about the status of education. From the earliest days of our republic, teachers have been the source of ridicule, condescension, or pity (Shulman and Sykes, 1983, p. 98). Not only has the field been denegrated in the public's view, but the teacher in the United States has always been seen as deficient. In 1932 Waller, a sociologist, characterized education as the "refuge of unsalable men and unmarriageable women." Perhaps the public view is best characterized by this cliche': "Those who can, do. Those who can't, teach. Those who can't teach, teach teachers." While teachers have always had to cope with criticism, Duke (1984) says, "my reading of educational history fails to find another era when their profession is so imperiled." In 1983, The National Commission on Excellence in Education published its report on the condition of education in the United States. It concluded that our nation was "at risk" because of its poor educational system. This report spurred a plethora of reports and books criticizing public schools and the teachers and administrators in them. Probably no other Western country exhibits such ambivalence about educators. One the one hand, we entrust them with our most precious resource, our youth; on the other hand, we castigate their intelligence, their skills, and their persons. We offer no respect or reverence; we offer few material inducements, few opportunities for advancement, and almost no rewards for professional service.

Curiously, the women's movement of the last few decades may also be putting the woman schoolteacher in a bind. Our past stereotypes about teaching as the "appropriate sphere for women may be suffering from a backlash. Our current understanding about sex segregation in the labor force may have created a mind-set against the traditionally feminized profession of today. Our concern about women's equal status in the society may, in fact, be driving competent women away from the profession of education. Adkison points out that in 1966 there were 760,000 women in colleges of education and in 1979, that number was reduced to 601,000 (1981). Adkison also points out that women in schools of business in those same years increased from 204,000 to 819,000. Women's "true profession" of teaching now competes with more lucrative and rewarding work because we have been successful in reducing the social restraints of women in other professional areas. As Sykes says, "No longer is teaching the zenith to which most college educated women can aspire" (Shulman and Sykes, 1983).

This fact was most poignantly illustrated to me during an undergraduate class, "Sex Bias in Education," that I taught at Lewis and Clark College in 1985. Two young women, both seniors and both excellent students, debated long and hard about their future work. They had been advised by their parents, their teachers, and their peers that they could do "more" than teach. They wanted to become teachers but felt the strong pressure to make another choice. They felt they would be "letting someone down" by choosing a career in teaching. Fortunately for education, they made an affirmative choice, but felt obligated to forcefully defend their choice. Not only is teaching no longer the zenith to which young women can aspire; it is often seen as the wrong choice for competent and capable women. The woman who chooses to enter and remain in education is seen as an anachronism in the eyes of her more liberated peers. Women who choose to teach are often seen as "unliberated," ones who have not freed themselves from the cultural stereotypes about women's place in the society. Perhaps a stereotype in reverse is operating; women who enter education do so because they are seen as adopting the denegrated position of women in the United States.

Efforts such as the Boston Women's Teachers Group (Freedman, Jackson, and Boles, 1983), the Research on Women in Education of the American Educational Research Association (Klein, 1985), the National Association of Women's Studies, and the studies on women teachers (Biklen, 1984) perhaps can restore a proper perspective to the study of gender as it relates to educational institutions. Perhaps, for the first time, we will have an educational reform platform which simultaneously recognizes the value of education and the value of women in our United States.

References

Adkison, Judy (1981). "Women in School Administration: A Review of the Research." *Review of Educational Research* 51, no. 3, (Fall), pp. 311–343.

Apple, Michael (1983). "Work, Gender and Teaching." *Teachers College Record* 84, no. 3 (Spring), pp. 611–628.

Bailey, Susan (1984). Correspondence from chief state school officers, Washington, D.C., April.

Barnes, Thelma (1976). "America's Forgotten Minority: Women School Administrators." *National Association of Secondary School Principals Bulletin* (April), 60, no. 399 pp. 87–93.

Bartholemew, Bernard, and Susan Gardener (1982). *Status of the American Public School Teacher.* National Education Association, Washington, D.C.

Biklen, Sari Knopp (1984). "Teaching as an Occupation for Women: A Case Study of an Elementary School." NIE Grant G-81-007, unpublished paper, Syracuse, New York.

Burstyn, Joan (1983). "Women in the History of Education." Paper presented at the Annual Meeting of the American Educational Research Association, Montreal.

Butler, Matilda (1979). *Education, The Critical Filter.* San Francisco: Women's Educational Equity Communication Network.

Byrne, David, Susan Hines, and Lloyd McCleary (1978). *The Senior High School Principal: The National Survey.* Arlington, Va.: National Association of Secondary School Principals.

Clement, Jacqueline, DiBella C., Ekstrom R, Fobras, S. Bartol, K. and Alban M. (1977). "No Room at The Top." American Education, U.S. Office of Education. pp. 20–26.

Collier-Thomas, Betty (1982). "The Impact of Black Women in Education: An Historical Overview." *Journal of Negro Education* 51, no. 3, pp. 173–180.

Council of Chief State School Officers. Newsletter, December, 1982. Washington, D.C.

Cubberly, Ellwood (1916). *Public School Administration. Boston, 1916. Boston: Houghton Mifflin. Reported in R. Callahan, Education and the Cult of Efficiency* Chicago: University of Chicago Press.

Donovan, Frances (1938). *The School Ma'am.* N.Y.: F. Slokes Company.

Duke, Daniel (1984). *Teaching: The Imperiled Profession.* Albany, State University of New York Press.

Ellenburg, F.C. (1975). "Elementary Teachers: Male or Female?" *Journal of Teacher Education* (Winter), pp. 329-334.

Flexner, Eleanor (1959). *Century of Struggle: The Women's Rights Movement in the United States.* Cambridge, Mass.: The Belknap Press, Harvard University Press.

Freedman, Sara, Jane Jackson, and Katherine Boles (1983). "Teaching: An Imperiled Profession." In *Handbook of Teaching and Policy*, ed. Lee Shulman and Gary Sykes. New York: Longman, pp. 261-299.

Goodsell, Willystine (1931). *Pioneers of Women's Education in the United States.* New York: Ames Press.

Gribskov, Margaret (1980). "Feminism and the Woman School Administrator." In *Women and Educational Leadership: A Reader*, ed. Biklen and Brannigan, Lexington, Mass.: Lexington Books.

Havens, Elizabeth (1980). "Women in Educational Administration, The Principalship.' National Institute of Education, Washington, D.C.

Hoffman, Nancy (1982). *Women's True Profession.* Westbury, N.Y.: The Feminist Press.

Jones, Effie, and Xenia Montenegro (1982). *Recent Trends in the Representation of Women and Minorities in School Administration and Problems of Documentation.* Arlington, Va.: American Association of School Administrators.

Kaufman, Paulie (1984). *Women Teachers on the Frontier.* New Haven: Yale University Press.

Kerber, Linda (1980). *Women's Place is in the School: The Impact of Women on American Education.* U.S. Department of Health, Education and Welfare, Washington, D.C.

Klein, Susan (1985). *Achieving Sex Equity Through Education.* Baltimore, Md.: Johns Hopkins University Press.

Lather, Patti (1984). "Gender and the Shaping of Public School Teaching: Do Good Girls Make Good Teachers?" Paper presented at the National Women's Studies Association Conference, June.

Lerner, Gerda (1979). *The Majority Finds Its Past.* New York: Oxford University Press.

Lightfoot, Sara (1983). "The Lives of Teachers." In *Handbook of Teaching and Policy*, ed. Lee Shulman and Gary Sykes. New York: Longman, pp. 241-260.

Lortie, Daniel (1975). *School Teacher.* Chicago: University of Chicago Press.

Los Angeles Unified School District (1976–77). *Guide to Schools and Offices.* Los Angeles: Los Angeles Unified School District.

Martin, Jane Roland (1982). "Excluding Women from the Educational Realm." *Harvard Educational Review* 52, n. 2., pp. 133–148.

Melder, Keith (1977). *Beginnings of Sisterhood.* New York: Schocken Books.

National Education Association (1983). *Estimated Statistics of Public Schools,* Washington, D.C. 1983.

Ortiz, Flora (1982). *Career Patterns in Education: Women, Men and Minorities in Public School Administration.* New York: Praeger, 1982.

Ortiz, Flora, and Catherine Marshall (forthcoming). "Women in Educational Administration." In *Handbook of Research on Educational Administration.* Baltimore, Md.: John's Hopkins University Press.

Paddock, Susan (1981). "Male and Female Career Paths in School Administration." In *Educational Policy and Management: Sex Differentials,* ed. Patricia Schmuck, W.W. Charters, and Richard Carlson. New York: Academic Press.

Schmuck, Patricia (1975). *Sex Differentials in Public School Administration.* Arlington, Va.: National Council of Women in Educational Administration.

Schmuck, Patricia, et al. (1985). "Administrative Strategies for Institutionalizing Sex Equity in Education Through Education in *Sex Equity Through Education,* Klein, Susan (ed). Baltimore, Johns Hopkins Press.

Schmuck, Patricia, and Spencer Wyant (1981). "Clues to Sex Bias in the Selection of School Administrators." In *Educational Policy and Management: Sex Differentials. New York: Academic Press.*

Sexton, Patricia Cayo (1973). "The Feminized Male." In Scientific Debate, ed. Stall New York: Addison-Wesley.

Shakeshaft, Charole (1982). *Women's True Profession: A Teaching Guide.* Westbury, N.Y.: The Feminist Press.

Shakeshaft, Charole, and Patricia Palmeiri (1984). "Goodby Miss Dove, Hello Ms ____: A Re-Evaluation of the Woman Teacher." Unpublished paper, New Hempsted, N.Y. Hofstra University.

Shulman, Lee, and Gary Sykes, eds. (1983). *Handbook of Teaching and Policy.* New York: Longman.

Steiger, JoAnn, and Eleanor Szanton (1977). *Women's Participation in the Education Division of HEW.* Washington, D.C.: National Advisory Council on Women's Educational Projects.

Tetreault, Mary Kay, and Patricia Schmuck (1985). "Equity, Educational Reform and Gender." *Issues in Education* 3, no. 1 (Summer), pp. 45–67.

The Woman Principal: A Fixture in American Schools. *School Life*, 1926, 11 (10), p. 190.

Tyack, David, and Elizabeth Hansot (1982). *Managers of Virtue*. New York: Basic Books.

Williams, Peg. "The Impact of Anti-Sex Discrimination Laws on the Employment of Oregon School Principals." Dissertation, Eugene, Or.: University of Oregon.

Woody, Thomas (1929) *A History of Women's Education in the United States*. Reprinted 1974, New York: Octogan Books.

Part II

Historical Perspectives On Women Educators

The five chapters in this section, representing five countries, focus on the authorities governing *whom* women could teach, *what* women could teach, and *where* women could teach. They illustrate the changing social ideology, institutional policy, and authority governing women's place in formal educational institutions.

Brehmer traces the role of women as teaching in German speaking countries from the religious schools of the Middle Ages to the political alignment of twentieth century West Germany. She provides a rich history of women saints, spiritualists, and religious orders that concentrated on education. The tapestry of women's lives as educators was certainly begun in these times. As Brehmer demonstrates, the basic issues of *who, what,* and *where* women can teach remain viable questions. Today, women educators in West Germany, as in all Western countries, teach in hierarchically sex-segregated institutions and concentrate on teaching basic skills to the young. Gribskov and van Essen, using original source material, document the lives of individual educators in their respective countries, the United States and the Netherlands. Their difficulty in finding archival material and secondary-source documentation of women who contributed to their teaching profession illustrates the devalued role women have played in our educational history (see also Hoffman, 1982 and Kaufman, 1984). Through the histories of individual women, Gribskov and van Essen recount the issues facing women educators in their time.

Moeller and Bystydzienski tell us about women's place in their professional associations: the teachers' unions. Moeller focuses specifically on the battle for equal pay in Denmark, and Bystydzienski offers a more comprehensive and comparative account of women's involvement in the teachers' unions of England and the United States at the turn of the century.

Several common themes about women emerge from all these historical perspectives. In all these countries, women are denied access to teaching in the public sector and to higher education and teacher-training institutions. In all these countries we also see wage differentials and differing social expectations and demands for change from the political activism of coalitions of women educators.

Though not a historian by training, I am sensitive to a paramount concern of historiography: how can we, with our twentieth century view, hope to understand and capture the times before us? How can we present historical material true to the context of its time? A fundamental issue facing feminists today is how to understand the underlying beliefs and conditions that faced women of times gone by. After all, access to schooling at all levels or teaching positions is no longer denied on the basis of sex. Wages are now equal for equal work, and women constitute the majority of educational professionals in most Western countries. What can we learn from past accounts?

An important theme, the bedrock of all these chapters about women's place in schools, is the debate about inherent gender differences or similarities. The debate continues into our time (see Maccoby and Jacklin, 1974; and Gilligan, 1982). Before the twentieth century, however, there was no debate (Rosenberg, 1980). The early Church fathers, as Brehmer points out, associated women with Eve and the fall of "man"kind. And the argument continued in the secular writings of the twentieth century. The social construct of women's place in the society of earlier times, and thus women's place in the schools, was based on a belief in the inherently different capacities of men and women and the inferiority of women. Implicit in ths argument was the fundamental right of men to conduct lives in the public and secular sphere, whereas woman's place was to be in the private and domestic sphere. Men were to govern women. This prevailing social ideology was also confirmed by "fact," that is, by the medical establishment and by philosophic discourses, well into the twentieth century (Rosenberg, 1982; Martin, 1982).

Our feminist sisters of a century ago, many of whom were involved in education, shared this belief in the inherently different capacities of women and men, despite their militarism for better access, more opportunities, and equal pay. Emma Willard, in her public address to the New York legislature (which was read by a man, since women were not allowed to speak in public), argued on the basis of gender differences. Women should be educated because they would be a "civilizing influence" on their husbands and sons—those who would live lives in the public sector. She said "Is it not in the power of our sex to give society its tone, both as to manners and to morals?" She further argued that the demise of previous republics was due to "frivolous women" who had not been educated properly to assist their husbands in the public sphere (reprinted in Kersey, 1981, p. 276). Thus women educators actively fighting for more participation and rights within the educational sphere used the argument of gender differences to make their point. At the same time, most of the male-dominated educational agencies used the same argument to prevent women from entering positions of public teaching, adding that if women were to teach, they should do so where their "natural abilities" would be put to best use—in the education of young children. They argued further that women's contributions could not be considered equal to the contributions of men. Each chapter in this section deals with the theme of inherent gender differences.

In some cases the argument about gender differences was used to prevent women from engaging in certain tasks and to encourage them to engage in other tasks once they "got their foot in the door." Moeller points out, for instance, that whereas the struggle for equal pay in Denmark "challenged the concept of women as physically and intellectually weaker than men," it was also asserted that "small children and girls would benefit from the special kind of teaching which only females could supply." Thus the sphere of the domestic domain was expanded to include public-sector reponsibilities for the young. This attitude has continued to the present day. Van Essen's chapter on the Netherlands in the nineteenth century shows how the argument of women's "natural feminine qualities and experiences of motherhood" served as grounds for denying women access to teacher-training institutions; it was argued that their "natural" abilities would translate into the classroom. While today all teachers of young children receive some training, in some countries there are different standards for elementary and secondary schooling.

One must remember that the social ideology of inherent sex difference, as the argument related to teachers, occurred in the context of the schools of the public sector controlled by men. Yet, Moeller points out that the male-controlled union would align itself with the women's cause for equal wages if it was in its best interest to do so. The men argued the case for equal wages for starting salaries (although supported pay discrepancies at later stages) so that they could remain competitors in the marketplace. They argued that "if the starting salary is the same, the *Kommunes* [local councils] will have no basis for calculating whether they can save money by employing a female instead of a male." But such alliances were not frequent, and the supremacy of the male teacher most often prevailed.

Bystydzienski points out that the argument about inherent sex differences had even been promulgated by historians of the teacher union movement. As she says, they "take the view that women are reluctant to participate in organizational activity because of their generally short-term involvement in the occupation and the dominant image of feminity favoring passivity and lack of interest in political matters." This stereotype of the woman teacher is given substance by most authors in this section. Bystydzienski goes on to argue, however, that this view does not stand up to the facts. It was women who urged the National Education Association to be less of a "debating society" and to concern itself with the lives of teachers; the insurgents of the more radical organizational change were more often than not female.

Women coalescing to bring about changes in their lives as educators, especially in the context of the nineteenth century feminist movement, appears throughout this section. Whether this political activism was the militancy of an Anna Jagd in 1904 in Denmark, who publicly confronted the union and organized with other women's groups to have representation in the union, or was the more decorous meeting held in 1910 in the Seattle home of Adelaide Pollock (eventually resulting in the National Council for Administrative Women in Education), there is evidence of political action taken by some women educators to change the circumstances of their professional lives, and their action benefited other women. Whether or not the academic debate on gender differences of similarities was important is not addressed by any of the authors. Whatever women's stand on this issue, it probably was not as important as other issues facing women in their time: low salaries, lack of job security, benefits, and the total subordination of women to male school authorities. It was these issues, and the feminist movement in general, that sparked the activism of the women in the union movement in Denmark, England, West Germany, and the United States and started the formation of women's associations which would speak out on behalf of women.

Certainly these feminist forerunners provide a model for twentieth century women educators—who have argued on the basis of similarity, rather than difference, between the sexes (Maccoby and Jacklin, 1974). Equal access and opportunity have been the hallmarks of the twentieth century demand for change. But although the demands have changed, they still echo the sentiment cited by Moeller and expressed by Luice Jensen in response to a 1899 circular in Denmark: "We only desire the right to up-to-date accommodation with two good rooms—without sloping walls . . . . It has always been a mystery to me why they give the woman teacher the most dismal housing, the lowest possible wage but the longest possible working hours—such is the courtesy shown towards the weaker sex."

References

Gilligan, Carol (1982). *A Different Voice.* Cambridge, Mass.: Harvard University Press.

Hoffman, Nancy (1982). *Women's True Profession.* Westbury, N.Y.: The Feminist Press.

Kaufman, Paulie (1984). *Women Teachers on the Frontier.* New Haven, Conn.: Yale University Press.

Kersey, Shirley (1981). *Classics in the Education of Girls and Women.* Matuchen, N.J.: The Scarecrow Press.

Maccoby, Eleanor, and Carol Nagy Jacklin (1974). *The Psychology of Sex Differences.* Palo Alto, Calif.: Stanford University Press.

Martin, Jane Roland (1982). "Excluding Women from the Educational Realm." *Harvard Educational Review* 52, no. 2, pp. 133–148.

Rosenberg, Rosalind (1982). *Beyond Separate Spheres: Intellectual Roots of Modern Feminism.* New Haven, Conn.: Yale University Press.

Chapter 5

Women Educators in German-speaking Europe: The Middle Ages to Today

ILSE BREHMER

W omen have always taught in the German-speaking countries of Europe. This chapter traces women's role as educators from the Middle Ages to the twentieth century: through the Reformation, the Enlightenment, into the Weimar Republic, and the Third Reich. Of course, until the Enlightenment, women taught only in religious institutions or in private residences. But their presence as educators is seen in art, in manuscripts, and in the sainthood of the Catholic church. It is a rich history, and the early part of that history in within the religious domain. This chapter will show that the place of women teachers, then and now, is bound by the social constructs of women's place in society.

The Middle Ages

The early Church fathers of the Middle Ages had a very low regard for women. For Tertulian women was "the Devels' Hoof." and for Augustine women was "the temple over the sewer." It was Eve who had tempted Adam to sin, and all women bore this responsibility. But there was also the opposite view, the Mary, the Mother of God, bore the Savior, thus giving "mankind" the possibility of deliverance from sin. In the Judgement Day vision of the Apocalypse, it is the Queen of Heaven who appears as the final vision, restoring harmony to the universe.

Within this panorama of medieval female ideologies, there are also the pictures of the *septem artes liberales*, almost invariably depicted as women, as, for instance, in *Hortus Deliciarum* by Herad von Landsberg. The representation of "Grammatica" from the fourteenth century in the Bavarian National Museum is probably the portrait of a secular woman teacher.

The patron saints of women teachers are St. Ursula and St. Katherine. Katherine earned her sainthood by defending her Christian faith against a colloquium of philosophers of the University of Alexandria. Ursula earned sainthood for accomplishing a journey down the Rhein to Rome with a bevy of virgins, converting many heathen on the way and finally dying a martyr in Cologne. Angela von Merici, who founded a teaching order in the sixteenth century, adopted Ursula as the patron saint for the Ursuline sisters. St. Ursula is often shown with arms outstretched, her copious cloak sheltering a motley group of individuals. This representation, usually reserved for the Madonna, indicated the great reverence for Ursula. She is shown, like Mary, with a book in her hand.

Mary and other female saints are far more often shown reading than are their male counterparts. This was a reflection, on the one hand, of the desirability of female preoccupation with the Psalms and the Holy Scriptures. On the other hand, literacy was derided by men as being an "unknightly" and a priestly virtue, and the devalued role of education was associated with the "unmanly"—women and priests.

The main center of female education in the Middle Ages were the convents and the Chorfrauenstifte (religious orders where litany singing was a significant part of the workshop). Cesarius van Arles (died in the sixth century) required every nun to learn to read and to occupy herself with the Holy Scriptured for two hours every morning. Nuns were also entrusted with the copying of manuscripts. In the so-called inner schools of these establishments, the novices received their training. In his letter "Epistulum ad latone", Hydronimus drew up the first Christian curriculum for girls' education. In 816, at the Reichssynode in Aachen, "De Institutio Sanktimonialium" was recommended as compusory reading to all convents.

During the Anglo-Saxon conversion missions to middle Germany (corresponding approximately to present-day Lower Saxony, Westfalia, and Hesse), Bonifazius called Benedictine nuns from

England and southern Germany. They were famous for their academic zeal, their high standard of education, and their cordiality. The lessons they have were based on the "septem artes liberales" (grammar, dialectic, rhetoric, music, arithmtitic, geometry, and astronomy).

The biography of St. Lioba, one of the early women teachers, has survived. She was educated in the convent of the Abbess Eadburga on the Island of Thanet in Kent, England. She was fluent in Latin, knowing the Holy Scriptures by heart, and was conversant with the writings of the early Church fathers, the *septem artes liberales*, and metric. She came to Germany in 735 at the request of Bonifazius and thereafter founded the convent at Tauberbischofsheim. In Fulda she is immortalized in a litany: "Oh mother of myriad spiritual daughters, Oh mirror of governesses, teacher of spiritual life, of feminine virtue" (Dauzenroth, 1971 p. 12). Her biographer, Rudolf von Fulda, praised her talent in forming each postulant as an individual, saying that "she had a soul as manifold and various as the daughters under her charge." Part of her teaching as also spreading the Gospel, which earned her the title "Apostolac Germanae".

In addition to the Bible and the writing of the early Church fathers, classical writers such as Virgil, Prudentius, Horatius, and Ovid were read in the late Middle Ages. Moreover, every nun was expected to be able to calculate the Church calendar and to have some knowledge of astronomy. Roswitha von Gandersheim composed plays and wrote saints lives. The nun, Herad von Landsbery (1140–67), also versed in the *septem artes liberales*, composed lyrics and set them to music and was fascinated by geometry and the "study of the Earth" (geography). and natural history. She collected "the fruit of her endeavours" together in a book "for the edification of her sisters," clerverly combining her work with the history of religion. To be sure of holding the attention of those young sisters who found it difficult to grapple with Latin, she added a German glossary and decorated the book herself with intricate illustrations (Specht, 1967, pp. 271–272). This is the first textbook we possess which was compiled by a woman for her female pupils. (Only a copy is now available; the original was destroyed by fire at the end of the nineteenth century.)

Another highly educated medieval lady was Hildegard von Bingen (1098–1179). She was only four years old when she had her first vision. At eight years of age she joined Jutta von Spannheim's hermitage, and she took her vows between 1112 and 1115. When she was forty-three she felt instructed by God to record her visions. At first she hesitated to follow this comand, but after becoming seriously ill, she finally wrote "Liber Scivias," which can be roughly translated as "Knowing the Way." She wrote with the assistance of a male secretary because she did not consider herself to be completely competent in grammar, but her account of her visions and other writings give the impression of one of the most learned women of the time. Hildegard's visionary powers were recognised by the pope. This fact is especially significant because women (and also men) with these powers were often suspected of heresy. In 1150 Hildegard founded the Convent of Rupertsberg for fifty nuns, two priests, seven poor women, serfs, and guests. Later she wrote works on nature study and natural healing, among them a study on the fish in the Mosel and a treatise on herbs. She corresponded regularly with the pope and the Emperor and she wrote choral works and opera. Hildegard also wrote her autobiography and spent a period as a wandering preacher, although this behavior was not officially allowed for a religious woman in the Middle Ages. In 1169 she cured a woman "possessed of the Devil" and found herself in a dispute with the Church after sanctioning the burial of an excommunicated nobleman in the Rupertsberger Convent cemetary. She was served with an interdict by the prelate of Mainz, which was later rescinded to enable her to receive last rites before her death on 17 September 1179 (Fuhrkotter, 1980). Hildegard was a visionary, a scientist, a poet, a musician, and the founder of a convent, a woman who negotiated with emperors and popes and preached when women were required to remain silent. She was unique in Germany, although there were similar women in Spain (Therese von Avila) and in Italy (Katherina von Siena).

Spiritual instruction in Germany varied from convent to convent and from period to period. In the course of the Middle Ages, it is especially noticeable that the use of Latin declined steadily. Grundman (1970) presumes that translations of Latin texts (Bible texts as well as saints' lives) were initiated for use in the convents, in which case it can be said that the convents supported the growth of German as a lingua franca.

The instruction offered to girls by the convents was either the instruction of postulants by the inner schools or that offered to girls in boarding establishments outside the convent walls. These girls would later return to secular life. From the tenth century onwards, the custom of sending daughters to the convents spread. In southern Germany in the eleventh and twelfth centuries, fairly extensive educational establishments seem to have existed for the daughters of nobility. The convents Neuberg and Indersdorf report the enrollment of three seven year old girls (Specht, 1967, p. 277). These boarders represented an important source of income for the sisters. Young ladies were taught to read the Psalter and some Latin, and to do practical and decorative handwork, in which the nuns excelled. They made vestments and alter cloths, tapestries, and many similar objects using both embroidery and weaving. There are some examples of this handiwork in the Weinhausen Convent in Celle. The events which these embroidered tapestries record are of both a clerical and secular nature, and the tapestries were actually made to order and were intended for sale. They depicted thems such as the life of St. Elizabeth, St. Anna, the love story of Tristan and Isolde, or a great hunting party. However, the education offered by the convents necessarily emphasized spiritual ideals and proved inadequate for the development of the required courtly skills.

In the late Middle Ages, governesses came from France to teach the girls French, different forms of needlework, and etiquette. French was the language of the cultivated classes. The playing of a musical instruments was also taught, along with games like draughts and chess. At the same time, the girls were initiated into the obligations of charity and mercy towards the poor.

In the towns another type of school was developing. Lessons were offered by the Beguine, an order of poor women who could not pay their dowry to Christ and were therefore outside the Church. In addition, individual women offered *Winkelschulen*, small private schools, for the daughters of the lower bourgeoisie. The burgesses of the artisan class needed some knowledge of reading, writing, and arithmetic to be able to carry out business transactions or to manage the business, either in their own name or their late husband (Wensky, 1980; Winter, 1975). With the addition of religious themes, these subjects remained the substance of the *Winkelschulen*.

Some of the original school directive have survived, for instance, from Mainz (1290) and Brussels (1320) where a separate school for girls is mentioned. A document from Speyer records the renting of a house by "Fau Elle," teacher, for the purpose of setting up a girls' school. There are reports of similar institutions in Frankfurt (1364). Emmerich (1445). amd Uberlingen (1456). In Nurnberg in 1461 we hear of girl pupils with their schoolmistress singing for the emperor.

The school regulations for German schoolmasters and mistresses of Bamberg dated 25 April 1491 laid down certain conditions, which included the requirement of "respectable and decorous conduct" for women. Schoolmasters' wives were only allowed to teach if they themselves were "schooled." In practice this meant that those teachers only had a bare minimum of education at their disposal, usually the rudimentary literacy skills. There were some regulations concerning the treatment of students, students were not permited to be sent on errands or gather firewood or fetch water. The teachers received a fixed fee for student tuition, which was partly paid in kind, and which often included lodging and wood and grain rights guaranteed by the city authorities. They also received a small fee directly from the pupil, which varies according to the financial status of the family. If women taught boys, they had to pay compensation to the schoolmasters. These schools were run along the lines of a "trade.' a fact that is quite clear from a tradesman's coat of arms painted for a schoolhouse in 1516 by Ambrosius Holbein. The school were also run as family businesses, with the schoolmistresses teaching the girls and the schoolmaster the boys.

In summary, there were several forms of education available in the Middle Ages to girls from the nobility, and in the later Middle Ages also for the daughters of the bourgeoisie. For those girls who intended to return to their own families, there were convent schools, the inner schools for the novices, and the boarding schools. A second possibility for educating aristocratic women was education by a governess, often from France, in their own court or in that of another high-born family. Generally speaking, there were more educational opportunities for men than for women in the Middle Ages and even the women of the feudal classes had a better formal education than the men.

The Reformation

In those areas of Germany where the efforts of the Reformation bore fruit, the convents lost their position as establishments of female education. This meant that for wealthy and poor women alike, the only remaining *Leitbild* (theme) was that of the "housewife and mother," just as Luther had intended.

Luther wanted education for women as well as for men, and even recommended it in his circular to the city fathers in all the towns in Germany. He suggested one hour of schooling a day for girls, and for boys three hours. Women, however, were to be educated for their proper roles in the home. He endeavored to promote girls' education by taking the "virtuous maiden" Else V. Kanity into his own household. In the 'maids schools' a schoolmaster was engaged for the girls (Stricker, 1929, pp. 7–8). The school regulations of Bubenhagen or Brunswick in 1528 give us insight into the curriculum. The girls were expected to be able to read and to know their catechism. (The Creed, the Lord's Prayer, the ritual of baptism, and the Eucharist). They were also expected to be able to recite parts of the New Testament and to know hymns and historical tales by heart. As Bubenhagen explained, "Maidens who have comprehended God's Word become useful, skillful, lighthearted, kind, obedient and respectful matrons neither superstitious nor stubborn—ruling their families with propriety and bringing up their children in obedience, honour and the fear of God" (Bubenhagen, quoted in Dauzenroth, 1971, ll. 34–35). Women's role was to be that of wife and mother. The curriculum varied somewhat from school to school. There was reading, writing, handicrafts, and religion, but it could also include nature study, practical physics, geography and economics, clerical skills, and modern languages.

These girls' schools were subject to church supervision and were inspected at regular intervals: "Every quarter according to the convenience of the pastor accompanied by his assistant and the envoy of the worthy commission, the maids shall be attended and duly examined in their catechism and their exercises. To which examinations the schoolmaster shall duly prepare and guide the girls. God have mercy on us in honour of His name (regulations of Naumberg Girls' School, Stricker, 1929, p. 20)."

Those teaching at the school received only a small remuneration. The male teachers had various possibilities for augmenting their income, but the women did not. Their salary was paid from the city exchequer ranged between twenty and thirty guilders, depending on the state of the city coffers. Occasionally living quarters were provided. Although the women also received an additional fee from each individual pupil, this fee was often waived for poor pupils.

Apart from these schools, which were under the auspices of the church and city authorities, there were also schools which only had to be registered to exist. The level of education of the teachers at such schools could not have been very high. For instance, we read that permission to teach was sought for "Behrendt Prens wife, he is a wheelbarrow maker, with some land for barley and turnips, she teaches girls and boys to read and write. Frau Kochen is a needlewoman and the wife of Hermann von Ohl can also spin and sew. Two seemen's wives also request permission to hold lessons" (Stricker, 1929, pp. 20–21). There were other women who applied for recognition: a cartwright's widow, a pastor's widow, housewives, the widow of a blind teacher, the widow of a nail-maker-journeyman, a cobbler's widow, a painter's widow, and other widows whose trades are not give. Other examples are unmarried women, the daughter of a teacher, the sister of a teacher, a maidservant, and a seamstress. How did they come to teach? Mainly financial necessity caused by war and sickness drove them to this work" (Strecker, 1962, p. 4).

These teachers were mainly the widows of schoolmasters. According to the school regulations of Pommern (1628), a widow had the right to carry on a school after the death of her husband. Daughters had the same right. This right was lost if they again married a teacher, who then took over the school. If the new husband followed another trade, the school had to be given up.

Similar cases of inheritance of the "trade" are noted for other countries. In the course of the social upheaval and penury caused by the thirty Years War, there was a strong tendency to put pressures on women to leave all guild trades. The German schoolmaster and the Latin schoolmaster also felt that women were a threat. The Herzog von Pommern in Stettin petitioned to remove two daughters of the late Schoolmaster Blummenew from school service because they were "not fragile but strong young girls, maids who could well go into service." This statement was followed by biblical quotations ostensibly showing that Jesus had only spoken to his disciples and not to the women when he had said, "Go throughout the world and teach" (Streicker, 1962, p. 7).

Starting in about the seventeenth century, examinations were required for teaching candidacy; from this time on we see fewer and fewer women teaching because they did not have the opportunity to acquire the required educational standards. Training seminars for women teachers were not available until the beginning of the nineteenth century.

In 1786 several academies for young ladies were founded in Germany following the ideas of Fenelon. They were residential schools and were usually in the countryside. In 1790, however, one of the schools was moved to Gotha by the Andre family, who considered the elocution of their daughters to be at risk from the "less pure vowels" of the country dialects.

The girls were trained not only as housewives through the practical tasks in the large family household, which gave the Schnepfentaler boarding academy its unique character, but also as "thinking housewives" capable of taking over other tasks, such as the formal education of their daughters (Blochmann, 1966, p. 90). These "Philanthropist" girls' schools in Kolmar, Muhlhausen, Darmstadt, and Frankenthal saw their main task as preparing girls for their careers as housewives and mothers. "The women whose sphere lies in the household" needs the true purity of heart that can only thrive on a delicate soul. Therefore the house where such a mother is in charge is equal to any educational establishment. This is a clear statement that the upbringing by the mother is equal to a formal school education, and perhaps superior.

The Enlightenment

The Enlightenment brought with it new trends. For instance, Gottsched, in his "Vernunftigen Tadlerinnen," recommended the foundation of an educational establishment for women. In Hippel's manuscript, "Uber die burgerliche Verbesserung der Weiber" (on the improvement of women of the middle classes; 1972), he explained the different abilities of men and women as having to do with God or nature.

The ideas of the Enlightenment were spreading across the continent; Oympe de Gouge wrote on the defense of women in France, and in England Mary Wollstonecraft campaigned for an improvement in womens' education. However, all their efforts, from the dawn of the Enlightenment to the French Revolution, found hardly any echoes in the educational establishments, neither in higher education for girls from the middle classes nor in elementary education of the masses.

In the wake of the anti-Reformation movement, several important teaching orders were founded. Angela von Merici founded the educational order of the Ursuline Sisters. In the course of the seventeenth century, schools were founded in Berlin, Breslau, Dorsten, Duren, Dusseldorf, Duderstadt, and Erfurt. Maria Ward also founded the Englischen Frauleins in the seventeenth century. Maria, a member of the English Catholic landed gentry, wanted to build an independent sisterhood of women based on the ideas of the Jesuits. She founded schools in Flanders, Germany, Austria, and Italy, and constantly and unsuccessfully endeavored to gain papal recognition for her schools. Although she was even regarded with scorn, her schools remained. However, it was only after the end of the nineteenth century that the Englischen Frauleins were able to acknowledge their founder as Maria Ward (Kohler, 1984).

Other teaching orders that were founded were the Augustiner Chorfrauen, the Devotessen, and the Armen Schulschwestern (Voss, 1952). During the period of secularization these convent schools were dissolved, but they became popular again in the second half of the nineteenth century. The educational aims of the convent schools were twofold: to achieve the ideal of a pious housewife and mother, and to instruct novices.

Training For Women Teachers in the Nineteenth Century

It was not until the nineteenth century that women began to recieve training to be teachers in secular schools. Initially it was adequate for women to offer proof of higher education and a good family background to gain employment in public schools and then later to be offered a permanent position. Gradually this requirement was superseded by examination requirements. Women were not required to attend a teacher-training institution but often used the services of private establishments to prepare for their exams. These services were offered by clerics, teachers, or courses available from the local government or girls' school, which ran from one to two years.

In some places so-called teacher-training crammers started their notorious activities. In many cases a two-year course consisting of six lessons a week was enough to satisfy the examination board that a teaching certificate should be issued. Moreover, the curriculum was completely geared towards the high schools, and emphasized English and French.

There was virtually no training for elementary-school teaching. In 1849 a Rhein newspaper recommended the establishment of teacher-training institutions in all the provinces. The number of female elementary-school teachers was relatively small at this time. An official education publication of 1859, which issued the first official statistics for women teachers in Prussia, lists 1,523 women teachers and notes that female teachers remain a complementary part of instruction, thereby keeping the word of the Bible that "Woman is Man's helper" (Gahling and Moering, 1961, pp. 24ff.)

In 1904 there were 133 state teachers' colleges for men in Prussia, but only ten states ran "seminars" for women. Nevertheless, about 1,600 of all teachers were women, and a directive from a minister in 1908 states that the "special feminine qualities" were not to be neglected. This meant that male teachers were not to be given preference over female teachers, since the good of the community as a whole depended on making use of women's "special characteristics." In 1905, however, the Ministry of Home Affairs in Prussia directed that the ratio of male to female teachers should be 2 to 1. At the same time, the inferiority of female teachers was underlined by the fact that women teachers were not required to take a "final" examination (Gahling and Moering 1961) The report also noted that because women gave fewer lessons per week than men, women were to be paid less. Women received only two-thirds of the male teachers' salary. Women teachers were independently organized to a high degree, despite the fact that women represented only about 5 percent to 16 percent of all teachers in 1905 and 1920 but pay differentials were not part of their agenda. Women teachers' demands were primarily about teacher training and the possibility of gaining further education to achieve higher qualifications.

Since women were excluded from grammar schools, they could not gain entrance qualifications to German universities. So womens' teachers association in 1889 began the Realkurse for women in Berlin. In 1893 these courses gave women the required grammar-school qualifications, thus providing women with the opportunity to gain university entrance. In 1893 private courses were started for senior women teachers; the participants were allowed to attend lectures at Gottingen and at Berlin University as "guests"—with special permission from a ministerial level. The foundation of classical grammar schools for girls quickly followed; in Karlsruhe (1893), in Leipzig (1894), and in Munchen (1900).

The Association of German Women Teachers and the Weimer Republic

In 1869 the Association of German Women Teachers and Governesses was founded, with Auguste Schmidt and Marie Kahn as chairs. In 1883 the Association of Christian Women Teachers was founded. Various local organizations amalgamated to form the Generala Association of German Women Teachers, headed by Helene Lange. Membership increased rapidly. In the following year it rose to 3,300, by 1900 to nearly 16,000, in 1913 to 33,000, and by 1933 to 40,000.

Existing alongside the General Association, was the Association of German Catholic Women Teachers. This association had 18,500 members in 1926. At local levels there were other small Protestant teacher associations. University entrance for women was finally achieved in 1908. Women also wanted to teach more classes and to take on "head teacher posts." The arguments against women taking on such responsibilities were that they were sick more often and more susceptible to mental illness.

The women's unions had an important social function: they set up insurance, provided job placement services, administered grants for students, set up retirement homes, advised teachers working abroad, and maintained holiday retreats. The General Association of Women Teachers official periodical was *The Women Teacher in the School and in the Home* and continued to be published until 1944. Didactical advice and pedagogic papers were published, along with legal advice and a job column. The Weimar constitution put the female teachers on the same level as her male colleagues; womens' pay was brought into line with male teachers so that wages were paid according to lessons given and qualifications held, regardless of sex. However, various exceptions were laid down which made it possible for women to be dismissed from service (Campaign for Dopelverdiener).

During the nineteenth century it was the law in some german provinces that women teachers had to give up their jobs upon marriage. This "celibacy law" was incompatible with the principle of equality as laid down in the constitution of the Weimar Republic and was therefore abolished. Nevertheless, various attempts were made with special rulings to exclude married women from the teaching profession. In 1937, during the Third Reich, the celibacy law was reintroduced. Not only married teachers, but also women teachers who could be supported by their fathers, could lose their status as civil servants and be dismissed.

The Catholic association of teachers survived until 1939 or 1940 as a religious organization. In 1947 the Working Committee for the Education of Women and Girls was founded as a successor to the General Association of German Women Teachers; however, it was to remain an ineffective shadow of its predecessor and was dissolved in 1967. Another section of the association was merged into the Union for Teachers headed by Emmi Bechmann.

The Catholic association of women teachers still exists today. However, it is fair to say that the tradition of the first womens' movements, with the active representation of women teachers through independent organizations, was not taken up again after World War II.

Education for Women in the Weimar Republic and the Third Reich

The endeavors of the first womens' movements, especially the organization of women teachers, had resulted before World War I in the opening of various higher lyceum study establishments and high schools. The high schools for boys in Prussia had always accepted a few girls among the pupils. In 1923 a reform of girls' schooling was introduced in the Weimar Republic which guaranteed the following school system of higher education for girls'. Four years of elementary schooling for all, followed by the possibility of a six-year high school education with *Obersekundareife*, approximately the equivalent of a high school graduation. The alternative was a modern high school leading to university matriculation. Parallel to this system were domestic-science schools with a three year postlyceum course. There were seven different forms of schools leading to university entrance.

Alongside these special educational establishments for girls were Gymnasiem (traditional types of grammar schools), which after 1924 were no longer representative of typical male-oriented education. In that year the Prussian Ministry for Science and Education set the following new guidelines: "The Gymnasium are to be available to both girls and boys. In all the higher offices men and women are needed who have drunk of the spiritual powers of our past and who are capable of leading us back to the source of German life" (Lundgreen, 1981, p. 72).

Efforts to introduce coeducation into the school systems were especially aided by educational reforms. "Coeducation of the sexes contradicts the point of national socialistic education. Therefore separate schools will be established for boys and girls" (Lundgree, 1981, p. 72).

The new high schools had a language section with English as first foreign language and French as second, and a domestic science section without any foreign languages. But the "womanly" subjects were taught in both language sections They were handicrafts, domestic science, child care, and nursing. The technical, and mathematical, and scienctific sections did not exist at girls' schools. The orientation towards the housewife and mother image was one of the anchors of National Socialism. Future mothers had to be familiar with the National Socialist theories on race and genetics, so they could choose a "racially suitable" husband and bear racially healthy children.

The ideology of the character of women which was taught in the schools at this time was following an age-old tradition (Wittrock, 1983). One of the common themes in the reading books was the self-sacrificing mother gladly giving her life for her son or heroically mourning his death. The other theme was the fighter engaged in war for her country and her follow citizens. This model woman made it feasible to use women in various positions in the war economy and behind the lines.

The BdM (Bund deutscher Madchen - Federation of German Girls) took on the most imaportant functin in the upbringing and education of young girls and boys. During *Heimabenden* (home evenings) and excursions, National Socialist ideology was propagated along with physical training. After the war, in the early phase of the federal Republic of Germany, the BdM was dissolved and a new educational system developed without explicit sex-stereotyped limitations.

Feminization of the Teaching Profession

Between 1967 and 1974 the number of women entering the teaching profession increased. In 1960 women accounted for 42.2 percent of teachers, and in 1982 for 54.6 percnet (Brehmer, 1982). These figures are only for full-time teachers; the majority of part-time teachers were also women. In 1935 women comprised about 35 percent of elementary school teachers, this rose to 65 percent in 1965. About 30 percent high school teachers were women in 1965. (Brehmer, 1982). But this increase of women in an academic profession has been connected with a loss of teaching status. Academics say that women see teaching as a "temporary job," are the *Gastarbeiter"* (guestworkers), consider teaching as a "part-time job with homework," and are unwilling to do their share of supervising extracurricular activities because of family obligations. Women give second priority to their career, are complacent, are less likely to join a union or become politically organized, show no interest in promotion, and have no desire to take on responsible positions. They tend to be emotional and show little capacity to "professionalize" their work. Their speech patterns reflect a lack of professional terminology and a preference for tangible, logical simplicity and spontaneity. The literature goes on to say that women's professional interest tends to center around music and literature and that women reject technical and scientific subjects. Becuase these stereotypes exist about the woman teacher, there is an effort to recruit men into teaching. Kingler, a sociologist, wrote, "The most important goal of status policy in the teaching profession should be to win as many men as possible over to the profession" (1970, p. 50). The fundamental error of studies on German teachers is their male bias; women teachers are often excluded from teaching samples, and when they are included, the authors present the stereotypic view even when the evidence is to the contrary (Boos-Nunning, 1979).

The sex biases that exist in school texts, curriculum, and practices are just now beginning to be recognized. But the level of recognition is much lower than in the United States and Great Britain. Some studies reveal male biases, for instance in textbooks (Hellinger, 1980), in the classroom interaction (Brehmer, 1982), and in differences in educational outcomes between boys and girls. In educational employment, women teach and men manage, and, with increasing teacher unemployment, the old argument is returning that each household should have only one wage earner. Of course, the assumption is that the woman of the household will not work.

The story of women educators in the Federal Republic is a story of limits and restrictions on what women can learn, what women can teach, where they can teach, and whom they can teach. Women's contributions to pedagogy have been ignored, despite the fact that there have always been independent organizations of women in unions and sacred orders attemting to change the patriarchial order. This chapter tries to rectify women's rightful place in pedagogy in the Federal Republic of West Germany.

References

Blochmann, Elisabeth (1966). *"Das Frauenzimmer" und die Gelehrsamkeit.* Heidelberg.

Boos-Nunning, U. (1979). *Professionelle Orientierung, Beruszufriedenheit, Fortbildungsbereitschaft.* Konigstein/T.

Brehmer, Ilse (Hg.) (1982). *Sexismus in der Schule.* Weinheim: Basel.

Brehmer, Ilse, and Uta Enders-Dragasser. *Bearbeiterin: Die Schule lebt. Frauen bewegen die Schule.* DJI Munchen.

Dauzenroth, Erich (1971). *Kleine Geschichte der Madchenbildung. Der verbotene Baum oder die Erziehung des anderen Geschlechts.* Ratingen: Hannover.

Fuhrkotter, Adelgundis (1980). *Das Leben der Heiligen Hildegard. Berichte von den Monchen Gottfried und Theoderich.* Salzburg.

Gies, Frances, and Joseph Gies (1978). *Women in the Middle Ages.* New York: Cambridge u.a.

Gahlings, Ilse, and Elle Moering (1961). *Die Volksschullehrerin. Sozialgeschichte und Gegenwartslage.* Heidelberg.

Gouges, Marie Olympe (1979). Politishche Schriften in Auswahl. (Hrsg.) Walter, Margarete. Hamburg.

Grundmann, Herbert (1970). *Die Frauen und die Literatur im Mittelalter. Ein Beitrag zur Frage nach der Entstehung des Schrifttums in der Volkssprache.* Archiv fur Kulturgeschichte. Bd. 16.

Hellinger, Marlies (1980). For Men Must Work and Women Must Weep." *Women's International Quarterly 3.*

Klingler, J. (1970). "Wird der Lehrerberuf ein Frauenberuf?" Kolner Zeitschrift fur Soziologie u. Sozialpsychologie 22.

Kohler, Mathilde (1984). *Maria Ward. Ein Frauenschicksal des 17.* Jh. Munchen.

Lundgreen, Peter (1981). *Sozialgeschichte der deutschen Schule im Uber-blick*, Teil II, 1918–1980. Gottingen.

Luther, Martin (1884). *An den christlichen Adel deutscher Nation, von des christlichen Standes Besserung.* Halle.

———— (1982). An die Ratsherren aller Stadte deutschen Landes, dab sie christliche Schulen ufrichten und halten sollen. 1554 in Bornkamm, K. u.a. Martin Luther ausgewahlte Schriften, Bd. 5, Frankfurt/M.

Power, Eileen (1975). *Medieval Women.* Cambridge and London u.a.

Specht, Friedrich, A. (1967). *Geschichte des Unterrichtswesens in Deutschland von den altesten Zeiten bis zur Mitte des 13. Jh.* Wiesbaden.

Stricker, Kathe (1929). Deutsche Frauenbildung vom 16. Jh. bis Mitte 19. Jh. Quellenhefte zum Frauenleben in der Geschichte, Heft 21.

Strecker, Dorothea (1962). *Kaiserin Auguste-Viktoria. Schule im Stettiner Madchenbildungswesen 1553–1945.* Marburg/Lahn.

Voss, L. (1952). *Geschichte der hoheren Madchenschule. Allgemeine Schulentwicklung in Deutschland und Geschichte der hoheren Madchenschulen Koln.* Opladen.

Wensky, Margret (1980). *Die Stellung der Frau in der Stadt Kolnischen Wirtschaft im Spatmittelalter.* Koln: Wien.

Winter, Annette (1975). "Studien zur Sozialsituation der Frauen in Stadt Trier nach Steuerlisten von 1364." In *Kurtrierisches Jahrbuch,* Jahrgang 15.

Wittrock, Christine (1983). *Weiblichkeitsmvthos. Das Frauenbild im Faschismus und seine Vorlaufer in der Frauenbewegung der 20er Jahre.* Frankfurt/M.

Wollstonecraft, M.A. (1972). *Vindication of the Rights of Women.* London.

Chapter 6

Adelaide Pollock
And the Founding
Of the NCAWE

MARGARET GRIBSKOV

To the educational task assigned to American women in the late nineteenth and early twentieth centuries—the task of creating a unified, educated citizenry—Adelaide Pollock brought the qualities desired by public school authorities of her time: decorous professionalism, American ancestry, partiotism, unfailing energy, Protestant religious beliefs, formal training, a liberal education and spinsterhood, for married women were almost universally banned from public employment.

Dedicated to her profession, to children, and to a still-young America, Pollock had other passions, too, among them wild birds and the working conditions of female school administrators, of whom she was one. Throughout her life, Pollock was a pioneer and a founder of organizations intended to support women and women educators, including one intended to promote and gain recognition for women administrators. Sadly, she is one of the many important women educators of her time who are forgotten today—by women, by educational historians, by her community, and even by an important organization she helped to found, the National Council of Administrative Women in Education (NCAWE).

Pollock's disapearance from history is but one illustration of the difficulties feminist historians face in attempting to reconstruct women's history. Until recently, American historians paid little attention to social and family history; instead, their focus was political,

economic, and military history at the national level—activities dominated by men. Historians have been even less interested in the history of education, although the transmission of culture has always been and still is one of the major tasks of each generation of adults within every society. The majority of American women, meanwhile, were working at the family and community level, where many women demonstrated leadership in civic, cultural, and educational affairs.

Women's history thus is much more than a history of the subjugation of women or of a few superwomen who somehow managed to excell in a man's world. In order to understand their own history, women must begin to question definitions of history which omit important aspects of commmunity life such as education, along with many other social arenas in which women have played a prominent part. For example, women's organizations were responsible for establishing most of the public libraries and other cultural resources in midwestern and western small towns and some cities, yet these accomplishments also are forgotten.

Because the traditional definition of history ignored education, little value was attached to official education records. In the West, at least, public-school documents were seldom preserved except those of the various state superintendents of public instruction; neither school districts nor county school offices maintained continuous archives. Recently some cities, such as Seattle, have belatedly instituted comprehensive archival programs, but the surviving records are fragmentary and yield only an occasional glimpse of even important, longtime employees such as Adelaide Pollock.

Pollock, fortunately, was a writer as well as an educator and seems to have been conscious of the significance of what she and other women educators of her time were attempting to accomplish. She wrote a brief history of the founding of the National Council of Administrative Women in Education which ended up in the archives of the Seattle Public Library. She was also socially prominent, with the result that her major achievements were recorded in 1927 *Who's Who in Washington State* as well as in several amateur histories of Washington schools. On the basis of these sources and others suggested by the first documents, it has been possible to reconstruct at least the general outlines of Pollocks's career and the events which led to the creation of NCAWE.

Sometime during the 1910 school year, Pollock, then principal of Queen Anne Grammar School in Seattle, invited other Seattle women administrators—elementary principals, vice-principals, and the female assistant superintendent—to dinner at her home. The purpose of the meeting was to provide the women with an opportunity to discuss educational issues and the special problems faced by women administrators, according to a historical sketch Pollock later prepared and the recollections of another woman was present. After talking over a recent education article entitled "The Teacher's Philosophy in and out of the School," the ten women decided to form a study group, without officers, minutes, a name, or dues. They agreed to meet regularly at various members' homes.[1]

Pollock does not describe the specific difficulties encountered by women administrators in Seattle, saying only that previously the women principals had "worked out the problems of their own buildings alone," with "little opportunity for any discussion of the questions which came to them as women."[2] For while nineteenth and early twentieth century policymakers—mostly men—struggled to create bureaucratic systems capable of accommodating growing numbers of schoolchildren, women educators, teachers, and principals daily confronted the diverse and multiplying mass of students in the grade schools. "Three-fourths of all the pupils are in the first four years' work of the elementary schools," the U.S. Commissioner of Education noted in his 1901 report, adding that, "women are to be preferred over men for instructional children under ten years of age."[3]

The children whom women educators were expected to mold into a literate, homogeneous citizenry were a heterogeneous mixture of native white Americans, native students of color, and the offspring of immigrant parents. Many of the immigrant children had been born in other countries and spoke languages other than English. Few of the pupils would graduate from or even attend high school, which was not compulsory, so the critical years were the elementary years, taught almost exclusively by women.

In 1910 American women were still relatively new to teaching and even newer to public school administration, and they were conscious of their recently gained status as professionals, educators, and administrators. Female educators had not been numerous in America in earlier times, although a few women had operated so-called dame school even during the colonial days. In the latter years of the nineteenth century, however, their numbers swelled at a time when the number of male educators was declining. Women began to dominate the education profession, at least in numbers, although men usually retained control over education policy. School administrators provided American women with their first large-scale opportunity to enter the ranks of management.[4]

The slaughter of young men during the Civil War was part of the reason that women almost totally displaced men as elementary teachers by the end of the nineteenth century. A surplus of women existed in eastern and southern states in the late 1800s, exacerbated by the outflow of young men from both regions who went west looking for farmland and economic opportunities.[5] Women moved into the elementary-school vacancies left by men, and also went west themselves into the many new schools springing up on the frontier. Some migrated west with their familities, as Pollock had done, but others went on their own, often but not always to join relatives who had resettled.[6]

Many of the women were suprisingly well educated for that time and place. American girls and women, in fact, were participating in education in large numbers for the first time in their history. By the late 1800s, public high school in the United States were graduating nearly twice as many females as males, and the two sexes were nearly equal among graduates of private high schools.[7] Increasing numbers of women attended colleges and universities after the 1870s, when prominent women's colleges were established and state universities, especially in the Midwest and West, opened their doors to women students. Women soon came to outnumber men in some midwestern and western state universities, at a time when teaching was one of the few professional fields open to women.[8] Teacher-training institutions, public and private, enrolled many more thousands of women, who far outnumbered men in the "normal" schools, as they were called.

The result was a bounty of educated women for public and private schools, while the number of comparable male candidates declined. By 1910, the Seattle district was receiving four times as many applications from women teachers as from men.[9] Long before 1910, school boards discovered that they could hire educated women for considerably smaller salaries than were paid to men, even to men with less education than women.[10] Few women had acquired as much education as Adelaide Pollock, who by 1910 had earned two degrees as well as a normal school diploma, but normal school graduates were common, and even women before 1900 women with bachelor's degrees were numerous.

By the end of the nineteenth century, women had gained access to elementary principalships and to some other administrative positions as well, in both rural and urban school districts. Teaching and school administration allowed women to use their educations and to achieve a measure of both professional status and financial independence, although their salaries remained lower than those typically paid to men in the profession.

Seattle's superintendent, Frank Cooper, had chosen Pollock to be the first women to head a graded grammar school, which was an elementary school in which classrooms were age graded, then still something of an innovation in American schools. Pollock was chosen soon after her graduation with Phi Beta Kappa honors from Stanford University in 1901.[11] The attendance area served by her school was one of the more fashionable areas of the time, with a clientele of upper-middle and upper-class families, a fact which may have influenced Cooper's selection of a principal for Queen Anne School.

Pollock was not the first woman principal in Seattle, however, as she herself was at pains to point out in her brief history of early women administrators in Seattle. Especially in frontier areas of the Midwest and West, women school administrators were numerous in the latter part of the nineteenth century and early twentieth century.[12] Women had headed at least five of six elementary schools in Seattle before 1900, and a woman had served as vice-principal of the city's first high school in the late 1800s.[13] Even more astounding, both Seattle and its neighbor in Oregon, Portland, had hired women superintendents at about the same time.[14] Seattle's pre-1900 women administrators included two who were graduates of Mt. Holyoke, as well as several educated in New England normal schools.[15]

Like most of the western women educators, Pollock was not a native of the West. She had come west with her parents from her birthplace in Cedar Falls, Iowa, in 1864, when she was four years old. Traveling by wagon train, the family settled in Oregon. Still unmarried at the age of twenty-six, Pollock entered the far west's first teacher-training institutions, San Jose, CA. Normal School, and graduated in December 1888. She taught in Seattle the following year and until sometime in the early 1890s, when she returned to California to become the first woman principal in the Stockton schools in 1895. [16] At least one other woman who participated in the 1910 meeting at Pollock's home was also a college graduate; the surviving personnel records for that era are too fragmentary to tell if there were others. Two of the women were graduates of eastern normal schools.

Professional or other higher education was not a prerequisite for administrative posts in most western school districts of the time. Urban districts, however, offering what most educators regarded as the most desirable and stable employment, could attract women with more extensive education and training. Urban teachers usually were at least high school graduates and thus were better educated than the majority of the populace; only 8.6 percent of Americans were graduating from high school in 1910.[17] Prior successful teaching or administrative experience was what urban school systems primarily sought in elementary teachers and in administrative candidates.

Suprisingly, high school teachers, women and men, were nearly all college graduates, and some held master's degrees.[18] Pollock was one of several Seattle school system employees who could boast more formal education than their superintendent a student from Cornell University.[19]

All the women attending that first meeting at Pollock's home were experienced educators, and most had almost as much administrative tenure behind them as Pollock. Soon after hiring Pollock, Frank Cooper selected several more women for elementary principalships and various central office administrative positions. He seems to have respected and admired his female subordinates. Later, Cooper would speak of himself as the "brother" of the organization started by Seattle women administrators in 1910.[20]

At fifty, Pollock appears to have been oldest of the group which met at her home, but all the participants for whom personal data still exist were middle-aged or close to it. Lydia Lovering, another elementary principal, had earned her University of Washington degree in 1896; therefore, she was at least in her mid-thirties.[21] Maxine Kelly, also an elementary principal, recorded her birth date as 1867 and so must have been forty-three. Almina George, assistant Seattle superintendent, was born in 1870, and so would have been forty. [22] Women teachers hired in Seattle also were older than might be expected: half were between the ages of twenty-six and thirty, and one-fourth betwen thirty and forty.[23] All the women educators, both teachers and administrators, were unmarried. The Seattle school board, like school boards throughout the country, explicitly prohibited the hiring of married women for full-time, permanent positions. Married women, it was believed, would have divided loyalties which would distract them from their work.[24]

Although Pollock says almost nothing about the specific problems the women administrators discussed, in 1910 or later, and does not use the term *discrimination* in her account, the women must have been concerned about certain discriminatory practices that were widespread in education. Women teachers and principals worked long hours, often for less pay than men. They were also considered less desirable than men. The all-male school board did not like the fact that men were becoming a minority among educators and had to be reasured by Superintendent Cooper in 1910 that "no male candidate of acceptable rating [was] denied."[25] Nor did women have high status in city school systems. In the local education hierarchy as well as in society generally, elementary education was considered less important than secondary and higher education. Even if the women principals did not view such attitudes as biases towards females, they would have resented such disparaging treatment of the field of elementary education.

Probably the women also talked about matters relating to their own economic security. In an era before Social Security, educators' employment offered them no pension plans, limited medical benefits (for example, sick leave at half-pay), and neither tenure nor unemployment insurance. Financial concerns as well as discriminatory pay practices must have concerned the women, not only for themselves but also for the women they supervised. Elementary teachers were paid less than high school teachers, and of course elementary principals' salaries were smaller than those of their secondary counterparts.

In addition, women were viewed as less effective disciplinarians than men, especially with boys, and were usually excluded from secondary principalships except in a few rural districts, although there were many experienced, well-educated women among high school instructors. Seattle, in fact, did not have a woman high school principal until the 1973–74 academic year.[26] A caste system existed within the education establishment throughout the United States which relegated women and the specialities they dominated to inferior and less lucrative positions in the educational hierarchy. In her history of the organization, however, Pollock cites only the principals' isolation from each other as the main motivation for bringing them together, and merely hints at discrimination. Except that hint, not a word of hers survives which suggests that she recognized the burden imposed on women by sexist practices, or that she harbored feminist thoughts.

The situation in which the women school administrators found themselves was not unique to their profession, and they may have been influenced by the examples set by other female professionals in the early 1900s. The year before Pollock held the meeting at her home, seven women journalism students at the University of Washington had organized an honorary society for female journalists, Theta Sigma Phi, the forerunner of the national honorary of the same name (now Women in Communications).[27] Pollock, who had earned a master's degree in history at the university a few years earlier[28], was the founder of the local Women's University Club;[29] therefore, she must have been aware of Theta Sigma Phi's existence. Both women doctors and lawyers had their own exclusively female professional organizations, the Women's Medical Society and the Women Lawyer's Association. Furthermore, Phi Delta Kappa, the most prestigious of the education associations, had never admitted women to membership[30], which must have rankled Pollock's pride. She was, after all, an experienced professional with a Stanford degree, Phi Beta Kappa honors, and a master's degree as well.

In addition, Pollock had already learned a bitter lesson, albeit vicariously, about the vulnerability of women educators to men's superior power and to their biases, no matter how high a woman's abilities and expertise might carry her in the school system hierarchy. During her first stint in Seattle, when she was fresh out of San Jose Normal School, Pollock had watched with dismay as Seattle's male principals, resentful and insubordinate, forced Superintendent Julia Kennedy's dismissal after a brief, two-year tenure. Pollock believed that Kennedy, who had been trained at the University of Chicago under the eminent Francis Parker, a leading educator of the day, "laid the foundation for our present ideals of education in this city."[31]

In the year following the meeting at Pollock's home, she and her female colleagues decided to formalize their group as the School Women's League, with a constitution, by-laws, and officers. Anna B. Kane, principal of Brighton Grade School, was elected president. Other women administrators in the superintendent's office and female heads of departments in high schools were invited to join them, in what appears to have been the first organization of Seattle school employees. Soon the group was expanded to included women holding administrative positions at the nearby University of Washington and at private schools.[32]

By 1915, other organizations of female educational administrators had sprung up in the state, perhaps inspired by the Seattle League. The League issued a call to "all administrative groups of women in Washington to attend a luncheon in Tacoma at the Washington State Educational Association" on 28 October 1915. Adelaide Pollock opened the meeting with a short explanation of its purpose, and Anna B. Kane spoke on "what the SWL of Seattle means to us." Then Miss Purinton of Spokane described the activities of the Ella Flagg Young Club organized by teachers in her Eastern Washington city.[33] Ella Flagg Young was a superintendent of Chicago city schools.

Other speakers included Elizabeth Clarahan, principal of Lowell School in Seattle, who described the "retirement fund," a topic on which Pollock unfortunately does not elaborate. The president of the Washington Education Association, a Mrs. Monroe, and State Superintendent Josephine Corliss Preston also addressed the audience, as well as several other Washington women administrators and college professors and a visitor from California, identified only as Mrs. Sweezy.[34]

"All agreed on the need for a state organization," Pollock relates, and a motion was approved "that Miss Pollock appoint a committee of five to plan for such organization." When the state organization became a reality, Pollock was elected as the first president. She and two other members, Almina George, assistant superintendent in Seattle, and Lucy K. Cole, music supervisor in Seattle, were instructed to draw up a constitution and by-laws. The name was altered to State Women's Educational League, soon shortened to "The SWEL's" according to Pollock.[35]

Later that same year or early in 1916, California and Washington women met in Oakland and formed a national association of administrative women with Lucy K. Cole as the first president. Cole, however, soon left the Seattle schools, for reasons Pollock does not explain.[36]

At the annual National Education Association (NEA) convention in New York in 1916, Almina George "saw to it that the organization did not die" and was elected acting president of the new national association, which was accepted as an affiliate of NEA. Pollock herself seems not to have attended that historic meeting: she lists "others who have also attended and kept us in touch," including Jessie Lockwood, principal of John Muir Grade School, Seattle; Helen Laurie, principal of Ross School, Seattle; and Elizabeth Sterling, a 1906 graduate of the University of Washington and Clarke County Superintendent of Schools. The name of the organization was changed to the National Council of Administrative Women in Education (NCAWE).[37]

Two years later, Pollock retired from her principalship to go with the U.S. armed forces in France, where she taught citizenship for the American Red Cross throughout World War I.[38] The change seems to have been motivated by patriotism, but it also suggests that she had some independent source of income, possibly inherited from her parents. She was only fifty-eight when she left her administrative position, an exceedingly early retirement age for women educators of her day. Most women teachers and administrators, unless they terminated their professional work by marrying, had long careers, in part because there were no pension programs. Emma C. Hart, for instance, served in three principalships for a total of thirty-six years in the Seattle District. Maxine Kelly, a principal in Iowa before she came to Washington State, added another twenty-nine years of administrative experience in Seattle, most of it at one school. Jessie Lockwood presided over John Muir School from 1910 to 1930.[39]

After her early retirement, Pollock continued to travel. At various times during her career and later, she visited Europe, South America, and Japan, and she had studied at Columbia University in New York,[40] another indication that she had independent funds, for her salary when she retired had reached only $3,000 per year, not a generous income even in her era.[41]

The organization she had started and nurtured, meanwhile, grew rapidly and eventually formed chapters in major cities in every state. No comprehensive history of NCAWE has yet been written, however, and precise decade-by-decade numbers of members and chapters are not available.[42] After World War II, the numbers of women administrators began to decline nationally, as older women retired and were succeeded by male administrators rather than women.[43] Current NCAWE officers and members are attempting to rebuild the organization from a strong grass roots base of local councils.[44]

Adelaide Pollock continued to be a female pioneer and a founder of organizations for women educators. After her retirement from the Queen Anne principalship, she served on both the Seattle Planning Commission and the Seattle Women Police Advisory Board, unusual roles for a woman of her time. She remained active in educational organizations, including the Seattle chapter of NCAWE, and served as its historian in 1932, when she wrote her history of women administrators. She was elected president of the Washington Pioneer Teachers Association in 1931–32, and was one of the founders of a home for retired teachers, the Ida Culver House on Queen Anne Hill (now located in Seattle's Greenlake district), where she lived until her death on 12 May 1938. While visiting at the home of a friend on Vashon Island and delighting in the birds on the island, she suffered a fatal stroke; she was seventy-eight.[45]

Pollock had been active in the community in other ways. An avid member of the Seattle Audubon Society, she wrote and lectured about birds. One of her books on birds, *Excursions about Birdland*, was published in 1925 and republished in 1930 as *Wings over Land and Sea.*.[46] She belonged to the Seattle Mountaineers, a hiking and mountain-climbing group still in existence, and regularly led troops of Boy Scouts up the slopes of Mt. Rainier. She also was a member of the Washingtion Federation of Women's Clubs, Daughters of the American Revolution, and the Queen Anne Fortnightly Club.[47]

Throughout her career and later life, she exemplified what her contemporaries—at least, the old-stock white Americans among them—regarded as the ideal woman educator. Descended from a revolutionary war soldier, David Pollock, she was thus at least a fourth-generation American at a time when American leaders were obsessed with the perceived need to Americanize immigrant children.

Many prominent Americans believed that only natives of the young republic could properly discharge this duty, and viewed the surplus, native-born single women of the eastern states, as well as other single females born in America, as a resource to be used in the task of teaching immigrant children American values, not least of all loyalty to the republican form of government.[48]

Some sense of how native white Americans viewed the immigrants and other systems of government, as well as how they saw the task assigned to the public schools, can be glimpsed in the 1891 address of Washington's superintendent of public instruction, Robert B. Bryan, a displaced New Englander himself. Bryan told an assemblage of county superintendents that most of the immigrants

> are from the haunts of vice and crime, having no sympathy for our political and social systems . . . . the violent Russian nihilist, the brawling German socialist, the poisonous French communist, the depraved and degraded Dago from the shores of sunny Italy, and the pest-breeding hordes from the shores of the Flowery Kingdon in far-off Asia . . . . these elements must be engrafted upon the tree of American liberty, and the whole must be molded and kneaded into one harmonious and homogeneous mass...[49]

Pollock also was a devout Protestant and a long-time member of the Plymouth Congregational Church in Seattle, where she taught a Sunday School class for boys[50], in an era when old-stock Protestant Americans became nearly "unhinged" over the large number of Catholic immigrants. Even before the Civil War, Catherine Beecher and other prominent New Englanders expressed dismay over the numerous schools being established on the western frontier by Catholic nuns and priests. ("West" in Beecher's day meant Ohio.) They urged single eastern women to assume the responsibility of teaching frontier children, and established the National Board of Public Education to train potential teachers and provide funds for their transportation west. Before the National Board's existence ended, it sent some six hundred women west, some as far away as Oregon, after training them in teaching methodology and Protestant theology.[51]

As Polly Welts Kaufman had pointed out in a recent study of the diaries of women teachers sent west by the National Board, their belief in significant religious purpose often strengthened women's determination to follow a professional career. The teachers sent west by the Public Education Society spoke not of financial gain or personal independence but of duty and social usefulness, although in fact their professional careers allowed them a measure of independence that few American women of that time enjoyed.[52] Other women educators probably shared those views, although the Protestant roots of the American public school system have received attention from educational historians only in recent years.[53]

Kaufman argues, furthermore, that pioneer teachers were often the daughters of the first generally literate American women.[54] Adelaide Pollock did not provide details on either her parents or grandparents, but it seems likely that her mother, Marilla Lucore Pollock, helped to inspire her daughter's educational and professional aspirations. Marilla Lucore may have been a teacher before she married, influenced by the entirely new expectation that it was *women* who should prepare an educated citizenry for the infant republic. It seems likely—although it would take much research to verify—that most of the early members of NCAWE also were native-born Protestants with above-average educational backgrounds and a sense of national and religious purpose.

Imbued with WASP values, the women educators of Pollock's generation were prominent among the architects and builders of the largest public school system in the world. They educated millions of Americans whose only exposure to formal education was in elementary school. They also helped design a curriculum to express the values of the fledging republic. And they participated in setting the course for American public education for several decades into the future. They achieved all this, furthermore, in spite of many discriminatory and restrictive laws and policies.

Women school administrators were not the only architects and builders of the American educational system. Pollock and other western women, soon joined by female administrators from across the nation, attempted with NCAWE to provide a foundation from which they hoped and expected that later generations of women administrators could progress beyond the founders' own achievements.

If some of their values now seem outdated and suspect, their accomplishments still deserve recognition. The opposite has happened, unfortunately; they are almost universally neglected, by women and by their communities. Although Adelaide Pollock was honored by the Seattle chapter of Delta Kappa Gamma in 1938 two weeks after her death,[55] now she is virtually unknown. Queen Anne School is no more, and no school in Seattle was ever named after her. Those Seattle schools named for individuals have usually been named for men, not infrequently for men who never set foot in a Seattle school building (for example, U.S. presidents). Yet a school board member said of

Pollock shortly after she died, "Personnaly I know of no one over the years, either man or woman, whom I would rate as high as a pioneer leader in education, in both the restricted and larger sense, other than Miss Adelaide Pollock."[56] NCAWE seems unaware of Pollock's role as founding mother; today only the Queen Anne Historical Society even recognizes her name.

Adelaide Pollock is lost to history both because she was female and because she was an educator. Women—and men—need to be concerned not only about the absence of women from what is defined as history, but also about historians' perennial silence concerning important social and community functions such as education and socialization. Women's work and leadership in these areas affected not only their own lives, but the lives of children and men as well. If what we call "history" is meant to provide a comprehensive view of society's past, then it must encompass events at the community level. History is not merely the story of what a few nationally prominent men—a tiny minority of the population—thought and did, or of the social arenas which that minority found interesting. Feminist historians also err if they unconsciously accept old definitions of history or view all of women's family and community activities, or their participation in important but traditionally female occupations, as merely evidence of women's subjugation.

Notes

1. Adelaide Pollock, "The Early Administrative Women in Education of Seattle, Washington" (typescript, Seattle Public Library historical collection); "Adelaide Lowry Pollock," in Joseph Hazard, *Pioneer Teachers of Washington* (Seattle: Seattle Retired Teachers Association, 1955), pp. 142–143.

2. Pollock, "The Early Administrative Women."

3. U.S. Commissioner of Education, *Annual Report*, 1901, (Washington, D.C.: U.S. Government Printing Office, 1902), vo. 1, p. x.

4. Margaret Gribskov, "Feminism and the Woman School Administrator," in *Women and Educational Leadership*, ed. Sari Knopp Biklen and Marilyn B. Brannigan (Lexington, Mass.: Lexington Books, 1980). See also Patricia Ann Schmuck, *Sex Differentiation in Public School Administration* (Arlington, Va.: National Council of Administrative Women in Education, 1975).

5. In the northeastern region, women outnumbered men from 1870 until 1900, while in the West, men outnumbered women from the earliest settlement until 1970. See the U.S. Department of Commerce publication, *Historical Statistics of the United States: Colonial Times to 1970*, 1975 edition, vol. 1.

6. Polly Welts Kaufman, *Women Teachers on the Frontier*, (New Haven: Yale University Press, 1984). My own research in thirteen western states also supports this statement.

7. U.S. Commissioner of Education, *Report*, 1894–95 (Washington, D.C.: U.S. Government Printing Office, 1896), pp. 38 and 49.

8. In 1907 women outnumbered men at state universities in California, Iowa, Kansas, Minnesota, Nebrska, Texas, and Washington. See Thomas Woody, *A History of Women's Education in the United States*, vo. 2 (New York: Octagon Books, 1974), p. 290.

9. Bryce Eugene Nelson, *Good Schools: The Development of Public Schooling in Seattle, 1901–1922* (Ph.D. dissertation, University of Washington, 1981), p. 73.

10. For example, the national average in 1894–95 was $46.82 per month for males, and $39.41 for females. Male teachers earned an average of $47.62 that year in Washington; females, $42.28. U.S. Commissioner of Education, *Report*, p. x/vi.

11. Stanford University, *Alumni Director*, IV, 1891–1931 (Stanford, Calif.: Standord University Press, 1932).

12. Gribskov, "Feminism."

13. Pollock, "The Early Administrative Woman," and surviving personnel records in the Seattle School District archives.

14. Julia Kennedy headed the Seattle School District from 1889 to 1891, and Ellen Clara Sabin was the Portland, Oregon superintendent from 1888 to 1891.

15. Pollock, "The Early Administrative Woman"; Angie Burt Bowden, *Early Schools of the Washington Territory* (Seattle: Lowman and Hanford Company, 1935), p. 197; Seattle School District archives.

16. Arthur H. Allen, *Who's Who in Washington State* (Seattle: Arthur H. Allen Publisher, 1927); Estelle Greathead, *The Story of an Inspiring Past: Historical Sketch of the San Jose State Teachers College from 1862 to 1928* (San Jose: San Jose State Teachers College, 1928), p. 314.

17. U.S. Commerce Department, *Historical Statistics*, Sec. H. 598–601.

18. Seattle School District, *Directory*, 1902–03 to 1921–22. In Seattle School District archives.

19. Nelson, *Good Schools*, p. 62.

20. Pollock, "The Early Administrative Woman."

21. University of Washington Alumni Association, *History and Alumni Directory* (Seattle: University of Washington Alumni Association, 1941). Lovering is listed as Lydia E. Forsyth, her later married name.

22. Personnel records, Seattle School District archives.

23. Nelson, *Good Schools*, p. 71.

24. Ibid. p. 72.

25. Ibid. p. 73.

26. Roberta Byrd Barr, a black woman, was named principal of Lincoln High School in 1973 and was the first women to head a Seattle high school.

27. June Handeland Lee, "The Birth of a Notion," *Landmarks*, no. 3 (Fall, 1984).

28. University of Washington Alumni Association, *History*; Bessie Bankhead, "Adelaide Lowry Pollock" (typescript prepared for Seattle chapter of Delta Kappa Gamma, copy in Seattle School District archives); transcripts of the registrar, University of Washington.

29. University of Washington Alumni Association, *History*.

30. Phi Delta Kappa did not admit women until 1974.

31. Pollock, "The Early Administrative Woman."

32. Ibid.

33. Ibid. Ella Flagg Young was superintendent of the Chicago school system from 1909 to 1915.

34. Ibid.

35. Ibid.

36. Ibid.

37. Ibid. University of Washington Alumnai Association, *History*.

38. Allen, *Who's Who*; Bankhead "Adelaide"; Seattle *Times* obituary, 4 May 1938; copies of Pollock's personal correspondence in Seattle School District archives.

39. Seattle School District archives, personnel records.

40. Allen, *Who's Who*; Bankhead, "Adelaide." At some time Pollock also stated that she earned a second master's degree jointly awarded by San Jose State Normal School and the University of Notre Dame in California, but I have been unable to find the date or official confirmation of the degree.

41. Seattle School District archives.

42. Telephone conversation with Mary Walsh, Pittsburgh, immediate past president of NCAWE, on 13 July 1985.

43. Gribskov, "Feminism."

44. Walsh, conversation, op. cit.

45. Bankhead, "Adelaide"; Seattle *Times* obituary, 4 May 1938.

46. *Excursions about Birdland* appears to have been privately published, perhaps by Pollock. *Wings over Land and Sea* was published by Lowman & Hanford of Seattle.

47. Allen, *Who's Who*, "Adelaide."

48. Kaufman, *Women Teachers*. See also Katherine Kish Sklar, *Catherine Beecher: A Study in American Domesticity*. (New York: W.W. Norton), 1973.

49. Robert B. Bryan, quoted in Alexander Pouw-Bray, *Changes in the Common School System of Washington State, 1889#1899*, (M.A. thesis, University of Washington, 1973), pp. 65–66.

50. Seattle *Times* obituary, 4 May 1938.

51. Kaufman, *Woman Teachers*; and Sklar, *Catherine Beecher*.

52. Kaufman, *Woman Teachers*.

53. For studies of religion in the schools, see Ruth Miller Elson, *Guardians of Tradition* (Lincoln: University of Nebraska Press, 1964); David Tyack, "The Kingdom of God and the Common School: Protestant Ministers and the Educational Awakening of the West,;; *Harvard Educational Review*, 36, no. 3 (1066), pp. 447–469; and Diane Ravitch, *The Great School Wars: New York City, 1805#1973* (New York: Basic Books, 1974).

54. Kaufman, *Women Teachers*, p. xxi.

55. Bankhead, "Adelaide."

56. Hazard, *Pioneer Teachers*.

Chapter 7

Female Teachers
In The Netherlands,
1827–58

MINEKE van ESSEN

Alberdina Woldendorp was one of the first published women teachers in the Netherlands; her manual for women teachers at infant schools and needlework schools was published in Groningen in 1827.[1] Her life, which has not been previously documented, is a remarkable one and illustrates the issues facing women and education in the early nineteenth century in the Netherlands. It is by way of briefly introducing her story that I will raise the issues of women's education and access to teaching roles.

In 1819 Alberdina Woldendorp, married at the age of seventeen, maltreated by her husband and finally deserted, had to find a way to earn a living. Teaching needlework (a valuable skill in Netherlands in those days) seemed an appropriate way to provide for herself, and she began teaching needlework at an elementary school operated by her brother-in-law. She obtained an official divorce (an exceptional feat in itself) and devoted herself to her new-found livelihood. Of course, she had no training in pedagogy, but began to investigate educational publications and visiting other schools. She quickly discovered that there were no Dutch publications for women teachers and began writing down her ideas and experiences. Well aware of her vulnerable position, in the book's introduction she noted the valuable assistance of her brother-in-law and acknowledged the public sentiment of female inferiority. She said, "To err is human and women err more easily than men, because it cannot be expected of them that they are men's equals where knowledge and insight are concerned."[2] The book was favorably received by the pedagogic press, and she continued her efforts to train women teachers, organizing regular meetings for women to exchange ideas and new methodologies. In 1831 she opened her own needlework school, having received a teaching certificate. She remarried but continued teaching until her untimely death at age thirty-five.

Alberdina Woldendorp has not been captured in hardly any educational text about education in the Netherlands; she and many other women who contributed to the development of pedagogy have been ignored. Only two women are mentioned in the history of nineteenth century education in the Netherlands—Barbara van Meerten, a headmistress of a boarding school for girls and author of many pedagogical texts, and Elise van Calcar, a Frobel advocate, active feminist, and author who lived in the latter part of the nineteenth century. By and large, women's contributions have been neglected and lost to history.

There is a paucity of materials about women teachers in general during this period. My original sources included manuals for infant schools and girls' schoolteachers[3] pedagogic magazines[4], annual government education reports[5], announcements of job openings for women teachers[6], and the minutes of parliament[7]. These sources provided an overall picture of vocational training and professional duties of women teachers but gave no pictures of individual women. To recapture the life of Alberdina Woldendorp and other women educators, I had to consult minutes and other documents from supervising agencies[8] and benevolent societies[9], as well as other archival material in many different locations (there is no central archive about women educators in the Netherlands). All the original source materials are not referenced in discussion, but a complete listing is available in the original Dutch manuscript.[10] It must also be noted that most Catholic schools are not included; although nuns were very much occupied in educating young children and girls, their position differed so much from that of professional school teachers that I excluded them from my research.

A General Picture of Education in the Nineteenth Century

In the nineteenth century Dutch society was characterized by a rigorous segregation of the different classes and little opportunity for social mobility. This class segregation was mirrored in the educational offerings available. Children from the lowest social class (unskilled laborers and charity cases) had some elementary education in free, state primary schools, where coeducation was the rule. Although they theoretically attended school from age six to twelve, in reality most students attended only a few years because they were needed to supplement their family's income. There were no secondary schools, and all vocational training took place through apprenticeships in the work setting. The children received the education considered appropriate for their social position—the fundamentals of reading, writing, and arithmetic and some history and geography. For these children, knowledge was considered less important than their spiritual well-being. The major mission of this class of children was to learn to be obedient and industrious.

Children from the lower middle classes (skilled laborers and shopkeepers) had no free education and usually went to inexpensive, private primary schools. Except in the Catholic sector, these schools were coeducational. The aim and content of the curriculum did not differ fundamentally from that available in the free public schools; it was the same basic fundamental knowledge with an emphasis on morality to produce obedient and industrious citizens who know their proper place. Most of these children also received only a few years of schooling, for most secondary schools were not available. Boys received their vocational training on the job; girls returned to the home or attended a needlework school.

Students from the middle classes (civil servants, entrepreneurs, and professionals) attended relatively expensive and usually sex-segregated private primary schools leading to about four years of secondary education in sex-segregated day or boarding schools. These schools had a full curriculum of reading, writing, arithmetic, history, geography, and language. Although some girls attended secondary schools, there were not many available, and curriculum consisted primarily of French and needlework. The upper classes received their primary education at home with a tutor and attended secondary school at exclusive, private, sex-segregated boarding schools.

Women as Teaching Professionals

In Alberdina Woldendorp's day, coeducation was the rule in most Dutch primary schools, and the teaching roles were filled by men. Women teachers populated only the infant schools, girls' schools (both at the primary and secondary level), and needlework schools. Some women tutored students at home or worked as governesses. These were the only roles available to women.

The social ideology concerning woman's role as teacher was directly related to woman's role as homemaker. It was appropriate for women to educate young children and girls, but it was not their place to educate boys after the very early stages. There was no training for women teachers because woman's "natural" role as mother was seen to translate to her professional role. Knowledge of child development and theories of pedagogy—which were seen as essential tools for male teachers—were thought unnecessary for females. The first Dutch Education Act in 1806 made no mention of requirements or standards for women teachers.

Although there were no legal standards for women teachers, the teaching manuals clearly depicted certain expectations about the character and capacity of women teachers. The model teacher should be loving, care giving, self-controlled, and of unquestionable virtue. She should prepare her lessons well, possess a wealth of knowledge, and teach in a sound, didactic manner. Obviously, a great many teachers could not live up to this ideal. They had received no training or poor training in content areas and often knew barely more than their pupils. In pedagogy there was no training, and many did not know the fundamental principles of teaching. The general view was that women, by virtue of being women, were trained well enough for the educational obligations they would face; this was belived to be true for both married and unmarried women who were accepted as teachers within this limited sphere. And women, such as Alberdina Woldendorp, who wanted professional training were left to find their own way.

In the early nineteenth century, however, the search for changes began. In 1827 the national authorities created a limited opportunity for the training of prospective women teachers at girls' schools. Ten scholarships were made available to middle-class, boarding school girls without means to train for the examination of teaching. This was the first opportunity for education beyond the secondary level and the first step toward the professionalization of women teachers. It was also the first recognition that some knowledge of pedagogy was important—even for girls' schools—and that women's "natural" knowledge was not sufficient for the role of teacher. Although many of the scholarship winners became teachers, some did not; this was the only opportunity for any education for girls without means, and some young women seized that opportunity.

The Infant-School Movement

At the same time that scholarships were being awarded to women teachers for girls' schools, there was a growing interest in the infant schools, which were taught primarily by women. Imitating the ideas flourishing in other European centers, an infant school was developed with clear pedagogical purposes. The dame schools had been the order of the day, but in the next decades the number of pedagogically sound infant schools began to grow (see table 1).

Table 1. Teachers in Infant Schools, The Netherlands, 1858

	Number of schools	Number of male teachers	Number of female teachers	Number of assistants
"Modern" infant schools	395	21	415	742
Dame schools	311		304	83

Source: Verslag van den staat der hooge, middelbare en lagere scholen in het kroninkrijk der Nederlanden (1858–1859), p. 200.

The rising concern over the education of young children led to the impetus to train women teachers at the infant schools. Between 1827 and 1858 the work of women teachers increasingly required some additional training. The topics of training manuals included pedagogy, didactics, and child development. The need for training supplanted the idea that women "naturally" had the capacities for teaching young children. Training centers, usually at the initiative of local supervising bodies, were established throughout the country. Part-time courses and practical training were offered. In 1844 the first (and for a number of years, the only) part-time training college for infant-school teachers was established in Rotterdam with a curriculum that combined traditional subject matter with pedagogic methods.[11] It was not until the end of the nineteenth century, however, that full-time training colleges were founded.

Women Teachers in the Girls' Schools

The professionalization of women teachers at girls' schools happened more rapidly than in the infant schools; rigorous examinations required subject matter knowledge as well as pedagogy. While in the 1830s female teachers of girls' schools were not examined in pedagogy, by 1840 the topic was obligatory in some states. National examination requirements for women teachers did not yet exist, however.

Most girls' schools were private businesses. The head was dependent solely on tuition fees and boarding fees. Sometimes there was an additional government subsidy. Yet all expenses of running a school—the purchase or rental of the building, heat, light, furniture, texts, and salaries of auxiliary and domestic staff—were paid for by the head. Some women proved to be excellent managers and provided well for themselves. In 1840 one headmistress in Groningen, for example, earned about 4,000 guilders which was a very comfortable salary and about 1,000 guilders more than the annual salary of some important civil servants. She invested wisely and helped provide for her relatives as well.

But not all women had such successful careers. Maria Johanna van Duinen, one of the scholarship winners for training in the infant schools, is one example of a less successful teacher. She was awarded the scholarship in 1836 and passed the teachers' examination in 1838. After eight years of practical training as an assistant teacher in different girls' schools all over the Netherlands, she opened a small boarding school for girls in a small town near Groningen, the city where she was born. With the help of an assistant teacher, she educated fifteen girls in ages ranging from six to fourteen in reading, writing, Dutch grammar, and French. But Maria was unable to provide for herself, even though the school inspectors and parents were highly satisfied with the school. She sought several other positions and at age of thirty-four was appointed head of a day boarding school attended by one hundred girls. She earned a salary of 1,000 guilders a year, a reasonable middle-class income for the time. But she was in poor health and had to give up the post. She therefore returned to her parents' home and earned a living by tutoring. She wrote a lesson book on natural science (which was not favorably received) and died at the age of thirty-nine.

Other women in girls' schools remained dependent on relatives, others were dependent (live-in) assistant teachers, and still others eked out an existence with home tutoring to supplement their salaries. Often headmistresses were assisted by husbands or mothers and other members of the family, so that the school assumed the character of a small family business. An example of such a family enterprise comes from Zierikzee, a small town on the North Sea. Adriana van der Velden, the twenty-year-old daughter of a village schoolmaster, was appointed head of the girls' school in 1853. Her three sisters all took on school responsibilities. One, who had a teaching certificate, became an assistant teacher; another, only fourteen years old, assisted in the household; a twelve-year-old began studying for the teachers' examination and became a teacher trainee. With the exception of the youngest, who left Zierikzee to obtain experience elsewhere, the sisters remained in faithful service for twenty-two years at the schools.

Most girls'-school teachers came from the educated but not highly prosperous middle class. In this class it was considered normal for girls to make their living before marriage and to continue some livelihood after marriage. They only had to make their independent way when fathers or other relatives could not support them if they remained spinsters or when they did not have a sufficient income through their husbands. In my investigations, however, I found the impetus of economic survival to be less a motivating factor than the sense of independent pride and self-respect that derived from teaching.

Women's Certification as Teachers

The number of certificates granted to women teachers at girls' schools rose sharply between 1827 and 1858 (see figure 1).[12]

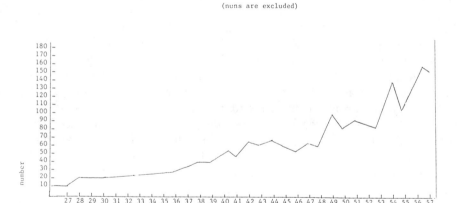

NUMBER OF CERTIFICATES GRANTED TO WOMEN TEACHERS

1827–1858

(nuns are excluded)

Figure 1

The rise in the number of women earning the teaching certificate cannot be explained solely by the availability of training opportunities. These opportunities were severely limited; the ten yearly scholarships and part-time courses available only in Amsterdam and Groningen were the only opportunities for women teachers. Most women prepared themselves through self-study. Yet despite the evident lack of training, the number of certificates granted to women continued to rise. Neither can employment openings explain the rise in certification; except in the girls' schools, men were still preferred over women. It is also interesting to note women's 102 percent gain in employment as headmistresses during this period (see table 2).

Table 2. Headmistresses and Headmasters, the Netherlands, 1825, 1848, and 1858

Position	Number in 1825	Number in 1848	Number in 1858	% increase
Headmistresses	181	257	366	102
Headmasters	2624	2964	3104	18

Source: Verslagen nopens den staat der hooge middlebare en lagere scholen in het koningrijk der Nederlanden (1816–40), pp. 140–141; (1848–49), p. 109; (1858–59), pp. 68–69.

Other factors must be used to explain this sharp rise in certificates granted to women. First, it became more customary for girls' schools to employ only qualified assistant teachers. Although not yet required by law, the jobs previously held by women now required certification. Many women teachers availed themselves of the limited training opportunities or studied on their own to earn the certificate. The certificates granted do not indicate the number of novices in the field but rather reflect the growing concern for training among women already teaching. Second, women came to regard the certificate as insurance; if they never married or were widowed, they would be able to earn a living instead of being dependent on relatives. And third, to be prepared for the teaching profession, with knowledge of child development, was seen as an admirable quality in a wife and mother. The Dutch minister for home affairs said in 1857, "Women trained to be teachers often appear to be the most desirable to choose as wives."[13] Thus the dictim about women's "natural" abilities translating to the classroom was reversed; the view changed from the idea that good wives made good teachers to the view that good teachers made good wives. This idea took hold, and the preference for young and unmarried women teachers became evident. Finally, earning the teaching certificate was the only higher education available to women, and some saw passing the teaching examination as a sign of their education and proof of their ability.

Women's Arrival as Teaching Professionals

The Education Act of 1857 finally recognized women as educational professionals and placed them, with a few limitations, on an equal footing with male teachers. Examination requirements were established and a legal minimum age was set. Unfortunately, the law did not apply to all categories of female teachers. Infant-school teachers remained exempt, as did needlework teachers. Although regulations were promised governing these exemptions, they were delayed for a century. Meanwhile, women could teach in these exempted areas on the basis of their "womanhood." Only recently have the last remnants of this inheritance from the nineteenth century concerning needleworka teachers vanished. In 1985 new standards were set for this exempt category.

While the Education Act of 1857 granted almost equal status in requirements for men and women teachers, there was a backlash. Young, unmarried women teachers were preferred (and were also cheaper than their more experienced counterparts). In the literature and in practice, the preference for unmarried women was already perceptible (see table 3). It was felt that domesticity was woman's natural role. Wives and mothers, it was assumed, had a role to perform at home which conflicted with the role of teaching. Thus, at the very beginning of the professionalization of women as teachers, again the idea of women's "rightful" place took hold and denied women employment opportunities in schools. By the end of the nineteenth century this idea was well established, and some decades later there were laws prohibiting married women from teaching. The last remnants of these laws were not to be abolished again until the second women's liberation movement in the 1970s. And the sex-segregation in employment grew; male teachers disappeared from the infant schools, and female assistant teachers were relegated more often to the elementary schools, where they would have a positive effect on younger students. Thus the advances made in the professionalization of women teachers achieved in the period of 1827 to 1858 led to some negative changes in the end of the nineteenth and twentieth century. While the argument about women's "natural" capabilities for teaching no longer holds true, there remains the image that women's contributions are best served with the very young, with daughters, and in subservient roles to men in the educational system.

Table 3. Married and Widowed Women Teachers, The Netherlands, 1827–57

Period	% female teachers
1827–33	26.0
1834–39	24.0
1840–44	15.0
1845–49	7.5
1850–54	9.5
1855–57	8.0

Notes

1. Alberdina Woldendorp, *Praktische handleiding voor onderwijzeressen der aanvange-of kinderscholen en die der vrouwelijke handwerken voor jeugdige meisjes* (Groningen, 1827.

2. Ibid., p. xv.

3. Between 1823 and 1858 nine manuals for infant-school teachers were published in the Netherlands. There of them were written by members of supervising bodies, three were translations from foreign manuals (under which a manual written by the Reverend Mayo and his sister Elisabeth, who both advocated the education of young children in England), and the remainder were written by teachers. Besides Alberdina Woldendorp, those teachers were her brother-in-law (his manual came out in 1847; in the book he did not even mention the existence of Alberdina's manual) and the principal of the training college for infant-school teachers in Rotterdam. For women teachers at girls' schools, only two manuals were published. One of them was writen in 1829 by the famous headmistress Barbara van Meerten and the other by an anonymous teacher in 1856.

4. I investigated twenty pedagogical magazines which appeared in the period under study. The most important of these was *Nieuwe bijdragen ter bevordering van het onderwijs en de opvoeding in het koningrijk der Nederlanden* (1816–63). This magazine also published lists of persons who received a teaching certificate. With the help of data on ages and domiciles mentioned in these lists, I managed to find the birth certificates of about 50 percent of the women who received a teaching certificate. Since the profession of the father was mentioned in the birth certificates, I could fix the social class of the teachers.

5. *Verslagen nopens den staat der hooge, middelbare en lagere scholen in het koningrijk der Nederlanden* (1816–58).

6. Most vacant jobs for male as well as female teachers at elementary and secondary schools were announced in the magazine *Nieuwe bijdragen ter bevordering van het onderwijs en de opvoeding in het koningrijk der Nederlanden*. This magazine also informed the readers about the names of persons who were appointed to vacant jobs and sometimes gave details about the application procedure and the school at issue. I collected all information available on the more than 500 vacant jobs for women teachers in the period under study (such as names of appointed teachers, salary, tuition fees, subjects that had to be taught, numbers of pupils, and demands that were made). With the help of a computer, I was able to make some generalizations for such topics as employment, demands, marital status, and income.

7. *Verslagen der handelingen van de Staten-Generaal* (1830–63).

8. For example, I consulted the archives of the Ministry of Home Affairs in the Hague and the archives of provincial and local supervisory bodies in Groningen, Deventer, Zwolle, and Rotterdam.

9. The most important benevolent society in the Netherlands in those days was the *Maatschappij: tot Nut van 't Algemeen*. I consulted the archives of this society in Amsterdam in Groningen.

10. Mineke van Essen, *Onderwijzeressden in Niemandsland. Vrouwen in opvoding en onderwijs* (Nijkerk, 1985, ISBN 90 266 1810 7).

11. On this training college, see Mineke van Essen, "A Dutch Traiing College for Infant-School Teachers in the Middle Nineteenth Century," *Conference Papers for the 4th Session of the International Standing Conference for the History of Education* (Budapest, 1982), pp. 407–417.

12. This diagram is composed on the basis of the lists of women who received a teaching certificate, as published in the *Nieuwe bijdragen ter bevordering van het onderwijs en de opvoeding in het koningrijk der Nederlanden. Verslagen nopens den staat der hooge, middelbare en lagere scholen in het koningrijk der Nederlanden* (1816–40, pp. 140–141; (1848–49), p. 109; (1858–59) pp. 68–69.

13. *Verslag der handelingen van de Staten-Generaal* (1856–57) p. 1047.

14. Table 3 is based on information collected from the announcements of vacant jobs (see note 6).

Chapter 8

Women's Participation In Teachers' Unions In England and United States

JILL BYSTYDZIENSKI

Teachers' organizations, and unions in particular, have been potential vehicles for teachers' economic and social advancement in the Western world. Women, who have constituted the majority of school teachers in many Western countries since the last quarter of the nineteenth century, have not benefited as much as men teachers from their union affiliation. Their position within the teaching occupation is still lower than than of their male couinterparts, and their involvement in running the unions and influencing policy is generally very limited.

Studies of teacher unionism typically blame women's "nature" or socialization for their failure to take part in union activity or to organize for better pay and working conditions. The image of women teachers as passive and nonpolitical has been perpetuated by many historians (Troop, 1957; Purvis, 1981; Tyack, 1967; Mattingly, 1975; Sugg. 1978) as well as sociologists (Lieberman, 1956; Etzioni, 1969; Lortie, 1975) and is frequently reflected in the unions' own publications (National Union of Teachers, 1981; American Federation of Teachers, 1982). Women teachers are consistently assumed to be non militant, inactive in union matters, and lacking in commitment to the occupation.

The history of women's participation in teachers' unions, however, has been very much neglected. Only recently have works begun to appear which suggest that periodically women teachers haven't taken an active role in their organizations and have even been moved to militancy (Partington, 1976; Ozga, 1981; Urban, 1982). Moreover, some have pointed out that to understand frequent lack of female teacher militancy and its occasional outbursts, one needs to examine structural and ideological factors rather than attribute conservative tendencies to the women themselves (Ziegler, 1967; Cole, 1969). If women teachers have indeed been passive and unconcerned, how does one account for their prominent role in the American Federation of Teachers during its early years or the actions of the National Federation of Women Teachers in England?

This essay compared the participation of women in teachers' unions in the United States and England. Historical evidence indicates that in many instances women were active in teachers' unions in both countries. There were many similarities in the role women played in the development of teachers' organizations in the two societies, yet a major difference existed in the levels at which activity was manifested. The history of women teachers in England reflects relatively high activity among the rank-and-file union members but little participation in union leadership, while the reverse is the case in the United States.

As will be shown, female socialization cannot account for the fact that many women teachers participated in union struggles; rather, wider societal context, and especially economic and social factors, influenced the ebb and flow of teacher militancy. Moreover, the structure of the teacher's unions themselves determined the extent to which women were able to participate.

Nineteenth Century Teachers' Organizations

Before the rapid expansion of public education in the nineteenth century in the United States, women constituted a minority of schoolteachers (Cremin, 1971), However, it was not long after the Civil War that women began to outnumber men in elementary education. Their proportion increased steadily, and by 1930 there were five times as many female as male teachers (Tyack, 1967, p. 470). A similar development occurred in England. With the passage of the 1870 Education Act, which established nonsectarian, local authorities to administer elementary schooling, women began to enter school teaching in greater numbers; by the turn of the century they had surpassed males (Gosden, 1972, p. 2).

The reasons for this influx of females into teaching in both countries were primarily economic. Women could be hired for considerably less than men. Moreover, teaching allowed for easy entry into uncertified posts compared with such options as domestic service or employment in factories, and so was relatively attractive to women with some education who needed or wanted to work (Butts and Cremin, 1953). At the same time, vigorous industrial and commercial expansion reduced the attractiveness of teaching for men (Ogburn, 1933). Men who entered school teaching at the end of the nineteenth century did so predominantly at the higher levels: in high school and administrative positions in the United States (Lortie, 1975, pp. 8–9) and in grammar schools and headmaster posts in England (Tropp, 1957, p. 18). Women teachers for the most part, filled the least prestigious, worst-paid, elementary-school positions.

The dramatic increase in the number of female teachers during the latter part of the nineteenth century and part of the twentieth century in the United States and England has been cited by many students of the occupation as largely contributing to teaching's depressed social status and as a significant deterrent to teacher professionalization (Lieberman, 1956; Tropp, 1957; Etzioni, 1969; Lortie, 1975). It is ironic that at the very time when women began to enter classroom teaching in large numbers, teachers' organizations increased in number and strength.

In the United States, local and state associations proliferated during the second half of the nineteenth century. In 1857 the first national teachers' association, appropriately named the National Teachers' Association, was established (Wesley, 1957). It was not until the 1880s, however, that the association (renamed in 1870 the National Education Association or NEA), began to draw large membership from among classroom teachers. But it would be wrong to assume that, as more and more women entered the teaching occupation and joined the NEA and its local and state affiliates, they began to gain power in teachers' organizations. As Elsbree (1939, ch. 20) points out, teachers' associations initially either barred women entirely or placed severe restrictions on their participation. Women were not admitted to membership in the NEA until 1866. Moreover, the NEA was organized to favor the dominance of school superintendents and college presidents. Since such positions were exclusively filled by males, women were effectively excluded from having a voice in policy matters (Bystydzienski, 1979, p. 71).

The policies developed by the NEA in the latter part of the nineteenth century ignored the welfare of classroom teachers. The NEA leadership, in its attempt to build a teaching "profession," shied away

from any pronouncements or activities which might have been interpreted as labor union tactics and concentrated on what it believed to
be more lofty purposes, such as the general improvement of American
education (Wesley, 1957). The association did not adopt unionist principles until well into the twentieth century; however, it remained the
only political vehicle for classroom teachers until the establishment of
the American Federation of Teachers in 1916.

The early developments in teachers' organizations in England
paralleled those in the United States. Until 1870, the English school
system was organized entirely on a denominational basis, and so were
the first teachers' associations. They were typically patronized by a
religious society or its leading members (Gosden, 1972, p. 2). With the
establishment of nonsectarian elementary schools in 1870, a national,
nondenominational organization, the National Union of Elementary
Teachers (NUET), came into being. Unlike its U.S. counterpart, the
NEA, the NUET recognized teachers' economic interests as among
its basic principles (Tropp, 1957; Locke, 1974). However, during its
early decades, the organization was reluctant to take action to improve teachers' salaries, secure tenure, or gain rights to appeal
employers' decisions (Tropp, 1957, ch. 8). Although presumably
representing elementary-school teachers, the majority of whom were
women, the NUET leadership was dominated by male headteachers
and principals (Purvis, 1981). By 1889, when the union dropped the
word *elementary* from its title, women constituted 75 percent of all
classroom teachers (Tropp, 1957, p. 118), and yet men were firmly in
charge of the organization.

Most historical accounts dealing with the development of
teachers' organizations in the nineteenth century in both England
and the United States acknowledge the influx of women into teaching
with the expansion of state-controlled education, as well as their vir-
tual absence from key positions and lack of voice in rapidly growing
teachers' organizations (see, for example, Elsbree, 1939, Tropp, 1957;
Wesley, 1957; and Roy, 1968). At the same time, these accounts take
the view that women were reluctant to participate in organizational
activity because of their generally short-term involvement in the occupation (between leaving school and marriage) and the dominant image of femininity favoring passivity and lack of interest in political
matters. A more careful examination of historical evidence, however,
reveals considerable activity among female schoolteachers and
numerous attempts to achieve equal status within the occupation of
teachers' organizations.

In the United States during the last quarter of the nineteenth century, the NEA came under the firm control of a conservative group of school superintendents and college presidents, popularly known as "the old guard" (Schmid, 1963, pp. 30–31). The control of this group, however, did not go unchallenged. It was classroom teachers who demanded that the NEA concern itself with their needs, and the leaders of the insurgents were more often than not female (Schmid, 1963). Women teachers at this time dominated elementary education, and despite the popular view that women were not committed to a teaching career, as well as a high level of turnover of primary-school teachers, women constituted a majority of the members of the occupation and formed a committed, career-oriented core group (Bystydzienski, 1979, p. 72).

The *Addresses and Proceedings* of the NEA from the 1880s and 1890s record numerous challenges by women members to prevailing policies of the organization. In most cases, the women argued for a greater role for women teachers in the NEA and for improving the economic conditions of classroom teachers. For instance, at the 1884 annual meeting of the association, a woman delegate spoke in favor of more involvement of women teachers in the decisions of the NEA (National Education Association, 1884, p. 112). In 1891 a group of West Virginia Education Association delegates, most of whom were women, described the campaign for higher salaries they had inaugurated in their state and encouraged other teachers to do the same (Lord, 1966, p. 53). In an address at the 1894 annual meeting of the association, a woman principal challenged the anti-union stance of the leadership by suggesting that the only way to raise the status of teachers was by organizing efforts for higher salaries (Donley, 1976, p. 12). Women were thus at the forefront of a movement to transform the NEA from a low-key, debating society into a union. It is interesting to note that the challenge came largely from female educators who had been promoted into higher ranks as principals, and increasingly, towards the end of the century as school superintendents.

Although many U.S. women teachers were active and vocal in their national organization, they did not speak out as a group against the policies of the NEA. Not until 1914 was a Department of Classroom Teachers established within the association which became a vehicle for the representation of elementary teachers' interests (Wesley, 1957, p. 23). The largely individual and isolated attempts of female educators to change the NEA were unsuccessful. At the turn of the century, "the old guard" remained firmly entrenched (Schmid, 1963), and classroom teachers began to organize themselves into alternative organizations—unions—in several cities and states. Women featured prominently in these efforts, particularly in Pennsylvania and Illinois (Donley, 1976, p. 13).

During its first three decades, the National Union of Teachers (NUT) in England was controlled by male headmasters (principals) and headteachers (Purvis, 1981). Despite the steady growth in the numbers of women elementary teachers, only a small percentage joined the NUT during the 1870s and 1880s (Tropp, 1957, p. 145). By the end of the century, however, union ranks had almost tripled—from 16,000 in 1890 to 43,620 in 1900 (Tropp, 1957, p. 169)—largely because of an increase in female membership.

The dramatic growth of women members in the NUT is directly attributable to the actions of the Equal Pay League. The league formed in 1896 by female teachers, worked as a pressure group within the NUT to recruit more women into the union and into leadership positions (Ozga, 1981, p. 21). It also wanted "to level up the woman's status to that of her male fellow-professionals and fellow citizens" (Webb, 1915, p. 8) by trying to achieve equal pay for woman teachers. Although unsuccessful in attaining the latter goal, the woman's league brought the issue of sex inequality within the teaching occupation and the NUT into public debate and was instrumental in gaining the support and participation of many female teachers. Spurred on by the efforts of the Equal Pay League, women teachers began actions at the local level to recruit more women into their organizations and to pass motions in support of equal pay (Phipps, 1928).

British women teachers at the end of the nineteenth century, like their American counterparts, became increasingly supportive of trade union tactics. Although the NUT defeated a motion in 1895 to affiliate with the Trades Union Congress (the British equivalent of today's AFL/CIO), many local associations continued attempts to work with trade councils and to support strike actions (Bystydzienski, 1984, p. 6). At the local level, women teachers during the 1890s often made speeches and proposed resolutions favoring unionization (Phipps, 1928). Despite the greatly increased female activity, however, men continued to dominate the NUT. In 1900 women were conspicuously absent from the NUT administration, and the union did not even consider debating the equal pay issue (Webb, 1915, p. 14).

As the developments of teacher organizations in the nineteenth century in the United States and England indicate, women teachers did participate in them and actively struggled to gain some control of their policies and effect some changes. Such evidence contradicts assertions that women teachers were docile and unconcerned and did not speak out or act on their own behalf. Particularly towards the end of the nineteenth century, female teachers in both countries became increasingly vocal and active. Reasons for this behavior cannot be found in the women themselves, but rather in the social and economic conditions of the time.

In both the United States and England, the last quarter of the nineteenth century was a time of rapid, though erratic, economic expansion. In the United States especially, and to a lesser extent in England, the growth of popular education came to be ideologically justified as providing able individuals with opportunities for social mobility in the increasingly diversified economic market (Karier, 1975). The job of public-school teaching thus in theory assumed relative importance. However, the employment conditions of teachers remained deplorable. Low salaries, lack of job security, and total subordination to school authorities characterized classroom teaching in the nineteenth century. As teachers' spokespersons at the time clearly indicated, public educators were convinced of the importance of the task they performed and deeply resented the lack of recognition from the society (Tropp, 1957, ch. 1;1 Wesley, 1957, p. 65). As teachers' organizations began to grow and prosper, expectations of better working conditions and higher status were raised but not realized. Teachers thus became increasingly radicalized—a condition clearly manifested in the growing teacher militancy at the turn of the century.

Since women constituted the majority of schoolteachers in both countries in the latter part of the nineteenth century, many must have been influenced by the general conditions affecting the teaching occupation at the time. Women teachers, however, also experienced a lower status than their male collegues, a situation which made it doubly difficult for them to function effectively as teachers and members of their occupational organizations. As female teachers' attempts to gain equal status with males within their occupation produced no changes, women educators became more militant.

Another factor which helped to encourage and support female teacher militancy was the suffrage movement. As women in the United States and England organized and lobbied to get the vote, the idea of ending sex discrimination, especially in pay, became more acceptable (Melder, 1977). Many of the suffragists were in fact schoolteachers (Cook, 1978).

In addition, specific conditions in the two societies encouraged different patterns of female teacher activity. In England, towards the end of the nineteenth century, teachers found themselves increasingly under attack from established sectors of the society. The old middle class in particular, resenting the growth of popular education and social services, used teachers as a scapegoat, blaming them for supposedly deteriorating morals and skills of generations of children and attributing teachers' failure to educate properly to their lower-class origins (Tropp, 157, pp. 147–149; Ozga, 1981, pp. 22–23). Since the expansion in British education in the nineteenth century occurred in elementary education and since the vast majority of elementary teachers were women of working-class background (Purvis, 1981), they deeply resented the public hostility directed towards them. The attacks on British elementary-school teachers appear to have had a radicalizing effect, bringing many into a closer alliance with the working-class trade union movement (Tropp, 1957, pp. 149–150). Since the NUT rejected an official alliance with the Trades Union Congress and most of its leaders remained opposed to union tactics, elementary teachers' unionist activities became largely confined to the local level.

In the United States, women teachers towards the end of the nineteenth century appear to have been more active at the national and state level than at the local level. Several factors may account for this pattern. After 1870, the United States experienced a massive growth in the secondary-education system (Trow, 1961), which began to draw in large numbers of women (Tyack, 1967). By this time, primary-school teaching was the exclusive domain of females, and an increasing number of elementary-school principal posts became available to women teachers (Wesley, 1957). Moreover, American women teachers had typically come from middle-rather than working-class backgrounds (Lortie, 1975, p. 35). School teaching in the nineteenth century United States was virtually the only socially acceptable occupation for educated women who wanted to work (Butts and Cremin, 1953). Middle-class, relatively well-educated women constituted the committed, active core of the teaching occupation (Bystydzienski, 1979, p. 72). Since local teachers' associations were dominated by conservative male superintendents (Donley, 1976, p. 18), women teachers increasingly began to turn to the larger and more fluid state associations, as well as to teachers' organizations in large cities such as Chicago, New York, and Minneapolis (Donley, 1976, p. 13). Female state representatives made frequent attempts to influence the national policies of the NEA.

With time, as American women teachers' efforts to gain power within established associations produced no visible results, they began to develop alternative organizations. Women teachers were thus at the vanguard of establishment of the first real teachers' unions in the United States.

At the turn of the century, many women teachers in England and the United States were active participants in their organizations and also worked towards improving their situation in those organizations and within their occupation. Their efforts continued and were strengthened in the course of the first decades of the twentieth century.

Unionization During the first Half of the Twentieth Century

During the first two decades of the twentieth century, the actions of women teachers in the United States and England intensified. Most notably, women teachers on both continents, failing to make inroads within existing, male dominated organizations, began to establish alternative structures.

In England, women NUT members through their Equal Pay League (renamed in 1906 the National Federation of Women Teachers, or NFWT) persisted in pressuring the union into accepting the principle of equal pay (Ozga, 1981, p. 21). At the 1904 NUT national conference, despite hostile remarks from male delegates, the group succeeded in putting forward a motion for equal pay, but the motion was voted down by a very large majority (Webb, 1915). The women did not give up, however, and year after year, despite demonstrations of opposition from the men, motions for equal pay were made (Ozga, 1981, p. 21).

In 1911, NFWT members launched a campaign to approve a NUT national conference motion of sympathy for unenfranchised women teachers. The women worked vigorously for several months so that the motion would be put to the full conference at Aberystwyth that year. When the motion was made, however, "all hell broke loose." "Hundreds of men, massed at the back of the hall, prevented Mrs. Croft from obtaining a hearing. They stamped, howled, hurled insults at the speaker and the suffragists, and utterly refused to allow Mrs. Croft's speech to proceed" (Phipps, 1928, p. 58). NFWT members, despite an overwhelming defeat, persevered. The "sympathy" motion was introduced at NUT conferences in 1912, 1913, and 1914, each time losing support by a large margin (Ozga, 1981, p. 22).

Failing to get their motion accepted by the national organization, NFWT members made attempts to have it passed at the local level.

However, because of the use of "subtle tactics that allowed for the revision of union rules so that local associations were released from their obligation to support the sympathy motion, and the last-minute changing of the dates of local associations' meetings so that no debate on such motions took place" (Ozga, 1981, p. 22), the group was unsuccessful in its attempts to gain support for the motion.

It seems that male resistance to the NFWT's attempts to be recognized on an equal basis within the NUT grew in proportion to the women's activity. Phipps (1928) details many examples of physical intimidation as well as descriptions of what were clearly shady practices to prevent the election of women executive members. For instance, at the 1913 national conference of the NUT, a certain Lord Haldane, outlining education of the future, referred throughout his speech exclusively to the education of boys. A Miss Cutten who was brave enough to ask the question "What about the education of girls?" was physically assaulted and, along with other women delegates, ejected from the meeting hall (Phipps, 1928, p. 32). Although women teachers increased their attempts to run for office, the strong control of the election machinery by men made such attempts extremely difficult. To keep women from getting power in the local associations, female candidates were often prevented from running for office by having their names excluded from nominating papers or being omitted from candidate lists (Phipps, 1928, p. 34). Such tactics, and the increasing frustration over the equal pay issue, eventually led the NFWT to sever its connection with the NUT.

The NFWT seceded from the NUT in 1919 and was renamed the National Union of Women Teachers (NUWT). Ironically, that very year, at its national conference, the NUT finally passed a motion for equal pay. Strong campaigning in local associations by members of the NFWT had finally prevailed; however, it was a hollow victory because a gap developed between official policy and NUT practice. Immediately following the pasage of the Equal Pay Amendment, the NUT endorsed a government report which stated that a salary scale which was adequate for women teachers was not adequate for men (Partington, 1976, p. 83).

As Ozga (1981) points out, increased female teacher militancy following World War I most likely alarmed the NUT executive into permitting the 1919 equal pay referendum, in the hope that token support through the adoption of the principle would prevent splits within the union. In the immediate aftermath of the war, as teachers' salaries became even more depressed, teachers' strikes were frequent and women teachers played a prominent role in their organization

(Phipps, 1928). When new salary scales announced in 1918 actually reduced salaries for women, the NFWT held a mass meeting in London's Trafalgar Square and threatened strike action (Partington, 1976, p. 58). Women teachers were exhibiting signs of a strong militant tendency which could no longer be dismissed by the male NUT executive. The NUT's halfhearted attempt to appease women teachers failed to work, and the women formed a separate union to fight for their cause. The NUWT was disbanded forty years later, in 1960, after it had finally won the battle for equal pay (Gosden, 1972, p. 16).

The NUT suffered another loss in membership as a consequence of the acceptance of the equal pay principle. In 1922, male teachers who remained most strongly opposed to equal pay for women broke away from the union and established the National Association of Schoolmasters, which was to represent the interests of male "career teachers" (Locke, 1974, p. 27). These men accepted the widely held belief that women teachers were not really interesed in teaching as a career and did not need to support families, and therefore did not merit nor need the same salaries as male teachers (Morris, 1969, p. 185). Hence, they completely ignored the struggles of many committed women teachers to gain recognition within the teaching occupations.

The first two decades of the twentieth century were also an active time for American women teachers. Higher and equal pay for teachers became the major focus of increasing challenges to the NEA administration made by female members. Women became vocal and conspicuous at the associations's annual meetings, advocating a strong public stance by the NEA on the salary issue (Donley, 1976, pp. 19–23) and often making eloquent arguments for equal pay (see, for example, Strachan, 1910). Women were also the first to suggest that classroom teachers, in contrast to superintendents and school board members, should have a role in guiding the policies of the schools. Prominent women educators such as Margaret Haley, Ella Flagg Young, and Mary C. Harris argued that teachers should have a voice in running the school system (Donley, 1976, p. 21).

The NEA's response to such challenges led to increasing frustration among women teachers. To be sure, nearly every year the association would pass a resolution calling for higher salaries, and in 1905 it inaugurated a series of salary studies (Donley, 1976, pp. 21–22). In 1914 the NEA officially adopted the equal pay principle (NEA, 1939). However, it did nothing publicly and actively to improve teacher salaries and other benefits. Teachers thus began to turn increasingly to the emerging unions in the hopes that their tactics would help improve teachers' economic position.

In Chicago, New York, and Minneapolis, women teachers were involved in large numbers in the new unions. Margaret Haley, who became the leader of the Chicago Teachers' Federation, served as a powerful role model and was successful in drawing the membership and support of many female teachers (Marsh, 1936). When the national American Federation of Teachers (AFT) was established in 1916, Haley became its first president. Largely because of her influence, the structure of the AFT was set up along democratic lines so that rank-and-file teachers could be elected delegates to annual federation meetings and could vote on policy matters (Donley, 1968, p. 73). This situation gave women teachers opportunities to be active at the national level, and indeed the ranks of the AFT increased, despite a strong opposition to teacher unionization by boards of education and the public at large (Bystydzienski, 1979, p. 117). By 1919, nearly 60 percent of AFT members were female (Donley, 1976, p. 102).

Faced with the threat of growing teacher's unions, the NEA began to make concessions to classroom teachers, By 1914 it had allowed for the creation of the Department of Classroom Teachers and in 1919 a change in the by-laws provided for automatic membership for all public-school educators upon payment of annual dues (Schmid, 1963, p. 246). In 1920 the NEA established a Representative Assembly of delegates to develop association policy, with delegates representing every state (Donley, 1976, p. 30). Such democratizing changes, for a time, gave classroom teachers a greater voice in the NEA and opened up top positions to women members. In 1919 Ella Flagg Young, principal of Chicago Normal School and formerly a classroom teacher, became the first woman president of the NEA (Donley, 1967, p. 21).

Whereas English teachers became increasingly involved in strike actions during this period (Coates, 1972, p. 61), very few American teachers resorted to strikes (Donley, 1976, p. 28). It seems that most AFT and NEA activity took place at the national and state level. At the level of local associations, there were very few unions, and in most NEA affiliates control firmly resided in the hands of male superintendents and often local politicians and businessman (Everett, 1942). Since such people had incomes which were typically much higher than those of teachers, they were rarely supportive of teachers' claims to higher salaries and usually were strongly opposed to union tactics (Donley, 1976, p. 33). The voice and participation of teachers (mostly women) at the local level was thus effectively limited.

The following three decades brought a steady decrease in union participation by teachers in both England and the United States. Although the NUWT in England continued to press for equal pay, even with the establishment in 1920 of the Burnham scales, which temporarily increased teachers' salaries, differentiation of pay on the grounds of sex continued (Ozga, 1981, p. 24). The NUT failed to sustain its militant female membership during the economic recession of the 1920s because it accepted cuts in teachers' positions. As unemployment grew, married women teachers were forced out of their jobs. The NUT did not oppose the hiring of untrained supplementary women teachers, who were paid very low wages (Phipps, 1928). Although strike actions were taken periodically by teachers during the 1920s and 1930s, women became less involved. Female teachers now confined themselves to protecting their jobs, and militancy among them gradually declined (Ozga, 1981, p. 24).

With the passage of the 1944 Education Bill, a uniform system of public education was established in England. Both elementary and secondary education were now under the control of the local education authorities, and a uniform system of salaries was developed for teachers at both levels, falling short, however, of equalizing male and female wages (Tropp, 1957, pp. 242–245).

With the expansion of secondary education, teaching once again became open to females, who came to the occupation in larger numbers during the postwar years. Women, however, did not flood the education market because many jobs in the growing service sector were now available (Tropp, 1956, p. 247). Despite NUT and government assertions that only certified teachers should be employed, uncertified women teachers were again being hired at very low salaries to accommodate the need to fill a growing number of secondary-education posts. The pay gap between men and women teachers thus remained in the postwar years (Partington, 1976, p. 249). It was only a matter of time before British teachers would again take action to improve their economic conditions.

A pattern of declining militancy among women teachers, beginning in the 1920s and continuing into post–World War I years, can also be observed in the United States. For one thing, women teachers' union activities were greatly curtailed throughout this period. During the 1920s, the unions experienced a time of decline and disintegrations, with 80 percent of the charters issued by the AFT inoperative by 1928 (Donley, 1976, p. 34). As opposition and hostility to teacher unionization grew, AFT membership dropped rapidly, and the organization barely survived into the next decade (Donley, 1976, p. 35). In the 1930s, as the depression made itself felt, union membership picked up, but women teachers did not join readily (Mesirow,

1966). As a result of the depression, many women teachers lost their jobs, and those who still worked were reluctant to jeopardize their positions (Donovan, 1938, p. 33).

While a large number of married women teachers were hired during a rapid educational expansion following World War I (Donovan, 1938, p. 57) thereafter, during the 1920s and 1930s a trend grew against employment of married teachers (Peters, 1934, p. 85). Several NEA studies found that local school boards routinely dismissed married women teachers despite the lack of state legislation specifying such dismissals (Peters, 1934; NEA, 1938; NEA 1939). In 1930, 77 percent of all female teachers were single (Donovan, 1938, p. 32). Since married female teachers were more active in teachers' oprganizations than single women (Peters, 1934, p. 84), their exit from the occupation greatly reduced women teachers' participation.

The NEA, meanwhile, after a short period of democratization, reverted back to its "old guard" days (Donley, 1976, ch. 3). School administrators were firmly in control once again. Despite teachers' continuing low salaries (which actually dropped during the late 1920s and in the 1930s), the association only rarely addressed the matter of teacher welfare and did not develop any mechanisms for improving teachers' economic and social standing (Bystydzienski, 1979, p. 123). Although a few women were to be found among the national and state NEA leadership during the latter part of the first half of the century (for example, Pearl A. Wanamaker, a school superintendent, was NEA president in 1947), female classroom teachers, for the most part, were absent from NEA discussions and debates and were also excluded from participation at the local level, where male school administrators continued to exert control (Everett, 1942).

The need for more classroom teachers after World War II, continued low pay, and postwar inflation created conditions for growing militancy among American public-school teachers. It is not surprising, therefore, that teachers became vocal again in the late 1940s and that strike actions were frequent during the 1950s (Donley, 1976, p. 36). Women teachers, once again, became increasingly involved in teachers' organizations and union actions.

As this account of women's participation in teacher organizations in England and the United States during the course of the first fifty years of this century indicates, economic and social factors greatly influenced the degree of female involvement. At the turn of the century, both countries experienced public-school expansion, which continued until the early 1920s. As more and more women entered the teaching occupation (elementary teaching in England and primary and secondary teaching in the United States), an increasing number became concerned about equal pay and better salaries. Supported by the suffrage movement, female teachers first tried to influence the policies of existing teachers' organizations, but, finding often insurmountable resistance from male colleagues and school administrators, began to establish alternative organizations (the NUWT in England and the AFT in the United States).

Economic recession, and eventually depression, took away many women teachers' jobs in England and the United States and further lowered their salaries relative to male salaries. In the United States, a growing anti-union sentiment during the 1920s and Communist infiltration scares in the 1930s (Mesirow, 1966) largely immobilized the teachers' union, while in England, the NUT failed to support the claims of its militant female contingent, and the NUWT did not have the power to negotiate with the government's Department of Education. Women teachers were thus increasingly left without effective organization.

Prevailing ideology, which defined the male as primary breadwinner, made it especially difficult for female teachers to fight for equal pay and power within teachers' organizations (Ozga, 1981, p. 25). The assumption that women have only temporary interest in teaching and that their primary allegiance lies with children and the home has persisted to the present (Lortie, 1975). The dismissals of married women teachers during economic recession in both England and the United States were justified by just such an ideology.

The different patterns of women's participation in the teachers' organizations in England and the United States that began in the nineteenth century appear to have continued into the first half of the twentieth. Female teachers remained more active at the local level in England, whereas their U.S. counterparts were more involved at the state and national level. The structures of the teachers' organizations seem to have accounted for this difference.

In England, the national union was tightly controlled by male headmasters and secondary-school teachers. Males also controlled the election process to the NUT executive. At the local level, however, teachers' organizations, which historically developed in a grass roots manner, were much more fluid and allowed greater participation to rank-and-file members. Officer turnover was frequent, and classroom teachers typically occupied the positions of president and secretary (Roy, 1968). Although female teachers encountered resistance from men at this level as well, they were nevertheless more successful in influencing local union policies.

In the United States a different structure prevailed. Within the NEA, local associations were dominated by school superintendents and typically "grew down" from the top instead of "up" (Everett, 1942). The NEA itself was for a long time controlled by school administrators and college presidents, although after the reorganization in 1920 it began to allow women into its top ranks (the women, however, were also school administrators). At the state level, NEA affiliates were more open and democratic, and it is here that female classroom teachers participated most often (Everett, 1942). The AFT national organization allowed for considerable involvement of the rank and file and thus had a high degree of participation of women members. Although a few of its local organizations in major cities attracted women teachers, the union established relatively few local organizations before its losses in the 1920s.

Generally, where the organizational structure allowed for democratic participation of members, women teachers exhibited involvement in teachers' organizations. The structures tightly controlled by select groups of males were the ones that proved most resistant to women teachers' struggles.

As evidence indicates, the decrease of female participation in teachers' organizations from the 1920s to the 1940s and women's failure to secure a better position within the teaching occupation can not be attributed to a lack of female teachers' commitment to their task or their reluctance to get involved. Given the opportunity and favorable societal conditions, women teachers in the United States and England participated in teachers' unions and associations and even fought relentlessly for their causes. As economic and social conditions once again began to change following World War II, so too female teachers began to exhibit more involvement and growing militancy.

Women in Teachers' Unions from the 1950s to the Present

Beginning in the 1950s schoolteachers in both England and the United States became increasingly involved in union actions. In the United States, over 100 strikes were carried out between 1949 and 1959, increasing to over 100 strikes per year in the late 1960s (Donley, 1976, ch. 5). In England, although actual withdrawal of teachers' labor was very rare during the postwar decade, demonstrations, "no-cover" protests (teachers refusing to teach classes of absent colleagues), and other actions (such as withdrawal of voluntary mealtime supervision) proliferated in the 1950s (Burke, 1971). During the 1960s and 1970s strike threats were frequently carried out by British teachers (Bystydzienski, 1984, p. 14).

Teachers' unions during this time began to take on a more militant stance. In England, the NUT, prodded by the more activist National Association of Schoolmasters (NAS) and the new Union of Women Teachers (created in 1967; it merged with the NAS in 1976), became more favorably disposed to striking as a bargaining tool (Partington, 1976). The 1974 affiliation of the NUT with the British Trades Union Congress made unionist strategies more acceptable to a large portion of its membership (Bystydzienski, 1984). In the United States, although both the AFT and the NEA did not officially approve of strike actions in the 1950s, they frequently provided unofficial support, and by 1967 both organizations voted approval of the right of teachers to strike (Donley, 1976, p. 107).

Although there is no doubt that many women teachers have participated in union activities in recent times, those who have studied the wave of teacher militancy during the 1960s and 1970s in the United States and England have not given women credit for the shift in teachers' behavior (for example, Hyman, 1972; Corwin, 1974; Lortie, 1975; Donley, 1976; and Lacey, 1977). On the contrary, an often-cited reason for increased teacher militancy is the post–World War II influx of males into the occupation. Although it its true that an increased number of males entered teaching following the war and that the proportion of women teaches had declined during the last three decades (Corwin, 1974; Partington, 1976), women have and still do constitute the majority of public-school teachers in both the United States and England (Ozga, 1981, p. 25; *Statistical Abstracts of the U.S.*, 1984, p. 151). Moreover, the assumption that females were less likely than males to be involved in union activity, including strike action, is not supported by available data.

In 1967, Ziegler reported that American women teachers took a more active role in teachers' organizations than their male colleagues. Cole's (1969) study of a New York City teachers' strike showed that women teachers were slightly less likely to be afraid of striking than men and that it was the structure of the school (elementary versus secondary) which accounted for the degree of support for strike action rather than a teacher's sex. Urban (1982) documented substantial female participation in a number of teachers' strikes during the 1960s and 1970s. Accounts of strike and other union activities in England during this time showed extensive female involvement, particularly at the local level (*The Teacher*, 1963–78). Thus, during the most recent wave of teacher militancy, women were again to be found participating in teachers' unions and taking an active role in the organizations' attempts to secure better pay and working conditions for their members.

The late 1970s and early 1980s again witnessed a drop in teacher militancy in both England and the United States. Declining birth rates and economic recession helped create an oversupply of teachers. Frequent attacks on public education and cuts in financial support by conservative governments in both countries resulted in a more cautious stance of teachers' unions (Bystydzienski, 1984). The constant threats of elimination of teachers' positions in England created an atmosphere of fear among employed teachers, while most temporary and supplementary women teachers found themselves out of work (Ozga, 1981). In the United States, although teachers' strikes have not ceased, they have become less frequent, and many public school teachers have become unemployed or underemployed (*On Campus*, 1984, p. 10). During the last few years, women teachers have been less active in the union movement (Cook, Lorwin, and Daniels, 1984).

Summary and Conclusions

An examination of the role women have played in the history of teachers' unions in the United States and England has revealed considerable participation and activity on the part of female teachers. Contrary to popular assumptions, women made periodic attempts to achieve, through teachers' organizations, equal and higher pay and status within the teaching occupation.

Women teachers appear to be most active during times of educational expansion and in democratically structured organizations. Thus, when their employment is relatively secure and the opportunity to participate exists, female educators are just as likely as males to take part in teachers unions if not more so. It is to these factors that we should look for an explanation of female participation in teachers' organizations, rather than attributing conservative tendencies to women themselves.

Despite many struggles, women teachers' attempts to achieve equality with male colleagues have not been realized. Even though in England and the United States both the unions and educational authorities eventually accepted the principle of equal pay and single salary scales for elementary and secondary teachers, women teachers' salaries still lag behind those of male public-school educators (Ozga, 1981, p. 25; *Census of Population*, 1980, p. 181). This difference in pay is today popularly explained by the fact that male teachers achieve higher levels of formal education (Kane, 1979). However, studies have found that sex discrimination persists in access to graduate education, resulting in more male teachers holding advanced degrees (Bystyzienski, 1979, p. 175).

The amount of power and influence women hold in teachers' organizations continues to be limited. In England, where in recent years more women teachers have attained positions of president and secretary at the local level, women remain conspicuously absent at the divisional and national executive levels (*The Teacher*, 1984, p. 13). In the United States, although women occasionally hold top administrative positions at the national and state levels, especially in the NEA, they are less likely to be found in local bargaining and grievance committees (Cook, Lorwin, and Daniels, 1984, p. 301).

It is interesting to note that as equal opportunity and affirmative action have become somewhat institutionalized in both countries, unions are making attempts to bring more women into those levels at which they are underrepresented. However, the direction of this effort has not been to make organizations more open and democratic, but rather to change women to become more assertive and to acquire "leadership skills" (*The Teacher*, 1984, p. 13; Stockdale, 1981, p. 12). Thus the view that characterized women teachers for over one hundred years as unable to participate by virtue of having the "wrong" attitudes appears to be alive and well even today.

If history is to be our guide, the current efforts to give greater voice to women in teachers' unions are doomed to failure. At best, a few token women will become actively involved. At worst, the present hierarchy will be preserved, and women teachers, alienated by increasing female unemployment, lack of equal salaries, and the inability of their unions to change the situation, will become even less active, until another demand for schoolteachers may stir them again to participation.

References

American Federation of Teachers (1982). *The AFT vs. the NEA*. Washington, D.C.: American Federation of Teachers.

Burke, Victor (1971). *Teachers in Turmoil*. Middlesex, England: Penguin.

Butts, Frank, and Lawrence A. Cremin (1953). *A History of Education in American Culture*. New York: Holt, Rinehart, and Winston.

Bystydzienski, Jill M. (1984). "Merging of Professionalism and Trade Unionism: The Case of the National Union of Teachers in England." Unpublished paper.

——— (1979). *The Status of Public School Teachers in America: An Unfulfilled Quest for Professionalism.*" Ph.D. dissertation, State University of New York, Albany.

Census of Population (1980). "Occupation by Industry." Washington, D.C.: U.S. Department of Commerce, U.S. Government Printing Office.

Coates, R.D. (1972). *Teachers' Unions and Interest Group Politics: A Study in the Behaviour of Organised Teachers in England and Hales.* Cambridge, England: Cambridge University Press.

Cole, Stephen (1969). *The Unionization of Teachers: A Case Study of the UFT.* New York: Praeger.

Cook, Alice H., Val R. Lorwin, and Arlene K. Daniels, eds. (1984). *Women and Trade Unions in Eleven Industrialized Countries.* Philadelphia: Temple University Press.

Cook, Blanche W., ed. (1979). *Crystal Eastman On Women and Revolution.* Oxford, England: Oxford University Press.

Corwin, Ronald G. (1974). *Education in Crisis.* New York: Wiley and Sons.

Cremin, Lawrence A. (1971). *The Transformation of the School.* New York: Random House.

Donley, Marshall D. (1976). *Power to the Teacher.* Bloomington, Ind.: Indiana University Press.

Donovan, Frances R. (1938). *The Schoolma'am.* New York: F. Stokes Company.

Elsbree, Willard S. (1939). *The American Teacher.* New York: American Book Company.

Etzioni, Amitai (1969). *The Semi-Professionals and Their Organizations.* New York: Free Press.

Everett, Ruth V. (1942). "From Regimentation to Self-Government in the North Carolina Education Association And—Back Again." Chapel Hill, N.C.: The University of North Carolina Press.

Gosden, P.H. (1972). *The Evolution of a Profession.* Oxford, England: Basil Blackwell.

Hyman, Herman (1972). *Strikes.* London: Fontana.

Kane, R.D. (1979). *Sex Discrimination in Education: A Study of Employment Practices Affecting Professional Personnel.* Washington, D.C.: U.S. Department of HEW, U.S. Government Printing Office.

Karier, Clarence J. (1975). *Shaping the American Educational State: 1900 to the Present*. New York: Free Press.

Lacey, Colin (1977). *The Socialization of Teachers*. London: Methuen.

Lieberman, Myron (1956). *Education as a Profession*. Englewood Cliffs, N.J.: Prentice-Hall.

Locke, Michael (1974). *Power and Politics in the School System*. London: Routledge and Kegan Paul.

Lord, Charles A. (1966). *Years of Decision 1865–1965: A History of the West Virginia Education Association*. Charleston: West Virginia Education Association.

Lortie, Dan C. (1975). *Schoolteacher: A Sociological Study*. Chicago: University of Chicago Press.

Marsh, Arthur L. (1936). *The Organized Teachers*. Boston: The National Association of Secretaries of State Education Associations.

Mattingly, Paul H. (1975). *The Classless Profession: American Schoolmen in the 19th Century*. New York: New York University Press.

Melder, Keith E. (1977). *Beginnings of Sisterhood*. New York: Schocken Books.

Mesirow, David (1966). "The AFT's Role in the Thirties." *Changing Education* 1 (Summer) pp. 30–32.

Morris, Nicholas (1969). "England." In *Teacher Unions and Associations: A Comparative Study*, ed. Albert A. Blum. Urbana: University of Illinois Press.

National Education Association (1884). *Addresses and Proceedings*. Washington, D.C.: National Education Association.

―――― (1939). *Progress and Problems in Equal Pay for Equal Work*. Washington, D.C.: National Education Association.

―――― (1938). *Status of the Married Woman Teacher*. Washington, D.C.: National Education Association.

National Union of Teachers (1981). *Equal Opportunities in Education*. London: College Hill Press.

Ogburn, W.F. (1933). "The Family and Its Functions." *Recent Social Trends in the United States* 1, pp. 661–708.

On *Campus* (1984). "Labor: A Tradition in Jeopardy?" 4 (September) pp. 10–11.

Ozga, Jenny (1981). *The Politics of Schools and Teaching*. London: The Open University.

Partington, Geoffrey (1976). *Women Teachers in the 20th Century in England and Wales.* London: NFER.

Peters, David W. (1934). *The Status of the Married Woman Teacher.* New York: Teachers' College, Columbia University Press.

Phipps, Evelyn (1928). *History of the National Union of Women Teachers.* London: National Union of Women Teachers.

Purvis, Jean (1981). "Women and Teaching in the 19th Century." In *Education and the State: Politics, Patriarchy and Practice,* ed. R. Dale et al. Barcombe, England: Falmer Press.

Roy, William (1968). *The Teachers' Union.* London: Schoolmaster Publications.

Schmid, Robert D. (1963). "A Study of the Organizational Structure of the NEA, 1884–1921." Ed.D. dissertation, Washington University, St. Louis, Missouri.

Statistical Abstracts of the United States (1984). Washington, D.C.: U.S. Government Printing Office.

Stockdale, James B. (1981). "The Principles of Leadership." *American Educator* 5 (Winter), pp. 12–15.

Strachan, Grace C. (1910). *Equal Pay for Equal Work.* New York: B. F. Buck and Co.

Sugg, Redding S. (1978). *Motherteacher: The Feminization of American Education.* Charlottesville: University of Virginia Press.

The Teacher (1984). "Equal Opportunities in Education" (February 24), pp. 12–15.

———— (1963–1978). London: National Union of Teachers.

Tropp, Albert (1957). *The School Teachers.* London: Heinemann.

Trow, Martin (1961). "The Second Transformation of American Secondary Education." *International Journal of Comparative Sociology.* 2, pp. 144–165.

Tyack, David B. (1967). *Turning Points in American Educational History.* Waltham, Mass.: Blaisdell.

Urban, Wayne J. (1982). *Why Teachers Organized.* Detroit: Wayne State University Press.

Webb, Bernice (1915). "Women Teachers in Elementary Education." *The New Statesman* (25 September), pp. 19–20.

Wesley, Edward B. (1957). *NEA: The First Hundred Years.* New York: Harper and Bros.

Ziegler, Harmon (1967). *The Political Life of American Teachers.* Englewood Cliffs, N.J.: Prentice-Hall.

Chapter 9

Danish Female Teachers And Equal Pay, 1898–1922

KIRSTEN MOELLER

This chapter deals with the history of womens' employment as teachers in public schools in Denmark and their struggle from 1890 to 1922 for equal wages[1] In this struggle, women were confronted with resistance from male teachers and educational administrators. This opposition arose from the economic, judicial, and ideological conditions of the society at that time, which resulted in conflicts of interest between the sexes and discrimination against women.

Of course, in some areas male and female teachers share the same labor interests—for example, in matters regarding the source of teachers' salaries, of tenure, and the structure and content of teacher training. However, in a capitalist patriarchy, the fact that women do not share the same material and legal rights as men is a source of conflict with regard to the structure of salaries and the conditions of employment.

Women's Access to Employment in Public Schools

The gradual change from a self-supply economy to a commodity economy brought about significant changes in the structure and function of the Danish household. The bourgeois and petite bourgeois household no longer required the same amount of female labor, but

173

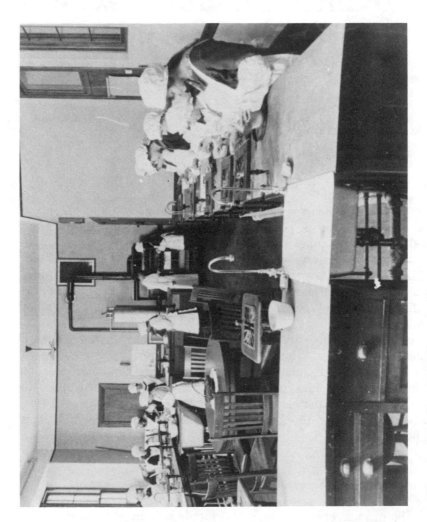

neither were they able to provide for unmarried female members. Therefore, single women had to secure an independent income by working outside the family.

Not all occupations were considered socially acceptable for women of the bourgeoisie and petite bourgeoisie. Factory employment was out of the question, as was going into service. However, genteel occupations such as nurse, governess, or private tutor were considered natural and socially acceptable as an extension of the functions women fulfilled in the family. In the nineteenth century and first half of the twentieth century, many unmarried women, especially from the petite bourgeoisie and the new middle class, earned their livelihoods as housekeepers, governesses, or private teachers. The wage they received was no more than an allowance and was not adequate as an independent livelihood. The Private teachers or governesses were often a part of the household where they taught and were thus prevented from having their own home or family. These forms of employments kept women as dependents upon the partriarchal family.

Nevertheless, these women subjectively may have experienced a form of independence in that they were able to manage for themselves and fulfilled a specific function which demanded special qualifications. This experience undoubtedly helped lay the groundwork for a new feminist consciousness that they could fend for themselves and need not marry solely for the sake of financial security. The conscious struggle for independence took shape as women experienced both the need for a more independent way of life and the possibility of attaining it. Thus, women began to formulate demands for the right to be educated and to obtain public positions.

Womens initial experiences in school teaching led to demands for better training so that they could carry out their duties satisfactorily. N. Zahle, the headmistress of a private teacher-training college for women, wrote:

> "I felt that I knew so indescribably little, miserably little, when I sat and prepared myself for the next day." "While I was teaching, I suffered under a constant feeling of ignorance and incompetence."[2]

The need for more and better training was not, however, felt by women alone. It accompanied society's needs for new qualifications and higher levels of training in general to accommodate new methods of production for national and international markets. The need for widespread education, combined with an explosive growth in the population,[3] could not be met because of a dearth of educated men in the teaching profession.

In 1858, it was recruiting problems such as these which first gave rise to a consideration of the possibility of employing educated women as teachers in the public schools.[4] At the annual national convention of teachers in Denmark on 25 May 1858,[5] the question of employing female teachers in the public schools was raised in a paper addressed to the convention by headmistress Pauline Worm, who argued for the right of women to sit for the teachers' examination and to be employed even in senior position in public schools.[6] A proposal was drafted whereby women could be employed in positions other than assistant teacher at larger village schools and in town schools, where there were at least two teachers positions. Women would teach the youngest children of both sexes and would teach older girls in needlework and possibly in other scholastic subjects. The arguments for the employment of women in the public schools ran as follows: Small children and girls would benefit from the special kind of teaching which only females could supply; females would be more stable than junior male teachers, who would inevitably apply for a better position; employment as a schoolteacher would be a suitable occupation for gifted women of limited means; and female teachers could be paid considerably less than males.[7]

The proposal concerning the employment of women teachers in the public schools was put before Bishops Brammer and Martensen and Hr. Borgen, the director of education in Copenhagen.[8] Both bishops rejected the proposal on the grounds that women's influence on children's upbringing should continue to be confined to the domestic sphere and that the participation of women in the educational system would not benefit children. Furthermore, they felt that women did not possess the qualifications necessary for teaching, such as the ability to maintain discipline and to teach larger classes of children methodically and stringently.[9] However, the bishops recognized that single women of small means should be afforded the opportunity of providing for themselves. Thus, they suggested that such women could be employed under homelike conditions as private tutors, governesses, housekeepers, or nurses. This meant that women could not take independent employment at a school, but they could be employed as assistants to male teachers that is, be under their guidance and associated with their households. The bishops did not want women to be employed in public positions nor to gain the ability to conduct an independent life. Women's place was in the home with family where she was subject to man's authority. Hr. Borgen, the director of education, did not agree. He was faced with a vast shortage of teachers and sought an economical solution. Therefore he supported the teachers' proposal, but on the condition that women teachers would be paid less than men.

Despite resistance from the bishops, the teachers' proposal led to the royal resolution of 4 November 1859, which gave women the right to sit for a teachers' examination and to seek positions in public schools.[10] The resolution did not demand that women possess an examination certificate, but merely that they demonstrate competence to the satisfaction of the local school authority. The resolution made no stipulation as to the female teachers' salary and no stipulations concerning teacher-training requirements. This was in answer to political pressure from farmers against any state control of education and their insistence upon local autonomy in determining teachers' competence and salary. Almost eight years passed before the salary of female teachers was established by law.

At the outset, most women teachers were employed in Copenhagen and had little or no teacher training. Attendance at private teacher-training colleges was financially prohibitive, and for the few who did train, the salary they subsequently earned was so low that they were frequently unable to repay debts incurred while training.

Salary According to Gender

The female teacher's salary was not legally established until 29 March 1867, seven years after the first women were employed in public schools. For the first time, Danish legislation explicitly stated the principle that public service appointments were to be remunerated according to sex.[11] Provincial towns were thus permitted to pay women teachers as little as two-thirds the salary received by men. In country schools, women teachers were to be paid the equivalent of the low-paid assistant teachers. An assistant teacher was a position for a newly trained male teacher; he usually held it for no more than a few years before obtaining a senior position as a schoolmaster (*forste-laerer, enelaerer*). Although the assistant teacher position was provisional for men, for women it was permanent. Thus, the female teachers was obliged to manage on almost half the male's salary for all her working life. The principle of payment according to sex formed the material basis for conflicts between men and women teachers which culminated during 1915–22.

Equal Pay for Equal Work

Women's experience of working life in the public schools and their growing awareness of their specific aptitude for teaching by virtue of their sex-differentiated socialization led women teachers to formulate demands for equal pay, adequate housing, and the right to state-financed teacher training. In connection with negotiations for a new Education Act the demand for equal pay for equal work was formally presented for the first time by Anne Brunn in 1898.[12] Female teachers had now been engaged in the same employment as men for some thirty-five years, yet access to teacher training and the salaries received for equal work remained unequal. Women had to finance their own education in private teaching colleges even though they had to take the same examinations as men, who could attend state-financed teaching colleges.

Women teachers, represented by Anne Bruun, presented their demand for equal pay to the Danish Union of Teachers (DUT).[13] Nevertheless, the DUT neglected to mention the women's demands in its petitions to the Ministry of Ecclesiastical and Educational Affairs, and to Parliament. Therefore, a lobby of some 229 female teachers presented their own petition calling for equal starting salary. A similar petition was presented to the government by the Danish Women's Society. Their demand was not met. The DUT ignored the petition, and the ministry refused to take it seriously, referring to women's well-known frugality.

The Teachers' Wage Law passed in 1899 stipulated that the starting salary for women should be less than men's and that male teachers' wages should increase on a more sharply inclined scale. Furthermore, the law legalized the principle that within the public services the wage structure was such that women were placed on the lowest pay scales and only men were at the top, despite the fact that male and female teachers usually carried out the same work and that women teachers in country schools often worked six to twelve hours more each week than men.[14]

The union achieved some general wage improvements in connection with the law of 1899; for example, it succeeded in gaining wage increases for already existing teaching posts. But wage levels for new teaching positions decreased, especially for the new positions held by women. The DUT itself was party to the introduction of a wage principle within the public sector which solved the problem of the lack of teachers. But the "salary according to gender" principle disguised that fact that, in general, many teaching positions were to be more poorly paid than before because the local councils (*krommuner*) converted good former positions to poorer positions in connection with new appointments, and may of the new positions in the countryside were converted into posts for women.

The background for this development was the law which gave local councils the right to freeze their educational expenditure, despite the fact that the need for education was growing and that the population had doubled from 1856 to 1899. The law allowed the local councils to recruit more teachers without being obliged to pay them more. In fact, women, who were used as a cheap labor force, enabled the necessary development of education and qualification to take place.

Mobilization of Female Teachers

For women teachers, the discouraging results of the negotiations leading up to the Education Act and the Teachers' Wage Law in 1899 made it clear that if any improvement were to be made in women's wages, social conditions, and working conditions, they would be gained only if women won the right to vote and to have their own representatives sit in the executive committee of the DUT. Actively supported by the Danish Women's Society and by many women teachers around the country, Anne Bruun threw herself into the fight for women's rights and improved working conditions. At meetings throughout the country and in letter to the press, she constantly agitated for women's suffrage, equal pay, and training colleges for women. She collected statistics proving that women spend more hours teaching than men without receiving any extra remuneration. In a rally cry to all female teachers, Anne Bruun wrote:

> "I wonder how long it will be before women teachers in Denmark—each and every one of them—will realize that as long as women have no political value, there is very little hope that our simple, justified demands will ever be met. The government runs four training colleges for men, which cost the State large sums every year. The State uses our labor—just as it does men's—(but unlike men) the abilities which that same state demands of us to teach must be procured on our own—at enormous personal expense . . . . This, they would not have dared to do had we had the vote. But—we will not sit idly twiddling our thumbs—next year we will be back and we will continue..."[15]

In the DUT journal for 1900, Anna Jagd called for a change in the DUT's laws so that two women could be represented on the executive committee, following the Norwegian example (which included four men and three women).[16] The DUT rejected the proposal.[17] Women teachers next tried to get Anne Bruun elected to the executive committee by urging all women teachers in Denmark to vote for her as one of women's two designated members, and to vote for a representative of assistant teachers in country schools as the other. In the

teachers next tried to get Anne Bruun elected to the executive com-
stragegy was met with great approval. The result of the election of
members of the executive committee was that Anne Bruun received
the majority of votes and, in 1902, became the first female member of
the DUT executive committee.

The Female Teachers' Electoral List

In order to secure increased representation at the subsequent
election in 1904, women drew up a "Female Teachers' List" with
Anne Bruun and Anna Jagd as candidates. Female teachers wanted
their own electoral list because of unjust disparity in men's and
women's conditions in the schools, which was the source of common
interest for female teachers. Women had also learned that they would
have to press forward their own interests because there had been no
indication that the DUT executive committee would do so.[18]

At meetings conducted throughout Denmark, Anna Jagd and
Anne Bruun were frequently met with questions about the necessity
for a separate electoral list for female teacher, and whether it was
wise for women to thus isolate themselves. They answered that the
separate electoral list was not a move toward isolation; on the con-
tray, it was meant as an attempt to break out of isolation in relation to
the activites and power relations of the DUT. Anna Jagd is quoted as
saying the following:

> "A Women's list is not drawn up with the intention of isolating
> ourselves from male teachers, but, on the contrary, to organize a bet-
> ter and more equitable collaboration with them. We women will get
> to know one another, learn to talk together and thus learn to advance
> our opinions at joint meetings, where—as we all know—female
> teachers have almost always remained silent . . . .While I have stress-
> ed our special interests here to some extent, I am by no means blind,
> by and large, to the common interests of our public schools. After all,
> I am in favour of the power which lies in cooperation, also in the work
> between men and women, of which we have seen far too little.[19]

The formation of the female teachers' electoral list was the source
of violent opposition, particularly from male teachers in provincial
towns. Those male teachers insisted that a separate female list would
damage their interests. They criticized Anne Bruun as being a female
teacher from Copenhagen who had little understanding of the position and needs of teachers in provincial towns.

> Miss Anne Bruun is a talented advocate for women's suffrage and for
> their eligibility at political and municipal elections. But such advocacy
> is unnecessary on this occasion; what is relevent here is the election
> of a male or a female teacher who has a thorough knowledge and
> understanding of the circumstances and conditions prevailing in the
> teaching profession in provincial towns. And in this regard, Miss
> Bruun has adequately displayed her lack of qualifications, both in her
> speeches and her writings.[20]

They failed to mention that teachers from the provincial town school
had eight male candidates on their electoral list and not one women.
The strategy behind their opposition was to engineer a schism between women teachers, thereby securing the votes of women teachers
in provincial towns for candidates forwarded by male teachers, all of
which were men.

Anne Bruun furiously answered her detractors in a long article
published in *The Public School*,[21] and many female teachers in provincial towns sent declarations in her support to the DUT journal:

> We do not doubt that Miss A. Bruun will also work for women
> teachers in provincial towns when the time comes. We women ought
> not to let male teachers continue as our representatives on the ex-
> ecutive committee. After all, we have no reason to expect much help
> from that quarter as long as they see nothing unjust in the hardest
> work and lowest wages being relegated to us.[22]

Once again, female teachers succeeded in getting Anne Bruun elected
to the committee, and Anna Jagd was voted in as an alternate. In the
years that followed, the female teachers' list was maintained and
received massive support, since female teachers represented a majority at the polls.[23]

However, male teachers in provincial town schools continued
their efforts to bring about schism in the women's ranks. At a
meeting of DUT delegates, they tried to alter electoral procedure for
the DUT executive committee. They suggested that the committee
should consist of an equal number of teachers from rural and urban
areas, thereby dividing the members of the DUT into two electoral
groups. This move was opposed by Anne Bruun because the women
teachers would thereby run the risk of losing their only representation. The suggestion was also opposed by the rank and file because the
proposed two-group representation did not reflect the actual distribution of teachers in the two prospective electoral groups.

The proposal was rejected but was forwarded again in 1909. On
this occasion, representation on the executive committee was propos-

ed to consist of six teachers from urban areas and nine from rural areas, corresponding to the actual distribution of teachers in towns and the country.[24] This time the proposal was adopted. For female teachers, the new electoral procedure meant that their nationwide electoral list was obsolete. Thus by means of the new procedure for elections, teachers from the provincial town schools succeeded in annihilating the long-opposed female list.

However, contrary to the female teachers' apprehension that they now would lose their representation on the executive committee, female teachers not only succeeded in maintaining that representation, but also in increasing it in the following years. This fortunate outcome was brought about by the continued forwarding of separate female electoral lists for both the urban and rural teachers' groups. In 1913, four out of fifteen members of the executive committee were women.[25]

The significant increase in female representation on the executive committee was due to a series of factors: first, to the increasing number of women employed in the public schools; second, to the political activity of the large group of women teachers who were especially active in the fight for female suffrage (which was granted in 1915); and, third, to the massive support by female teachers for the separate female electoral list.

The Male Concern over Low Female Wages

The wage law of 1899 was generally unsatisfactory, particularly because increases in the cost of living had effectively cancelled any wage improvements it provided. By 1905, teachers' wages were completely out of keeping with the times. At a long series of meetings, both men and women teachers forwarded demands for a radical wage reform. At the fourth meeting of delegates in 1905, teachers' living conditions were discussed. According to the minutes of this meeting, only conditions relevant to male teachers were discussed while the specific living conditions of female teachers were not raised. The problem confronting male teachers was that the local councils preferred to use the cheaper labor force composed of women. Therefore, male teachers proposed an equal starting salary for all teachers, regardless of sex, thus preventing economy from being a motive for hiring.[26] Concerning this situation, Kjaergaard, a member of the executive committee, remarked:

> If the starting salary is the same, the Kommunes [local councils] will
> have no basis for calculating whether they can save money by

employing a female instead of a male teacher when setting up new positions, but will pay solely in keeping with the interests of the school...In the context of the female teachers' final salary as being set at two-thirds of that of the male teacher, due consideration has been paid to the male teacher's position as family provider.[27]

At the meeting of delegates, female teachers were poorly represented (consistituting 8 out of 135 participants) and had no real possibility of defending their own interests. Female teachers therefore ensured that the position of Danish female teachers, in relation to the law of 24 March 1899, was one of the items on the agenda at the ninth Nordic School Convention, a public convention for all teachers which took place in Copenhagen on 8–16 August 1905.[28] Before the convention, Anne Bruun and Anna Jagd had called upon all Danish female teachers to attend and participate actively in negotiations. These negotiations ended in a resolution in which female teachers made, among others, the following demands: that needelework should be included in the school's normal teaching periods; that if the teaching in this and other subjects exceeded thirty-six hours weekly, needlework should be remunerated with fifty kroner per class annually; that wage rates for male and female teachers would be equalized; and that government training colleges, would be established for women.[29] However, these demands were not included or even mentioned in the DUT's later proposal for a new wage law.

In December 1906 the executive committee sent a petition to the Ministry of Ecclesiastical and Educational Affairs asking the minister to take the initiative in bringing about a radical wage reform for all public-school teachers. The petition was favorably received by the minister, who promised to propose a new wage law the next year. When the negotiations began in earnest between the ministry and the DUT, proposals for a new wage law were forwarded both by the DUT executive committee and by the provincial town teachers' organization. Except for a point concerning the calculation of seniority, these proposals were largely identical.[30] Both proposals contained only the demands of male teachers, as forwarded at the fourth meeting of DUT delegates. On 9 October 1907 the minister presented "the law on wages for male and female teachers in public schools." The bill was in close agreement with the wage principles formulated by the DUT executive committee.[31] While it contained wage increases for both men and women teachers, the greatest increases were for headmasters and schoolmasters all of whom were men.

Until women's enfranchisement in 1915, conditions for female teachers remained more or less unchanged. On the other hand, male teachers were generally afforded new possibilities for improving their living conditions: first because they were generally better paid than female teachers, and second because the DUT policy worked for the creation of new senior and leader positions which bore considerable wage increments. These positions laid the ground for a new administrative hierarchy and power structure among teachers in the school system and gave teachers new career opportunities considered desirable both by the DUT's masculine faction and by the ministry. However, these new positions were created solely for men.

As to the vast disparity in wages between urban and rural areas, and between men and women, no real changes had been effected. The law was met with violent criticism, particularly from assistant teachers in rural areas and from female teachers. The chair of the DUT called for solidarity from the rank and file and advised against internal dissension while the law was being negotiated. He felt that any schism among teachers would undermine the union's position while it was negotiating those parts of the law which were considered unacceptable by the DUT members. At the first meeting of the executive committe immediately following the proposal of the bill by the minister, it was decided that the chair, vice-chair, and Anne Bruun should endeavor to effect changes in the proposed law. These changes included remuneration for the teacher of needlework, calculations of tenure, and increases in the lowest pension levels.

After another year of negotiations in the DUT and Parliament, the Wage Law of 1908 was passed.[32] The wage principles in the law were still those suggested by and favoring male teachers: the same starting salary for both sexes, with a more quickly rising scale for male teachers and a final wage level for female teachers which corresponded to two-thirds of the male teachers' wage.

Male teachers in schools in provincial towns and schoolmasters in village schools thoroughly approved the new law. However, female teachers, particularly those in rural areas, had yet to achieve any improvement in their conditions in terms of salary or accommodations. Women teachers had only one demand partly fulfilled. The payment for teaching needlework was fixed at fifty kroner a year. However, this remuneratin bore no relation to the actual number of teacher hours. The women's housing conditions remained those fixed by the original law of 1856. In a circular form from 14 February 1899, it was recommended that assistant teachers and female teachers be allotted two attic rooms with a cooking stove, but with neither larder nor wash house. Since accommodations for female teachers was a permanent home, and not just a provisional arrangement as it was for the assistant teachers, it was particularly imperative for women to win the right to better housing. Luice Jensen, a representative for women teachers in country schools, wrote:

> We only desire the right to up-to-date accommodation with two good rooms—without sloping walls—and as much room as necessary for us to be able to house someone who can help us should we fall ill or become infirm. Moreover, as in any other (decent) home, there should be a kitchen, larder or cellar and a washroom. It has always been a mystery to me why they give the woman teacher the most dismal housing, the lowest possible wage but the longest possible working hours—such is the courtesy shown towards the weaker sex.[33]

Once more the majority in the union and Parliament stipulated that teachers should be treated unequally according to sex.

The Appointing of the Wage Commission

As a result of the sharp price rises of up to 70 percent which accompanied World War I, the effective income of civil servants and other public employees fell drastically compared with that of private employees. Salaries received by public employees were totally insufficient to maintain the previous standard of living. In the period 1908–16, the average income in the private sector increased by 88 percent (277 percent for fisherman, 123 percent for farmers, 200 percent for lawyers, and 30 percent for workers), whereas teachers, as one group of public employees, only marked a 9 percent increase .[34] The unacceptable situation for public employees was discussed at meetings and in numerous articles.

In 1917, public employees' organizations decided to form a common representative body. Their aim was to gain a stronger position for negotiations with public employers and to effect a new wage reform. Thus, both the common representative organ and individual professional organizations brought pressure to bear on the ministry and parliament. Parliament decided by law in 1917 to appoint a Wage Commission. It was the task of the Wage Commission to investigate conditions of employment for public employees and to forward a proposal for a radical wage refore applying to all public employees. The commission consisted of twenty-one members, two of which were appointed by the DUT's executive commitee—Carl Dige, a declared opponent of equal pay, and Thora Pettersen.[35] Thora Petersen was appointed not only to represent 4,000 female teachers out of a teaching force of 10,000, but also to represent 1,400 women who were in other areas of public service. She had been actively engaged with the wage question for a number of years, both in the DUT and in the Danish Women's Society, and was therefore considered an able representative.

The DUT's Proposal for a New Wage Reform

As early as 1915, the DUT had set up a committee to draw up a concrete proposal for a wage reform for male and female teachers. Both Thora Peterson and Carl Dige were members of this committee. Within the committee, opinions were strongly divided on the principles which were to form the basis for a new wage law. Thora Peterson insisted on "equal pay for equal work," whereas the men on the committee wanted a wage differentiation. They found it reasonable that, as family providers, men should receive a higher salary than women. These men opposed the equal pay principle, despite the fact that men and women teachers performed the same work in the schools, primarily because it was a flagrant challenge to the general idea of women as dependent, and as constituting a less valuable labor force. In short, the principle challenged the concept of women as physically and intellectually weaker than men. Equal pay also threatened the concept of man as provider and the rights connected with that role, including his right to maintain a person (wife or housekeeper) to manage his household and minister to his needs.

At the same time, male teachers had an interest in seeing the profession attain a financially and socially higher position in the community. Therefore, they also had an interest in preventing the local councils from exploiting the cheap labor force which female teachers represented. If this situation was the prevented, it would be strategically unsound to continue supporting the idea of lower wages for female teachers, particularly since female teachers were generally recognized to be quite capable when possessing the same amount of education as men and also to be committed educators—in short, to constitute a reliable labor force. It was not only male teachers who assumed this ambivalent position, but all male wage earners. On the one hand, men had an interest in maintaining their position as "providers"; on the other hand, as wage earners they were interested in preventing cheap labor from effectively keeping wages down and from women being preferentially hired as a cheap and willing labor force.

However, male dominated organizations and the state maintained men's traditional position as breadwinners.[36] This concept of the patriarchal provider formed the basis for the policy and legislation on unemployment, pay, and conditions of appointment for public employees, as well as for fiscal legislation developed by organizations and the government in the 1920s and 1930s[37]

After two years of work, the consensus of the DUT wage reform committee was that an equitable standard of living should be secured for both male and female teachers. Thus both the basic wage as well as the senior increment would be the same for all. However, an extra allowance should be paid to teachers who were classed as providers. Thora Petersen felt that support allowance should only be granted to teachers with children, while men on the committee insisted that it be give to "providers", that is, *married men* with or without children. However, the committee decided that *single women with children* (usually widows) could also receive a support allowance.

The DUT wage committee presented their draft of the reform at the DUT's convention of delegates in Copenhagen on 8–9 August 1917.[38] The proposed reform contained significantly new wage principles, for example, assessment of the value of work, support allowances, and equal pay for equal work.[39] These principles touched off a heated debate. The men in the assembly wanted neither equal pay nor support allowances in the form suggested by the committee. The debate was characterized by violent and insulting attacks against women and the women's movement. The principles were called a "lamentable manifestation of the confused and despairing women's movement." Women teachers were called "old spinsters," and women were blamed for wanting "payment for children." These attacks were answered in sharp terms by Signe Veilgaard,[40] and, despite the reactions of the assembly, Thora Petersen insisted on the principles of equal pay.

At the conclusion of the debate, a majority in the assembly demanded, in a resolution, that the executive committee was to make no final decisions about wage reform until the reform had been discussed at all levels in the DUT and a new convention of delegates had taken place in which a final decision could be reached on the kind of wage principles for which the DUT should work.

Resolutions against Equal Pay

Subsequently, various resolutions were passed by many different groups in the DUT.[41] The majority demanded that disparity between salaries of men and women teachers should continue to be valid as established by the Wage Law of 1908, that is, by wage differentiation according to gender. Thora Petersen defended the wage reform proposal in DUT's journal, by arguing that remuneration should be for work performed, She said:

> It is from the standpoint of "providers" that male teachers are demanding higher wages; consequently, it must also be from this standpoint that a settlement will be reached, if one does not accept [the principle] that a salary represents a remuneration for work performed, and for nothing else. [42]

But the men in the DUT insisted that, because they were providers, they should have higher wages as long as men and women were to share the same standard of living. The men felt that a difference in wages according to gender was also justified by other considerations. Their arguments in favor of differentiation in wages ran as follows: if women were to receive the same wages as men, it would mean that men's wages generally would be reduced; only men are providers; women do not, in fact, perform the same work as men; women cannot be used to the same extent as men; and women are more frequently ill than men.[43]

Because of the heated debate between men and women teachers, the executive committee decided to put the new wage principles to a vote among the rank and file. The result of the ballot was that, among those entitled to vote, 68 percent called for wage regulations following the main principles of the law of 1908, that is, "wages according to gender." Almost all the women teachers (1,678 individual) in the towns protested and forwarded a resolution to the DUT executive committee and the Wage Commission in which they demanded a wage reform on the principle of "equal pay for equal work."

Attempts to Oust Thora Petersen from the Wage Commission

At the next convention of the DUT delegates in Odense in December 1917, it was questioned whether the DUT's representatives in the Wage Commission still represented the DUT's interests, since the majority of the rank and file were opposed to the equal wage principle and to support allowances for both men and women. However, Thora Petersen refused to work for any other principle than that of equal pay for men and women doing equal work. The DUT delegates then demanded that she withdraw from the Wage Commission. She refused to do so on the grounds that she not only represented the women teachers, but also other women in public service, and that she had no intention of letting them down. The result was that the Wage Commission was urged to develop other wage principles.

The equal pay issue threatened to disrupt the DUT. This situation forced the chair, Hr. Svane, to find a workable solution.[44] He succeeded in convincing the Wage Commission to allow Thora Petersen to work for the interest of female teachers and their demand of "equal pay for men and women," while Carl Dige was to forward the men's standpoint, "a different scale for the two sexes." If the women's demand to the Wage Commission for equal pay threatened to depreciate men's wage levels, Carl Dige was to oppose such proposals for reform. Hr. Svane's proposed solution of the conflict about the equal pay issue was represented at the convention of delegates in the summer of 1918 and was adopted. Thereafter, Thora Petersen continued to work in the Wage Commission as the only women among the commissions's twenty-one members.

Thora Petersen's Work in the Wage Commission

Thora Petersen ably fought against the many prejudices attached to women as a sex. She demanded that evidence be forwarded to substantiate the allegations that female public servants were not as able, useful, or responsible as their male colleagues and that they were ill more frequently than men.

An ad hoc committee was constituted with Thora Petersen, Carl Dige, and three other men as members to investigate the allegations. All four men were opponents of equal pay. Thora Petersen took it upon herself to begin an investigation of the allegations concerning female civil servants, and it was decided that a questionnaire concerning men's and women's work should be sent to all sections of public administration.

The completed questionnaires were available by the end of 1918. They indicated that in cases where women's employment was basically identical to men's, the difference in the usefulness of women as opposed to men was based on the public administration's special provisions limiting women's participation in certain roles and upon the fact that women were not trained in all the service areas that men were. In general, the evidence showed that *given equal conditions, men and women were equally useful and able.* Furthermore, evidence showed that female public servants were more often absent because of illness than men. Thora Petersen insisted that women were more frequently ill than men because they were generally subject to poorer financial, housing, and working conditions than men were.

During negotiations within the Wage Commission, Thora Petersen was strongly supported by the Danish Women's Society and other organizations of the women's movement. The Danish Women's

Society held large public meetings with support from other women's organizations. At the meetings, resolutions demanding equal pay were adopted and sent to the Wage Commission and to Parliament. These women were particularly active during the period preceding the general elections in 1918, the first national election in Denmark in which women participated. They demanded that all candidates for Parliament should state their position in regard to the equal pay issue.

Following women's enfranchisement, the new political pressure which women's organizations and the women's movement were able to bring to bear upon representatives in Parliament ultimately succeeded. The legislation which stipulated the "equal pay for equal work" principle for public employees became a reality. The Wage Commission concluded its activity on 27 June 1919. A majority of fifteen of its members summarized their conclusions regarding illness, responsibility and early retirement from the public service in the following remarks:

> When taking actual conditions into consideration, an argument for different wages for men and women is considered untenable.
>
> Such provisions exist in present legislation even for areas where full equality in regard to the kind and quality of work performed is acknowledged. These provisions have undoubtedly been based on considerations which are irrelevant in determining the actual value of work performed.
>
> Of such considerations, the following may be mentioned:
>
> 1. women as a rule do not have the same obligations as men in regard to providing for others,
> 2. by virtue of their sex and mode of being, women are assumed to be able to manage their affairs more economically than men.
> 3. that, on account of these and other reasons, women are, to a great extent, both willing and able to take up employment and work at a lower wage than men.
>
> A majority among us concede that a certain relevance can attach to the first point, in that we consider it desirable that public employees carrying out the same line of work should also enjoy the same standard of living. This means, however, that the unmarried male and the unmarried female employee should enjoy the same conditions of employment.
>
> With regard to the second and third of the above-mentioned points, the committee feels that the State cannot be justified in taking advantage of the fact that financially needy female public employees, driven by necessity, are often obliged to work in their free time, a circumstance that does not apply for men. In the final analysis, the State can derive no real financial advantage from the surplus labor of these women, due to the fact that the effects of insuf-

ficient rest and recreation upon them adversely influence the quality of their work. Furthermore, the committee feels that the negative assessment by public authorities of female public employees' health and stamina is consistently misleading, as it fails to take into account the effects upon these women of excess overtime work and the consequent lack of sufficient rest and relaxation.

Therefore, and on the basis of the above-mentioned, this committee concludes the correctness of establishing equal salaries for men and women occupying the same positions.[45]

With this, the commission adopted the principle of equal pay for equal work.

When wage law proposals were raised in Parliament in the summer of 1919, all parties accepted the principle of "equal pay for equal work." However, certain reservations were voiced. The Liberal Party expressed concern that higher wages for women would lure them away from the home. The Social Democratic party felt that equal wages might result in a reduction in hiring women for the public services, a consequence which would scarcely be in their interests.

The Wage Law of the New Education Act for public-school teachers was passed on 4 October 1919 and formally ratified *equal pay for men and women*. However, the new law still operated with the following provisions:(1) there would be two different wage levels for teachers of different seniority at country schools, that is, for assistant teachers and for schoolmasters (only men); (2) there would be two different wage classes for teachers with different levels of training, that is, for teachers (male and female) with full three years of training and a teacher examination, and for teachers with one and a half years of training and no examination, but with the right to teach children six to eleven years of age and to teach girls in nedlework (mostly women); and (3) there would be two different wage classes for married teachers (mostly men) and unmarried teachers without children (mostly women). The law did succeed in abolishing the principle of salary according to gender. In fact, however, differing circumstances and working conditions for men and for women meant that an inequitable economic basis for women was maintained, despite the formal principle of "equal pay for equal work" and despite the fact that men and women teachers carried out the same work.

Resistance against Equal Pay

During the period of negotiations about the new wage reform (1917–19), vigorous resistance to equal pay had been expressed by a majority of the DUT male membership. Paradoxically, it was precisely in an organization where the greatest equality existed in the nature of the work, training, and responsibility of its male and female members that the heftiest opposition to the establishment of equal pay for equal work was to be found. Within the DUT, feelings ran high in the years that followed, and the equal pay principle was repeatedly under attack.

The opposition attempted to undermine female teachers' right to equal pay in various ways. It tried to create a schism between domestic working women's organizations and the female teachers' organizations. The opposition also tried to prove the, in fact, women now constituted a more expensive work force because of their frequent illness and earlier retirement. Furthermore, the opposition tried to belittle women with blatantly sexist arguments concerning women's and men's relative abilities as teachers.

In the DUT's journal, the provincial town teachers' journal, and the daily press, a constant stream of articles appeared in which men tried to demonstrate that equal pay was a mistake. In an election editorial, the editor of *The Towns School* warned his colleagues against reopening the conflict surrounding equal pay, while at the same time lauding the innate superiority of the male. He wrote:

> The legislative powers in this country have settled the conflict once and for all. Now it is experience—the facts—which must determine whether society is best served by men or by women in various positions. Those men who cannot reconcile themselves to the present situation should pull themselves together and say to their fellows: "Men, let us rejoice that in the future we need no longer fear cheap competition from women. We are the stronger sex, with the larger brain and greater physical strength, and through out work we can prove to this society that we are more suitable and worthy . . ."[46]

This election editorial is followed by other articles about the size of women's brains, the strange feminine logic which consistently misses the point, and women's unsuitability for leading positions and their difficuly in making a satisfactory effort. Statements such as the following may be found:

> Without the support and cooperation of teachers [men], a great many of them [women] are not up to the mark in certain areas . . . I think that those who have fought for the equal pay principle, and succeeded in getting it implemented, have done the Town school's women employees a terrible disservice."[47]

"We are the best suited for leadership and in all of the leading positions we acquit ourselves better than women."[47]

There is little difference between the patriarchal and sexist opinions of the town school teachers in 1919 concerning women's suitability as teachers and those of the bishops in 1856.

Gradually, as the debate spread to trade journals, the daily press, and public meetings, the "provider principle" was raised again. Not all opponents of equal pay principle dared declare publicly that they supported "salary according to gender." Instead, they tried to forge alliances with groups of married women who were dissatisfied with the existing structure of support allowances but not with equal pay. In this connection Copenhagen's school commissioner made the following remarks: "It is a matter of indifference to me whether the result within the educational sector turns out to be a wage difference according to sex or according to the provider principle."[48] At this time he also contrasted married male teachers' poverty and hardship to female teachers' material and existential well-being.

In 1922 a violent conflict developed between opponents of equal pay, notably Mr. Kaper, Copenhagen's school commissioner, and female teachers. In connection with the budget debate on November 1921, the Copenhagen school commissioner had requested that an estimate be made of the additional expenditures incurred by the city as a result of using women teachers instead of men. He claimed that because of women's greater incidence of illness, earlier retirement with pension, and longer life span, the employment of teachers created extra expenses for the *kommune* (Copenhagen).

This criticism of the employment of women teachers was met with violent protests from the city's female teachers, who resigned en masse from the Pedagogic Society chaired by Commissioner Kaper. Hedvig Baumgarten, the president of the Union of Women Teachers in Copenhagen, prepared another accounting, which for the 1922–23 fiscal year revealed that the employment of female teachers would earn savings amounting to 198,331 crowns (equivalent to a yearly salary for approximately sixty teachers).

But the commissioner continued to work against equal pay for the city's female teachers. In 1925 he conducted a lecture on the subject of women's public employment conditions, in which he presented new figures for both male and female absences due to sickness (see table 1). These statistics and those covering pension conditions were used to support the commissioner's claim that women were more expensive than men.[49]

Table 1. Sick Leaves Statistics Presented by Commissioner Kaper, Copenhagen, 1922–25

	Personnel, excluding teachers		Teaching personnel	
	Women	Men	Women	Men
1922–23	17.2	14.4	26.7	13.5
1923–24	16.2	15.2	24.2	14.4
1924–25	14.9	14.0	21.6	13.7

As a counterattack, the Union of Women Teachers in Copenhagen, together with the Copenhagen chapter of the Danish Women's Society issued a small pamphlet called "Misleading Statistics: Figures Regarding Illness and Pension Conditions".[49] First, they criticized the base of calculation used by the council and, second, the manner in which the council's sick leave and pension statistics were being used. The pamphlet was submitted to the Ministry of Education, and copies were forwarded to Copenhagen's city council, the press, and all chapters of the Danish Women's Society.[49]

The arguments raised by the pamphlet were later substantiated by figures provided by Copenhagen's Office of Statistics, which calculated sick leave percentages for men and women employed by the city. The Office of Statistics proved that *the highest percentage of sickness was among the lowest-paid men and women*; that 52.3 percent of women had no sick days whatever; and that the average age of female teachers was higher than that of male teachers, and that therefore females would naturally account for more days of sick leave than males.[50] Moreover, the figures revealed that, since the introduction of equal pay, there had been a general reduction in the amount of sick days among female personnel, and that there was no longer any significant difference in this respect between male and female employees. The relative difference in the incidence of illness among teaching personnel, however, was considerably greater, but here the figures showed that the number of sick days among female teachers had also declined following the introduction of equal pay. All these findings also supported Thora Petersen's earlier arguments when she had fought for equal pay in the wage Commission (1917–19).

The many persistent attempts to annul the equal pay principle during the course of the 1920s did not succeed. Female teachers were well organized and active in the Danish Union of Teachers, in the Danish Women's Society, and in political parties. Any attempts to question the right to equal pay for equal work in the 1920's were met with counterattacks from women.

Summary

The development of the capitalist mode of production in Denmark resulted in radical changes throughout the society. The family patriarchy in which the man of the house held absolute sway over wife, children, and domestics was gradually dissolved, although patriarchal power structures and ideology remained. Men now developed *collective dominion* over women on the labor market. They did this through (1) male-established and male-dominated interest organizations, (2) the establishment of a labor hierarchy with women at the bottom and men at the top, and (3) an increasingly comprehensive and male-delineated process of state intervention in the functions of the family.

The capitalistic modes of production also bore other changes. Because of new production methods and expansion to meet the demands of the national and international market, a labor force with qualifications to meet these new conditions became necessary, and that in turn called for generally higher level of education for all citizens. The necessity for more education, combined with an explosive growth in the population, resulted in a dearth of teachers in the last half of the nineteeth century and the beginning of the twentieth century. General problems in recruiting an adequate number of trained teachers among men therefore gave rise to discussions concerning the possibility of employing women as teachers in the public schools.

As we have seen a proposal concerning the use of women as teachers was forwarded to the Ministry of Ecclesiastical and Educational Affairs. It led to royal resolution in 1859 and later to a law in 1867 on the employment of women in the public schools. The law determined the principle that those employed in public services were to be paid according to gender. Women could not be paid more than two thirds the salary of men (many women were paid less).

The unequal conditions for male and female teachers were the result of the economic and political situation, which required a low level of public expenditure from the school system, and the patriarchal ideology which defined women as second-class citizens and as naturally subordinate to masculine domination. The fact that women did not have to have any training and the ruling that they could only work in inferior positions emphasized their subordinate position and value as subject to authority of male teachers and as citizens with the primary function of furnishing maternal care to small children and training older girls to be wives and mothers.

These conditions formed the material and ideological basis for the conflicts of between female and male teachers which culminated fur-ing the period 1918–22. Because female teachers in fact shared the same work as male teachers, it became apparent to women that unequal pay for equal work was unjust. The self-confidence which many female teachers gained through their more independent working life resulted in their ability to protest openly against such inequality, forwarding demands for the franchise, equal pay for equal work, and state-financed training colleges for women. With the franchise of 1915 female teachers gained new political power, and after thirty years of struggle, they succeeded in 1919 in gaining equal pay.

Notes

1. Danish public schools (*folkeskolor*) are publicly financed by the state and local councils (*kommuner*). Today 90 percent of all Danish children attend public schools.

2. Nathalie Zahle *Mit liv* (My life) (Copenhagen, 1914, p. 66.

3. The Danish population increased from 1,523,000 in 1850 to 2,594,000 in 1900.

4. Before 1858 very few women were employed in public schools. Women were employed as teachers, but only in needlework school in Copenhagen and some of the provincial towns. Private schools made use of female teachers, but the training these women had received was quite superficial and was often no more than the education they themselves had received at similar private schools.

5. Beginnning in 1834, Danish teachers convened at national meetings where educational matters were discussed. In 1841 teachers in Copenhagen formed The Society of Teachers, and in 1874 they formed the national union, "The Danish Union of Teachers" (DUT) was thus the first trade union in Denmark.

6. Pauline Worm was headmistress for a private girls' school. She was also extremely active in the newly formed Danish Womens' Society. Her letter is reproduced in *Bog og nal* (Book and needle) (Copenhagen, January, 1917), pp. 6–7.

7. J. Larsen, "Documents Concerning the Setting-up of the Female Teachers' Examination and the Employment of Female Teachers in Public Schools," in *Bog og Nal*.

8. Ibid, pp. 8–12. The bishops' replies are included here. The Church was always involved in educational concerns because it superintended the public school system.

9. Female teachers could take examinations in arithmetic, German, French, English, and needlework, but not in mathematics, physics, or gymnastics. The subjects were weighed differently for women and men. Needlework weighed triple for women, while arithmetic weighed double for men.

10. In 1861, women also gained access to teaching positions in public schools in Copenhagen. They taught girls in almost all subjects, and boys in the lower classes. By 1879, female teachers were carrying out 53 percent of all the teaching work in Copenhagen public schools, and in 1887, 54.6 percent.. The costs involved were only three-fifths what they would have been had male teachers performed the same work.

In 1895, there were 6,458 teachers in Denmark, with the breakdown as follows:

Place	Male teachers	Female teachers
Copenhagen (capital)	447	549
Town	726	597
Country	3,488	651

Source: J. Larson, *Bidrag til den danske folkeskoles historie fra 1818–1898* (The history of the Danish public school from 1818 to 1898) (Copenhagen, 1899).

	Male teachers		Female teachers	
Year and place	Total	With teacher training	Total	With teacher training
1895				
Town, ex-cluding capital	746	616	616	338
Country	3,507	3,238	647	183
1905				
Town, ex-cluding capital	1,118	950	956	675
Country	3,748	3,530	1,208	240

Source: 'Folkeskolevaesenet," 1904–1905, *Danmarks statistik* 1908 (Danish Statistics 1908), p. 246.

11. The law set down a difference in the salaries of male and female teachers which was far greater than that between the salaries of men and women employed in other areas of public service.

12. Born in 1853, Anne Bruun worked as a teacher in Copenhagen. She was extremely active in the Danish Women's Society, for which she edited the periodical *Women and Society*. In 1900 she became the first women to sit in the executive committee of the Danish Union of Teachers, in which she continued until the 1915 election, when she declined the nomination because of failing health.

13. The teachers formed the DUT in 1914. In 1919 it received the right of collective bargaining. In 1900 union membership numbered approximately 6,000 (of which 5,000 were men, and 1,000 were women).

14. Female teachers in the rural areas taught needlework, but since this subject was not included in the standard curriculum, it was taught after normal school hours, which usually meant an additional six to twelve hours of work per week for the women. There was no stipulation made in the wage law concerning how this extra work was to be remunerated.

15. *Danmarks Laererforenings Medlemsblad* (DLM), nr. 10 (1901) (journal of the DUT).

16. Born in 1851, Anna Jagd was an extremely active member of the Danish Women's Society. She was employed as a teacher in Svendborg and sat in the DUT's executive committee from 1905 to 1906.

17. There were twelve seats in the executive committee. Five of these were up for election in 1900. The following year, the remaining seven would be up for election, and so on.

18. That teachers made no particular effort to alter wage discrimination against women was confirmed at the DUT delegates' conventions and by negotiations concerning a new wage law for teachers in 1907–1908.

19. DUT's journal (DLM), nr. 9 (1904), p. 53.

20. DLM, nr. 14 (1904), p. 89–90.

21. *Kobstadsskolen* (The Town School), nr. 2, (1904).

22. DLM, nr. 19, (1905), p. 125.

23. In the election of the executive committee in 1906, for which five representatives were to be chosen, almost all the women backed the female teachers' list. Female teachers accounted for 50 percent of election participation at this election. Average election participation was 41 percent. All female teachers voted for the female teachers' lists. *Folkeskolen*, nr. 26 (1906), p. 203 (DUT's n w. journal). As a result of this election, female teachers won additional representation in the executive committee. Female teachers in the rural areas won one more representative, and female teachers in the towns won three representatives.

24. The proposal made by the DUT and the Town Teachers' Society advocated the formation of a national union with an executive committee consisting of fifteen members. The term of office was to be three years, and the

committee would retire en masse at the expiration of this period. The first election was held in 1909, with the fifteen members being chosen from two groups: group A—teachers from country schools, and group B—teachers from towns, excluding Copenhagen. Group A elected nine members and group B six members.

25. There were 7,200 members in the union in 1915, of which 59 percent were men and 41 percent awere women. In the executive committee, women held 27 percent of the seats. As of 1985, women accounted for 56 percent of the membership and men for 44 percent , but the women have only 19 percent of the seats in the executive committee (five out of twenty-seven seats.

26. *Folkeskolen*, nr. 28 (1905), p. 169.

27. Kjaergaard (1966–1927) was a member of the DUT's executive committee from 1905 to 1915 and a central figure in discussions concerning the matter of salaries and seniority. He was especially prominent in educational circles as editor of *Folkeskolen* from 1906 to 1927.

28. All speaches delivered at the convention are reproduced in full in the DUT journal *Folkeskolen* , 1905–1906.

29. The resolution appears in full in *Folkeskolen*, nr. 30 (1905), p. 92.

30. The principles of the proposal, among others, were as follows: local councils should increase starting salaries (the basic minimum wage), and all supplements should be paid by the state; state wage supplements should commence immediately upon employment; starting salaries were to be identical for men and women, but salaries of male teachers were to increase on a more sharply-inclined scale.

31. *Folkeskolen*, nr. 28 (1905), p. 169.

32. For minutes from these negotiations, see *Folkeskolen*, 1907–1908.

33. *Folkeskolen*, nr. 1 (1909), p. 9.

34. *Folkeskolen*, nr. 25 (1918), p. 239.

35. Carl Dige (1873–1954), was a member of the DUT's executive committee from 1916 to 1928 and was chairman for the DUT from 1927 to 1928. Thora Petersen (1885–1954) was a member of the DUT's executive committee from 1916 to 1929.

36. On the whole, state policy with regard to women is rife with contradictions. One one hand, it attempts to keep women in their traditional roles as wives and mothers, supported by the male, while on the other hand, women are encouraged to enter the labor market, thus enabling them to provide for themselves, or at least affording them the opportunity of so doing.

37. The distinction between "providers" and "the provided for" is reproduced in a series of legislative amendements in the unemployment law of 1919; in laws dealing with the salaries of public servants and teachers in 1919,

by which married men were considered providers regardless of whether or not there were children in the marriage; and in social legislation by which, according to the rules covering sickness benefits, the married man, as provider, could claim higher benefits.

38. The draft of the bill presented by the Wage Reform Committee is reproduced in *Folkeskolen*, September 1917.

39. In a capitalistic society, wages are established in keeping with the market value of the labor force, and not with the needs of the workers, that is, in relation to how he or she has to provide for.

40. Signe Veilgaard (1867–1962) was a member of the DUT's executive committee from 1924 to 1936.

41. These resolutions are reproduced in *Folkeskolen*, 1917.

42. *Folkeskolen* nr. 37 (1917), p. 13.

43. The debate is reproduced in *Folkeskolen* and *Kobstadsskolen* (The Town School) from 1917–1919.

44. O. Svane (1869–1948) was a member of the executive committee in the Copenhagen Teachers' Union from 1895 to 1910. He was a member of the DUT executive committee from 1910 and chair for the DUT from 1915 to 1927.

45. Reproduced in *Lading, Agot: Dansk Kvindesamfunds arbejde gennem 25 ar* (The Work of the Danish Women's Society during 25 years) (Copenhagen, 1939), pp. 78–79.

46. *Kobstadsskolen*, nr. 16 (1919), p. 96.

47. Ibid. nr. 20, p. 139.

48. Ibid. nr. 23, p. 161.

49. "Misleading Figures: A Statement of Accounts," Copenhagen's Union of Women Teachers and Danish Women's Society (Copenhagen branch), 1926.

50. V. Jespersen, "Accurate Figures." A reply from Department Head V. Jespersen. Copenhagen's Union of Women Teachers and Danish Women's Society, 1926.

References

Borchorst. A. *Arbejdsmarkedets konsopdeling—patriarkalsk dominans eller kvinders valg?* (Sexual devision at the labor market—patriarchal dominance womens' choice?). Aalborg University Press, 1984, Denmark.

Borchorst, A. and B. Siim. *Kvinder i velfaerrdsstaten.* (Women in the welfare state). Aalborg University Press, 1984, Denmark.

Dahlstrom, E., and R. Leljestrom. "Patriarkat och kvinnoforskning" (Patriarchy and Women Research). *Sociologisk Forskning* (Sociological Research), no. 2, Goteborg, 1981, Sweden.

Danmarks Laererforenings Medlemsblad (Journal of the Danish Union of Teachers), Copenhagen, 1900–1906, Denmark.

Folkeskolen (The Public School), Copenhagen, 1907–1928, Denmark.

Hartmann, H. "The Unhappy Marriage between Marxism and Feminism." In *Women and Revolution,* ed. L. Sargent. Boston, 1981.

Kobstadsskolen (The Town School), Slagelse, 1908–1922, Denmark.

Kvinden og Samfundet (Woman and Society). Copenhagen, 1878, 1885, 1898, 1900–1922, Denmark.

Lading, Aa. *Dansk Kvindesamfunds arbejde gennem 25 aar* (The work of the Danish Womens' Society during 25 years). Copenhagen, 1917, Denmark.

Larsen, J. "Aktstykker vedrorende oprettelse af laererindeeksamen og laererindernes ansaettelse ved Folkeskolen." In *Bog og Naal* (Book and Needle). copenhagen, 1917.

—— *Den Danske Folkeskoles Historie 1818–1898* (The history of the Danish public school 1818–1898). Copenhagen, 1899, Denmark.

Lemche, G. *Dansk Kvindesamfunds historie gennem 40 aar* (The history of the Danish Womens' Society during 40 years). Copenhagen, 1912, Denmark.

Rasmussen, H. "Laerernes uddannelse, deres okonomiske og sociale stilling siden 1814" (The teachers' educational, economical, and social conditions since 1814). In *Den Danske Folkeskole gennem hundrede aar, 1814–1914* (The Danish Public School during one hundred years, 1814–1914). Copenhagen, 1914, Denmark.

Ravn, A., B. Rosenbech, and B. Siim (eds.) *Capitalism and Patriarchy.* Woman Studies Series, no. 13. Aalborg University Press, 1983, Denmark.

Zahle, N. *Mit liv* (My life). Copenhagen, 1914, Denmark.

Part III

Feminist Perspectives
On Schooling

F eminist scholarship places women at the center of inquiry; it provides a new framework for the study of institutions and lays the groundwork for the transformation of knowledge (Biklen and Shakeshaft, 1985; Tetreault, 1985). The three chapters in this section illustrate feminist perspectives on schooling: women are at the center of their inquiry, and a new lens is presented to investigate school policies and work realities. Enders-Dragasser presents a current policy issues on homework in the schools in West German and its effect on women as teachers and mothers, Reynolds investigates the policy debate concerning married women teachers in Ontario in the 1940s, and Biklen documents the work lives of contemporary women elementary-school teachers in a school in the United States.

Ender-Dragasser focuses on the privatization of schools and the homework policy in West Germany. She shows how the fiscal problems of West German schools have resulted in a shorter school day and an increased reliance on the unpaid labor of parents—primarily mothers. The homework policy, to compensate for fewer hours in the school day, requires that students engage in many school tasks at home under the supervision of parents. Thus, children's success in school becomes increasingly dependent on the available help and supervision at home. This policy has direct implications for women as mothers and teachers. First, women become, in part, a hidden subsidy to the schools; their unpaid labor becomes expected as part of the national schooling process. The phenomenon of women's labor supplementing schooling represents a long-standing tradition in education; historically women teachers were paid less than their male counterparts and were an economic advantage to the formal school systems. Although current laws require equal pay for equal work, again, in the privatization of schooling, women provide the hidden economic subsidies.

Enders-Dragasser also shows the effect of this policy on the social expectations for women at home and in the workplace: "good mothers" are at home after the shortened school hours to provide the necessary supervision and support for their children's education. Although the author does not give statistics on women's employment since the inception of this policy, one might expect to see a decrease in the numbers of women with school-age children in the work force. She also points out the "double bind" that is created in the interactions between women teachers and mothers, a theme also addressed by Biklen. The homework policy creates an inherent conflict between women: since mothers who teach are employed outside the home, they do not uphold the image of the "good mother," and thus tension is created between unemployed mothers and employed teachers who are mothers. Furthermore, women teachers who are mothers of school-age children must encourage mothers to assist in homework, and at the same time be available to their own children at home. The policy has other implications for equal access and opportunity: whatever "leveling" function schools have played for students from different language, cultural, and social-class backgrounds has been eliminated; the educational outcomes of students become increasingly reliant on the educational levels of their parents; and children with German-speaking and educated parents will receive more able assistance than students from non-German speaking or poorly educated parents.

Reynolds elucidates the cultural assumptions about gender that were evident in the 1940s debate over the policy excluding married women from the teaching force in Toronto. Most Western countries have had policies restricting married women as teachers; Reynolds show the debate and demonstrates the underlying assumptions surrounding it. She goes beyond the obvious facts to ferret out the meaning of what happened and "tries to explain, why, out of a range of possibilities, a particular choice was made." Women teachers in Toronto were fairly active on behalf of their sex and founded the Federation of Women Teachers as early as 1880, but it was an up-hill battle for equality for many decades. Danylewyxa and Prentice, in a history of Ontario teachers, point out "It would be many years after the First World War before the women teachers of Ontario were able to take a more militant stand of to begin to recognize the factors that worked to create the unequal status in the profession" (p. 170, 1984). During the 1940s, their efforts seemed to take a turn for the better when the school board rescinded a policy excluding married women from the teaching force. Reynolds goes on to explore the limiting "liberation" of this new policy. She presents similar themes already presented in other chapters: the division between the public and the private sphere, the belief in the inherent differences and social obligations of women and men, and the concern that women would take jobs away from the male breadwinners. She recaptures the patriarchal views and the articulated misogynist arguments used to support the seeming newly "liberated" policy for married women as teachers.

Biklen studies the work lives of women elementary schoolteachers in one school in the United States. Her chapter adds to the newly emerging literature about women, teachers, such as that by Lightfoot (1983), Freedman (1983), Lather (1984), and Acker (1984). Biklen's chapter lays to rest some of the assumptions about women's career motives and priorities. She closes the gap between the cultural stereotypes and the realities by focusing on women as subjects for study. She shows, for instance, that women have a strong career orientation—contrary to the myth that teaching is a lower level of priority for women teachers. She shows that women resent the bad press about elementary teaching as simple and unimportant work—contrary to the myth that women do not have professional identities. She demonstrates that women elementary teachers want intellectually stimulating and rewarding professional development—contrary to the myth that they want to be "told what to do" and not be intellectually taxed. Biklen also raises the issue about the relationships between mothers and women teachers and the double bind created between women employed as teachers and the "good mother" who stays home with her children. She illustrates the demeaning experiences women teachers have with administrators in the central office, with parents, and with the press which reproduce the cultural stereotypes and present elementary teaching, and women, in a devalued role.

Educators have always had to answer three basic questions: Who should be taught? What should they be taught? Who should teach them? The answers to these questions have changed over the years. It is now generally assumed that girls should be educated, that there should be equal opportunities for learning in our schools, and that adult women and men should be educated and trained in the skills and artistry of teaching and educational leadership. Since the days of the cloistered nuns in German-speaking Europe, there have been significant changes for girls as students and for women as educational employees. But the fact remains that gender plays a significant role in the opportunities, experiences, and outcomes of students and adult professionals.

References

Biklen, Sari Knopp, and Charole Shakesshaft (1985). "The New Scholarship on Women." In *Handbook for Achieving Sex Equity Through Education*, ed. Susan Klein. Baltimore, Md.: Johns Hopkins University Press, pp. 44–52.

Danylewyca, Marta, and Alison Prentice (1984). "Lessons from the Past: The Experience of Women Teachers in Quebec and Ontario." In *World Yearbook of Education 1984: Women and Education* ed. London: Kogan Page, pp. 163–172.

Freedman, Sara (1983). "Teaching: An Imperiled Profession." In *Handbook of Teaching and Policy*, ed. Lee Shulman and Gary Sykes, New York: Longman, pp. 261–299.

Lather, Patti (1984). "Gender and the Shaping of Public School Teaching: Do Good Girls Make Good Teachers?" Paper presented at the National Women Studies Association Conference, June.

Lighfoot, Sara Lawrence (1983). "The Lives of Teachers." In *Handbook of Teaching and Policy*, pp. 241–260.

Tetreault, Mary Kay (1985). "Feminist Phase Theory: An Experience-Derived Evaluation Model", *Journal of Higher Education* 58, no. 4 (July–August), pp. 364–384.

Chapter 10

Mothers' Unpaid Schoolwork in West Germany

UTA ENDERS-DRAGASSER

The elementary school system in West Germany demands a great deal from its students and their parents. Through the extensive use of homework, schools have become "privatized," requiring the involvement of parents (usually mothers) in the education of their children. It is a system that reinforces sex stereotypes and fails to make the best use of its teachers. This chapter examines the effects of "privatization" on women in German society and discusses the need for change.

The West German School System

West Germany has a compulsory, federal school system, administered by the states, which traditionally has been highly selective (for example, all states have special schools for handicapped, elementary-school drop-outs, etc.). Since success in elementary school determines the choices available to the student at higher educational levels, the pressure to succeed academically begins early and affects students and parents alike. After completing four years of elementary school, children are assigned to one of three types of upper-level schools. (Assignments are based on school performance, teacher recommendations, and the parents' wishes.) The schools, a heritage of prewar times, are the *Hauptschule* (basic school), which grants the

Hauptschulabschluss certificate; the *Realschule* (middle school), with *Realschulabschluss*; and the traditional *Gymnasium*, which grants the *Abitur* or *Hochschulreife* certificate and which leads to the university.

Generally, elementary-school hours are 8:00 A.M. to 1:00 P.M., though a few afternoon lessons may be held one or two times a week. Classes are often dropped, however, because cost cutting has eliminated teaching positions—and thousands of teachers are unemployed. This inefficient system flourishes only because students are required to do extensive homework after morning classes. Each state school system has its own regulations fixing the whereabouts and the amount of time permissible for these afternoon homework sessions, but in every case they are considered a private, parental affair. The homework policy has become established practice—with little criticism or public debate—even though schools are not fulfilling their responsibility for educating students.

The drawbacks of such a system are numerous. If children do not understand what they are taught in the morning, they cannot reproduce it correctly in the afternoon. Parents (that is, mothers) then fail to accomplish their task, which is to help the child learn. And when mother fails, teachers—and fathers—are upset. This "homework problem" surfaces from time to time in the media, producing a spirited debate of its pedagogical implications and numerous helpful hints. Inevitably, though, public interest fades, and the problem remains unsolved.

The roots of the problem lie in the German school system's history of discrimination against women, though in this century women have fought for and achieved important goals: the right to study (1908); coeducation (after World War II); equal rights—achieved after a mass protest by women— (Article III, 2 of the Constitution of the Federal Republic, 1949: "Men and women have equal rights"); and finally, unlimited access to general education (1980).

Over the years, teaching has become an acceptable profession for women and, since the 1950s, for women with children. It is the only profession open to large numbers of academic women. Female teachers are trained and examined in the same institutions as men. They receive equal pay but tend to remain in the lower ranks. They represent a majority in lower-paying elementary schools and a minority in the higher-paying Gymnasiums.

The management, administration, and development of the compulsory state school system is in the hands of men. Only a small percentage of those working in administration, especially in the higher ranks, are women (currently, only about 10 percent of all heads are women), and they seldom participate in important developments and decision making.

The current high unemployment rate among teachers has fueled the resurrection of the Third Reigh's *Doppelverdiener-Klausel* (double-income clause of the civil servants' regulations) of 1933 to 1937. The law would secure the few open teaching positions for men while pressuring women to leave teaching. From 1933 to 1950 the double-income clause was the basis for mass dismissal of women: wives, mothers, and daughters were removed from the civil service if their husbands or fathers had a regular income. Now, in the 1980s, the clause is again being publicly discussed. Men are preferred, states the rationale, because they need an income, and married women are refused positions because they don't need a "double income." This position clearly violates the equality article of the constitution and places unrealistic restrictions on married women, who apparently should stay home and let men do the breadwinning.

The West German school system, like the double-income clause, continues to promote images of women which do not fit with reality nor with equality regulations. Neither the federal constitution nor any state school acts prohibit sex discrimination in school, or even mentions it. (In the state of Hessen, however, women fought for and won an antidiscrimination provision in 1984.) In textbooks and other teaching materials, girls and women are not represented in accordance with their numbers or by their importance in society. Instead, they are shown as they relate to men: as wives, daughters, mothers, sisters, nurses, secretaries, assistants, etc. No strong, creative, independent, opinion-making women act as positive role models. Women are shown as dependent beings in need of help—who do all the housework. Criticism of this situation, until recently, has had little effect. But in three federal states—Bremen, Hamburg, and Hessen—textbook sexism has become a political issue. In Hessen, curriculum revisions were scheduled to begin in 1985.

The accepted rules of behavior in schools permit male students and teachers to discipline female students and teachers by exercising various forms of sexism, including physical violence and sexual harassment. As a consequence, girls and women are affected physically, psychologically, and intellectually. They quickly discover that their assets are their bodies, appearance, and nice manners: not personality or creative and intellectual potential.

Young girls learn to accept sexism and female inferiority as normal. Their perceptions and experiences undergo a shaping which influences their view of life, their plans for the future, their wishes, and their hopes. They wait for the fairy tale prince and forget to rely on their own strength. Their lives are firmly rooted in the sexist experiences of family and school.

Finally, girls generally perform better in school than boys, but because of these pervasive role orientations, they often underachieve in mathametics, the natural sciences, and technology. They learn to avoid success in male-dominated subjects and vocational training, and this avoidance results in a lack of competent women to teach such subjects. Rapid advances in technological development have drawn public attention to this issue, but the necessary changes in administration and the curriculum have not yet been made.

Unfortunately, both teachers and mothers, as credible and loving authority figures, unknowingly pass on society's sexist attitudes and expectations. Some of this lack of understanding can be attributed to the failure of women in schools and universities to critically analyze their gender status or to study the history and social situation of women. Women's studies programs are considered one-sided and do not exist at the university level.

The Role of Mothers in the School System

When I began, in 1980, to analyze the West German homework practice as a researcher, mother, and teacher, I was surprised and disturbed by my findings. Mothers produce an enormous amount of unpaid work for schools, and because of it they face tremendous problems which school researchers have failed to notice. Researchers have ignored the personal involvement of mothers (and some fathers), and have failed to consider the question of what "parental help" really is. The hours of unpaid labor hidden within the privatization structure made it not a pedagogical problem, but an important social issue.

Four years ago no one seemed interesed in these social implications, but today the situation is changing. While debate still centers on the pedagaogical problem, more and more women are discussing the homework issue publicly and perceiving it as an exploitive and misognist practice. A 1973 study showed that 80 percent of mothers (but only 1 percent of fathers) spend daily time with their children because of homework. (2. Familienbericht, 1975, p. 31). The privatized afternoon "shadow school" is discriminatory in other ways as well. It is not available to the nearly 40 percent of school-age children who have working mothers or the more than 10 percent whose mothers' native tongue is not German. Children in these two categories are therefore likely to be educationally disadvantaged, making the homework practice an important class and ethnic issue as well.

Because the unpaid schoolwork of mothers is an accepted part of school life in West Germany, it is also an integral part of the workday of women educators. Most of these women consider the practice "parental help," forgetting that as paid educators they demand and control the unpaid work of other women. Why do female teachers fail to understand what this means? Three of the many aspects of this complex problem are of special interest.

1. When homework must be directed by mothers, it affects the way they plan and organize their lives. No one can do paid and unpaid work at the same time, and mothers lose time they might otherwise have for paid work, vocational training, or other opportunities. Their participation in political, cultural, scientific, and social life is limited. Their family's economic situation and their own chance for economic independence is hampered. They system prevents mothers from entering the labor force and from contributing to other areas of society.

2. The labor of women in homework "shadow schools" influences the quality and quantity of their social contacts and limits daily contact with other adults. Through homework, the school exercises an enormous amount of control and ideological influence on mothers, their children, and other family members. Within marriages a subtle hierarchy of work and control may develop. Because mothers are responsible for their child's success in school, they may actually do the schoolwork, while the father, it he chooses, can rid himself of both the responsibility and the work. In some cases he may even unite with the child against the mother, weakening or undermining her authority.

3. The privatization of schoolwork impedes reforms in school and youth welfare. Those who might protest are silenced by their responsibility because they are blamed when their children fail. And they are misused as role models—forced by social pressure to act according to a picture of "normal" motherhood which is partly fiction and partly exploitation.

Research has given us no clues as to when and why this long-established practice of "privatized afternoon school" began. But the words *parents* and *help* are effectively used to mystify the personal involvement of mothers and reinforce their socialization by schools. It is agreed that children must work at home with the help of their parents, and because teachers are not directly invovled in the process, they are not held accountable. Scholastic success or failure becomes the parent's (that is, mother's) responsibility, effectively putting in private hands an immense amount of otherwise expensive and strenuous supervisory, educational, and instructional work.

If schoolwork had not been transferred so effectively into mother's work, society might look quite different. The job situation for teachers and social workers might be much better. But a vicious circle has been created: the teacher shortage creates exhausted teachers, who demand that parents work for the schools. While student-teachers ratio is increased and the number of lessons per course is reduced, the number of lessons per teacher remains the same. School costs are cut but working conditions deteriorate, leaving the teachers demanding, more than ever, the help of parents. The invisible competition between paid and unpaid teachers means that positions are eventually lost.

What effect does this situation have on female teachers? The division of labor into paid and unpaid categories generally leads to competition between teachers and mothers. However, this competition is not perceived as being related to proficiency, but to their role as females. According to the patriarchal double standard, teachers "work" while mothers, even when doing identical work, "help" their children out of love. Thus, unpaid work is not work; it is love. This double standard seems to strengthen the teacher's position, but it also allows the administration to pit the female teacher against the other, and vice versa. Eventually, this sitution results in fewer teaching positions, making teaching in West Germany a closed shop for women.

Privatization also means that teachers lack a way of measuring their effectiveness as teachers. They cannot differentiate between what they achieve during class and what children learn at home from their mothers. When teahers set an idea in motion, they often do not know where it ends. They cannot always determine which conflicts originate in school and which in the family, or what effects these conflicts might have on their students.

Teachers who are mothers must deal with the fictitious reality that "Mothers don't work, they stay at home." Of course mothers do work, both inside and outside the home. For female teachers and mothers, this is a double bind situation, with each role imposing an element of unreality on the other. A women who is both teacher and mother of a school-age child may believe she is not the good mother represented as "normality" to her students. She has not renounced her paid job and dedicated herself to the well-being of her child. At the same time, she expects other mothers to do so by demanding that homework be done properly putting the burden on the mother, thereby denying her own accountability, as a teacher, for a student's success or failure in school. This paradoxical situation may strengthen her mistrust of other women and create unnecessary rivalries, instead of permitting her to handle the situation in a professional manner.

As long as this conflict is not fully understood, the paradox and the problems will continue. The social distance between women teachers and mothers will widen, and the teacher's tendency to blame the mother will increase.

We must look for ways to change this situation. Female reality must be made visible to be analyzed. We must face our actions and understand the consequences those actions have for other women—even if it leads to a crisis. After the first intense reactions and attempts at justification, such a crisis may lead to better understanding between women, and eventually to female solidarity. If that happens, the division and isolation of women, which make it so difficult for them to act collectively in their own interest, will be overcome.

References

Enders-Dragasser, (1984). "Divided Schoolwork—Divided Women: Women Working as Paid and Unpaid Educators for the Compulsory School System of the Federal Republic of Germany." Paper presented at the Second International Interdisciplinary Congress on Women Groningen, the Netherlands, April.

Enders-Dragasser, Uta (1981). "Die Mutterdressur." *Eine Untersuchung zur schulischen Sozialisation der Mutter und ihre Folgen am Beispiel der Hausaufgaben.* Basel, 1981.

Familienbericht (1975). Zweiter Familienbericht. Familie und Sozialisation—Leistungen und Leistungsgrenzen der Familie hinsichtlich des Erziehungs-d und Bildungs-prozesses der jungen Generation- Erster Teil: Stellungnahme der Bundesregierung Zweiter Teil: Bericht der Sachverstandigenkommission, herausgegeben vom Bundesminister fur Jugend, Familie und Gesundheit, Bonn-Bad Godesberg.

Chapter 11

Limited Liberation: A Policy on Married Women Teachers

CECILIA REYNOLDS

The relationship between feminism and teaching, which is primarily a woman's occupation, is a curious phenomenon. Within the feminist movement there are those who seek equal access to established insititutions and those who believe that feminist ideology should serve as a mechanism for transforming those institutions.[1] Much of the literature on women in education is firmly rooted in liberal arguments for equal legal and social status within the profession.[2] In this chapter I will take the alternate view and argue that an exclusive focus on women's integration into existing institutions is too limited a liberation. I argue that the institutions to which women seek access are fundamentally flawed. I will illustrate this point through a historical case study of a policy concerning married women teachers in Toronto in the 1940s where the dominant view regarding women's place was reconstructed in the "liberal" policy. As a result, the patriarchal nature of the teacher hierarchy was maintained rather than transformed.

The initial entry of women into publicly funded state schools was constructed so that men took superior work roles while women took subordinate role. In the same way, when married women became teachers, male teachers remained primary workers, largely because they were seen as breadwinners, and females were designated as secondary workers and supplementary wage earners, whether or not

they actually fell into those categories. When we examine the discourse about women teachers and the speech and language used, we observe ways in which that discourse was altered as demands for teachers increased, but the underlying patriarchal assumptions about gender roles remained the same. Thus, it is clear that in the past, even when women teachers gained access to teaching roles, they remained disadvantaged.

The Policy on Married Women Teachers

During a routine check of the names of teachers who were returning from a leave of absence in 1922, Mr. Powell, one of the trustees of the Toronto Board of Education, objected strenuously to the reinstatement of a Mrs. F.M. Hicks because she was a married women. That objection led to an official policy adopted by the board on 19 March 1925 which required the resignation of all married women teachers.[3] All principles were instructed to make a list of the names and addresses of female married teachers. Those who could not claim to be "breadwinners" were notified that they must resign. According to the policy, female teachers automatically ceased to be employed as teachers for the board on the date of their marriage.

In January 1946, with World War II over, a newly elected board, with an unprecedented six female out of a total of twenty members, had to decide what to do about the eighty-eight married women teachers who had been given temporary teaching jobs because of a teacher shortage during the war. On May 10, the Management Committee of the board voted to return to the old policy, which would force the eighty-eight married women teachers to resign. The committee soon learned that there were many individuals on the board, the teaching staff, and the community who were ready to oppose their decision.

The Debate

Members of the committee used arguments against hiring married women teachers which echoed those which had been used in the nineteenth century against hiring any women as teachers. For example, Trustee Roxborough stated that since the war was over, "the time has now arrived when women should find their place in the home. A married women's place is in the home taking care of the responsibilities she has chosen to take on her shoulders."[4] Other female teachers also were heard espousing this view of women's proper place. A member of the Federation of Women Teachers' Associations of Ontario said: "No one can do two jobs well. A married women is responsible to her family."[5]

Those who argued against women teachers in the nineteenth century had stated that women were "naturally" unable to cope with the teaching role in the state schools. Those arguments were later turned around, and women were said to be quite "naturally" the best persons to teach children, particularly young children. Thus a division of labor in schools developed: men taught older children while women taught "the little ones." In the twentieth century debate over married women teachers, it was argued that married women were unable to adopt teaching roles because their duties as wives were "naturally" more important and precluded their ability to teach well. These arguments were also turned around, and it was said that married women would make good teachers because they understood children and the problems families could encounter. Thus, a division of labor developed whereby men taught as their primary occupation but married women taught in conjunction with their responsibilities as wives and mothers. Unlike men, women were expected to undertake dual roles if they married, and therefore their commitment to their teaching role was viewed as something secondary. The underlying patriarchal assumptions about women's "natural" roles in both centuries placed women in school roles which were largely subordinate to those occupied by men.

But it was not only women's natural abilities which were under debate. There were those who claimed that married women should not be allowed to teach because their teaching would create unfair competition to war veterans, who should be given top priority for available jobs. In addition, older married women were accused of taking work away from young women. As a member of the women's federation stated: "No married women, except in exceptional circumstances, should be teaching now that there are single girls out of a position."[6] The belief revealed in such arguments was that men and single women had a greater right to jobs and that only secondarily should married women be considered for employment. Such arguments buttressed what has been described as the "back to the home" movement following World War II, in which an attempt was made to encourage women to leave the paid work force and to lessen competition for male war veterans. Married women were seen as a threat to men and single women in the labor market. They were also a threat to the status quo of the teacher hierarchy. In that hierarchy in the past, female had largely been young and inexperienced and males had been able to claim greater shared of adminstrative posts, partly because of their greater stability as mature and experienced members of the occupation. Married women teachers were a potential threat to such a division of labor.

The side of the debate which favored a rescindment of the old policy on married women teachers was led by Trustee E.A. Hardy. He was a former principal and in his fiery rhetoric he called for social justice. He declared: "Women nobly won the right to work during the war years. We were happy to attain their assistance at that time. Now, why should marriage disqualify them?"[7] Other trustees, particularly the female ones, agreed with Hardy, and Trustee Conquergood called the old policy a "needless restriction" which was a "handicap on personal liberty"[8]

Statements such as these reveal underlying assumptions about women's rights to employment. The arguments stressed that because women had contributed to the war effort by joining the paid labor force, they should be permitted to remain as a form of reward for service. However, Dr. Hardy took the argument further into the realm of social justice when he claimed: "The shackles imposed on women by the stronger sex have been somewhat shaken."[9] Hardy called for progress and the removal of "old-fashioned regulations." He cited the example of Britain and some cities in the United States where married women had been allowed to teach.

The arguments which appear to have carried the most weight, however, were those of a pragmatic nature. One member said: "It is very doubtful if the board can replace the eighty-eight married women teachers with equally good single teachers for some time."[10] If the board wished to maintain the calibre of its teaching staff and especially if it wanted to initiate junior kindergarten programs and vocational schools,[11] it had to be assured of a supply of qualified teachers. Moreover, in an educational system in which the extension of education was purported to be an asset in the job market, it was difficult to sustain a policy which failed to recognize or use married women who were well qualified. Forcing them to resign was a "great waste of ability, training and education."[12]. As one of the female trustees also pointed out, in the rapidly expanding and urbanized school board, it was become increasingly difficult to enforce the old policy on married women, and some women were marrying "on the sly" anyway.

A long-standing goal of teachers' groups in the province had been an increased reliance on teachers' credentials rather than one their personal characteristics. From a liberal perspective, reliance on credentials facilitated "equality as sameness" and appeared to safeguard the rights of the individual. Dr. Hardy stated "Women have equal franchise and have the same right to life, liberty and the pursuit of happiness as men. If a married women's pursuit of happiness could be attained in the teaching profession, it is not the right of any school board to rob her of it."[13] Yet, equality as sameness, when male careers were taken as the norm, still left women at a disadvantage unless they could claim to be like men. Married women throughout the twentieth century have had difficulty arguing that they are the same as men largely because they have consistently been seen as the persons primarily responsible for the maintenance of the home and the care of children.

On 19 May 1946, the motion to rescind the old policy on married women teachers was passed by the Toronto board by a vote of fourteen to four. Dr. Hardy claimed that married women would be given "equal opportunity along with single men and women."[14]. But, director, Dr. Goldring, stated that the policy of the board would be to "give preference in empolyment to men and unmarried girls, and fill other vacancies with married women."[15] Trustee Conquergood commented, "After a few years of teaching combined with marriage, the teachers will have the good sense to leave and set up a home."[16]

The Meaning of the Debate

The discourse of this policy debate reveals the outcome of attempts to simultaneously accommodate demands to "liberalize" women and yet uphold patriarchal views of women's roles in the home and the work place. The outcome was the maintenance of a pool of male teachers who were afforded relatively well-paid and secure teaching jobs which were seen as likely to lead to further advancement into administration. Concurrently, female teachers were afforded jobs with lower pay, and because they were under pressure to leave those jobs if and when their reponsibilities in the home dictated, their positions were less secure. Moreover, relatively few women could hope that they would advance to administrative roles in schools. This dual labor market for teachers was largely based on gender and was economically advantageous to employers, who could be sure of a supply of qualified and yet relatively inexpensive female teachers.

As married women joined the teaching ranks, the militancy of single women teachers for equal wages was dealt something of a blow. Divisiveness was created between married women and single women teachers. And the demand for equal wages from single women teachers ended in public criticism leveled at all female teachers—they were not committed to their role as teachers. Women teachers were fragmented rather than brought together as a homogeneous collective. Thus the seeming liberation of the policy which allowed married women to teach was in actuality more limiting and did little to alter the division of labor in schools, a division largely based on gender.

Today, women teachers in Canada, as elsewhere, are increasingly vocal about their desires for equal access to administrative roles in schools. This examination of the debate around the policy on married women as teachers suggests that access alone may be insufficient as a goal. Unless the division of labor in schools is transformed and patriarchal assumptions about women's roles in the home and the school as a work place are addressed, the teacher hierarchy may remain essentially unchanged, despite an influx of some females into administrative roles. Until women are appointed to roles which carry the same weight in the organization as those given by men, they will have little impact. When women gain access "as women" and are not forced to appear to be like men, then gender inequity will be removed. Considerations of the past must be used to develop plans for the future. Women must come to speak about their own experience within a discourse which they can claim as their own. Without the insights provided by their own history and apart from such a feminist discourse, women teachers, like women everywhere may be forced to offer the lament of Samuel Becket: "I am walled around with their vociferations, none will ever know what I am, none will ever hear me say it. I won't say it. I can't say it. I have no language but theirs."[17]

Notes

1. Kathy Ferguson, *The Feminist Case Against Bureaucracy,* (Philadelphia: Temple University Press, 1984), p. xiv.

2. Margaret Berry (ed), *Women in Educational Administration.* (Arlington, Va.: National Association of Deans and Counselors, 1979); Sara Knopp Biklen and Marilyn Brannigan, *Women and Educational Leadership* (Lexington, Mass: D.C. Heath and Co., 1980); Patricia Schmuck, W.W. Charters, Jr., and Richard Carlson, *Educational Policy and Management: Sex Differentials* (New York: Academic Press, 1981).

3. The following policy was adopted by the Board: (1) That all principles be requested to make a report to Senior Principal Smith of Chief Inspector

Cowley setting forth the names and addresses of all female married teachers on their staff. (2) That all female teachers in our employ who marry on and after this date, shall, by reason of such marriage, automatically cease to be a teacher on our staff and her salary be paid to her on the usual date of payments of such salary up to the last day of her teaching prior to the date of such marriage. (3) That a committee be appointed to investigate and report regarding the teaching contracts of all married female teachers who are now in the employ of the Board, save and except only as follows: (a)widows, (b)married women who are not living with and are not supported by their husbands, (c)married women whose husbands are disabled either physically or mentally and by reason of such disability are unable to and do not earn a livelihood sufficient for the maintenance of such married women teachers, and it is of necessity that such a married women teacher provide for herself and her family, (d)a special teacher, the retention of whose service have been specifically recommended by the Chief Inspector on account of high efficiency. (Source: The Toronto Board of Education Archives.)

4. *Toronto Daily Star*, "State Lifts Ban," 17 Mary 1946.

5. Quoted in Doris French, *High Button Bootstraps*. (Toronto: Ryerson Press, 1968), p. 13.

6. Ibid., p. 134.

7. *Toronto Daily Star*, "Board Lifts Ban," 17 May 1946.

8. *Toronto Telegram*, "Married Women Eligible," 17 May 1946.

9. Ibid.

10. *Toronto Daily Star*, "Should Married Women Teach?" 10 May 1946.

11. The minutes of the board for 1946 indicated that the board did not initiate both of these programs in 1946.

12. Ibid.

13. *Toronto Daily Star*, "Board Lifts Ban," 17 May 1946.

14. *Globe and Mail*, "Give all Women Equal Chance," 8 May 1946.

15. *Globe and Mail*, "Married Teacher Status A Problem," 23 April 1946.

16. Ibid.

17. Quoted in Ferguson, *The Feminist Case*, p. 30.

Chapter 12

Women in American Elementary School Teaching: A Case Study

SARI KNOPP BILKEN

It seems to me gentlemen, that none of you quite comprehend the cause of disrecpect of which you complain. Do you not see that so long as society says woman is incompetent to be a doctor, lawyer or minister, but has ample ability to be a teacher, that every man of you who chooses that profession tacitly acknowledges that he has no more brains than a woman?

Tyack and Hansot, 1982, pp 64–65

How far we have progressed since 1852? Recent concern over educational reform has inspired educational leaders to develop ways of attracting "smart" and "talented" people to the teaching profession. Since women's occupational horizons have expanded, bright women no longer flock to the teaching profession as they once did (Schlechty and Vance, 1982). And why not? School teaching is demanding, low paying, and publicly unappreciated; it carries low occupational status. Moreover, elementary schoolteachers generally spend their day in a room with two dozen or so children, isolated from other adults. Finally, and most importantly, teaching young children is women's work. As feminism has enabled women to choose more

freely among occupational options, they have found that what former-ly presented an opportunity is now less appealing.

I will examine these problems from the perspective of women who are themselves teachers and in light of the new scholarship on women. The social contexts will be a group of elementary teachers in a northeastern city in the United States.

Women in Elementary School Teaching

Traditional Literature

When gender has figured in the literature on elementary school teaching, it has generally diminished rather than expanded our understanding of this occupational role and of the women occupying it. What women do must be accounted for in the larger context of male activity. Men represent humanity, while women are "the other" (de Beauvoir, 1974). There is no honor in teaching as a life-along com-mitment: "To persist in teaching is, in a sense, to be 'passed over' for a higher position or marriage" (Lortie, 1975, p. 89). Women are perceived to have low occupational commitment and to be subor-dinate, and all women's occupations "appeal more to the heart than to the mind" (Dreeben, 1970, p. 181). Teachers of young children, in other words, represent sentiment rather than intellect.

Labeled "semiprofessions" (Etzioni, 1969), teaching, nursing, and social work are diminished in their professional standing by shorter training, a lack of control over technical knowledge, lower status, less of a right to privileged communication, and less autonomy from supervision or societal control than are the professions. It is no coincidence that these jobs are mostly done by women. Teaching, like the other "semiprofessions," is women's work.

Sociologists have rarely explored elementary schoolteachers' in-tellectual interests. According to Dreeben (1970), women's occupa-tions "appeal more to the heart than the mind." The language of other researchers is almost identical: "The main intrinsic appeal of the semi-professions is to the heart, not the mind," and women have a "lack of drive toward intellectual mastery" (Simpson and Simpson, 1969). More than a hundred years after Susan B. Anthony's words, we find sociologists mouthing the same assumptions.

Sociologists have also related the lack of professional autonomy to the number of women in an occupation. The public is "less willing to grant autonomy to women than to men" particularly because women often accept the cultural norm that women should defer to men (Simpson and Simpson, 1969). Dreeben (1970) explains that women's occupations tend to be subordinate, and that in these occupations supervisors have firm control over their subordinates' work. "In some ways, the school principal resembles, not so much the administrator in the world of business and industry, as the patriarch presiding over a harem. The duties differ, but the structure is similar" (Hall, 1966).

The literature on occupational commitment has approached women in elementary school teaching in a similar manner, comparing women's inadequate performance to men's. Dreeben (1970) found that women have low occupational commitment to teaching. Simpson and Simpson (1969) argues that women are less "intrinsically" committed to work than are men. Hall (1966) argued that women do not see teaching as a career; they see it as an adjunct to domestic life, "something they can slip into, and step out of, as it suits their interests in their homes and/or families." These recent findings simply reaffirm those of earlier works (Mason, Dressel, and Bain, 1959; Grambs, 1957).

This literature maintains that expectations and stereotypes about women's roles carry over into the occupational setting. It views teaching as an extension of the female role at home and represents stereotyped views of women. As feminists challenged these stereotypes, a different literature emerged.

The New Scholarship

The new scholarship on women is undertaken from an opposite perspective. (Biklin and Shakeshaft, 1985; Stimpson, 1980). This appraoch suggests that our examination of women's working lives inadequately represents and misleads because it it based on stereotyped assumptions about women. Scholars working from the new framework resist taking the lives of men as the norm. The traditional literature accepted the traditional images of women as subordinate and in the organizational hierarchy because of their pliable, deferent, and passive attitudes. It accepted family and work interests as opposing commitments. The new perspectives challenge these values.

We can divide this scholarship into two categories. The first approach provides a different analysis of data: it searches for a theoretical framework by which to understand women's work, and it criticizes scholarship that is infused with sex stereotypes. The second approach consists of new research undertaken to find out how women behave in the work place and what they think about their work. These two approaches are not opposing strains of inquiry; rather, the second has built upon the first.

Feminist scholars have challenged stereotyped studies of working women (Coser and Rokoff, 1970; Epstein, 1976; Kanter, 1975, Laws, 1976, Lightfoot, 1983; Feldberg and Glen, 1979). Studies of women in the labor force have focused on male-female inequality and usually concentrated on positions (such as administrators) where women are absent. Women were viewed as "deviant" because they did not fit the male career norm. Or women's absence was seen as a "social problem." (Kanter, 1975; Laws, 1976). Researchers formerly paid little attention to what women actually did on their jobs. Characteristics of women's work such as income and status, hours and demands, and occupational culture have only recently become subjects for study.

Another component of the traditional analysis of women at work has been the belief that women show low work commitment. Epstein (1976) has noted that it is the belief that women lack career commitment which has constrained their advancement possibilities, no matter what the occupational sphere. I have argued elsewhere (Biklen, 1985) that our traditional means of measuring career commitment should require both internal commitment and external expression of that commitment. Career and family life are posed as mutually exclusive alternatives for women; but interestingly, many women do not consider family and maternal commitment as naturally opposed to work commitments.

Other new research examines women's perspective on their working lives freed from stereotyped notions about what women value. Marrett (1972) has questioned the traditional portrait of women as acquiscent and uncommitted at work, and has presented studies in which differences between men and women were found to be less than expected. If studies were controlled for job level, education, and age, what men and women look for in their work would not be different. Another study of men and women in a "research and development" unit found that women and men are highly similar in their motivations and involvement with their jobs, in their job satisfaction, and in their perceived conflict between the demands of work and home (Saleh and Lalljee, 1969). These findings contradict the traditional portrait of women.

Grandjean and Bernal (1979) compared work orientations of male and female teachers working in coeducational and single-sex Catholic schools. They examined what they called "assumed" differences in the work orientations of men and women; specifically, they explored whether women like a tight structure, are more interpersonally oriented, and lack "intrinsic" interest in their work. Men and women teachers showed the same concerns for extrinsic and intrinsic aspects of teaching, though there were stronger concerns among women on some issues, such as having adequate facilities, an appropriate course load, and evaluative feedback. Male and female teachers also showed remarkably similar work orientations. And when men's and women's characteristics diverged, their differences contradicted prevailing stereotypes: it was women for whom professional autonomy was slightly more important, and it was men who were more concerned with keeping students under control.

As these studies indicate, the new researchers take great interest in the psychological impact of occupational conditions. Miller, et al. (1979) examined how women's work conditions affected their psychological functioning and found no evidence that employed women are in any sense psychologically disassociated from their working lives. These authors studies which working conditions offered the most support. The job conditions that encouraged self-direction enabled women to behave in more open and flexible ways with others and to think more effectively.

Miller (1980) examined which characteristics determine job satisfaction for male and female workers. She found that the actual job conditions themselves, rather than gender, have the greatest effect on worker satisfaction. One gender difference, however, was described as "dramatic":

> It seems to be the autonomy associated with complex work that produces job satisfaction for men. For women, complex work does not necessarily imply autonomy; their subjective rewards come from the challenge and interest inherent in the tasks themselves, not freedom from control.

Miller emphasized, however, that "although there are differences in the particular occupational determinants of job satisfaction for men and women, the broad range of job conditions that influence affective responses to work is impressive for each."

All these studies of women's work commitment reinforce the idea that women do take their work seriously and that their working identity is an important part of their personal identity. We must search for new ways to study women's work commitment. Measuring their commitment to teaching by asking how many of them plan to leave teaching within the next five years (Dreeben, 1970, p. 181) may simply not be an accurate measure. Such an approach pits work against motherhood; it is a way of conceptualizing commitment which may not reflect how which women actually frame the work-family continuum.

These general studies of women's work have been recently supplemented by research which examines women in elementary school teaching from the perspective of the new scholarship on women. These studies give increasing attention to the importance of locale. Studies of women who teach in Vermont (Nelson, 1983), Ohio (Quantz, 1982), in other midwestern states (Spenser, 1986), Oklahoma (Patrick, Griswold, and Roberson, 1985), and Boston (Boston Women Teachers' Group, 1980) all examine the meanings that teachers derive from their work.

The Teaching Reputation:
How Teachers Think They Are Perceived

How do teachers view the social value of their work? This section examines how teachers consider their work in the eyes of three groups: the public at large, their supervisors, and parents. The particular teachers whose views are represented here were part of a two-year study funded by the National Institute of Education. I observed and interviewed teachers, principals, and parents in two schools in a middle-sized city in the Northeast over an eight-month period. The primary site was an elementary school which had seven hundred students, a reputation as a "good" place to work, and high student achievement levels as measured by test scores. Racial integration in the school was achieved through busing; the faculty and administration were also integrated. The purpose of the study was to examine how women elementary schoolteachers look upon their work, what they value and criticize about their occupation, and how they negotiate work interests with family and sex-role expectations. Data were gathered using the qualitative methods of participant observation and in-depth interviewing (Bogdan and Biklen, 1982).

The women's movement has helped create rising expectations among women for job opportunities with higher status and better pay. Teachers have been caught up in this tide as well. One feature of social life which undermined the willingness of the women to identify proudly with their teaching role was the social devaluation of teaching. This low status was an issue even to those women who announced their lack of sympathy with feminism.

This phenomenon was not, of course, unique to the city in which the research was conducted. The popular press has carried articles noting teachers' low social esteem. Women studying to be teachers at Yale before the master of teaching program was dropped revealed that while they were interested in the program, they "dreaded the 'intellectual insult of being undergraduate education majors' " (Sarason, 1982, p. 65). A similar feeling has been observed in other places.

The Public at Large

In the study, teachers felt that "teachers ususally get a lot of bad press" partly because the public did not understand the work of teachers.

> How difficult it is to be a teacher. Teachers are underpaid and undervalued. How many people end the day after working nine to five at XXX Corporation and go home and just sob because their work was so hard. Nobody understands what it's like to work around children all day, how hard it is and what it does to you. (Kindergarten teacher)

> Teaching looks easy from the outside. I went into the bank the other day a little after 2 [o'clock] and the teller said to me, "Ha, how do you like that—2 o'clock and here you are out and my wife has to stay downtown and work until 5:00." I said, "Yeah, but you don't know what I do all day." That's what it looks like from the outside: the hours, the summer vacation—and people don't know what it's like to be responsible for thirty kids for six hours every day. It's very, very difficult.   (First grade teacher)

> People emphasize the bad part of teaching too much these days. You know, it's hard enough teaching a class when you don't have discipline problems. That's what the public doesn't understand.
>   (Second-grade teacher)

The teachers in this study felt resentful because they were not sure that the public viewed them as serious workers. Teaching well, as one of the teachers said, is challenging even when the class is not filled with discipline problems. The teachers in this city did not want teaching to be undervalued (or underpaid). They wanted the recognition that they worked diligently at challenging jobs, and they wanted the status that such a reevaluation would bring.

Yet they did not suggest that the status of elementary school teaching was related to the fact that work with young children is categorized as women's work. Usually they were too busy defending and explaining the seriousness of their work. So although they spoke to this issue, they appeared unaware of their devalued role as conducting "women's work" for example, than they did of the issue of, hours. Other reasons offered for the lower status of teaching included the view that teachers were "powerless" public servants (in contrast to politicians). They also argued that the many mediocre people in teaching detracted from the reputations of those who were "more professional," that is, better at their work. Some teachers did suggest, however, that working with children was not socially valued and that consequently it was difficult "to make money" in teaching or to have people value their work.

Occupational camouflage was another indication that teachers recognized the social devaluation of their work. Some teachers said they never revealed what they did in settings that were not clearly receptive. One teacher whose husband was a corporate executive said that she would lie about her occupation when people discussed work at parties. As she said, "when people make terrible comments about teachers, the last thing I'm going to do is tell everybody I'm a teacher."

Increased consciousness about women's roles also affected teachers' occupational evaluations. A second-grade teacher, for example, said that the women's movement made her more conscious that teaching had low status as a profession and that she could do something "better" like being in "business management" or administration, where the "pay is more and the status is better." She felt uncomfortable that people looked down on women who taught, "now that there is an impetus for women to do more."

A music teacher felt torn between understanding this negative evaluation and still enjoying her profession. She said that she know that there was "very little status in teaching," and that if she were choosing a career again, she did not know if she would want to be a teacher. As she put it: "It's a funny thing. I'm caught in this. I love my work. I love teaching, but I wish that teaching had more recognition and that people cared more about it."

Teachers handle their dilemma in different ways. Some try to convince themselves that their self-evaluations are the most important. A kindergarten teacher, for example, said: "Other people don't consider us professionals like doctors or lawyers. But I do!" Others complained and wished for an alternative: "I want respect from others about what I do. You know, I'm in my forties now, and I know I can do this well, and I want other people to value what I do." Still others argued with friends who denigrated teaching. To teasing about short hours and long vacations, one teacher reported:

> You get to go to the bathroom whenever you want to. If you're not feeling so great one day, or if you're feeling down in the dumps, you can take a two-hour lunch. We don't have the flexibility to arrange our lives that way. When we're in bad spirits, we still have to come in and be 100 percent there for the kids.

The Central Administration

Most if not all teachers in this study felt that "downtown's view of teachers' competence was evidenced by the low level of staff development programs. Many teachers commented on a particular in-service program. All elementary schoolteachers had met in a large auditorium for a session on the importance of writing in the curriculum. At the start of the session a new curriculum was handed out to the "1,000 or so" teachers sitting in the audience, and they were told to open to the table of contents. They did so, and the speaker then read down the table of contents. After he had finished that, he read the curriculum for the fourth-grade level. The teachers, with the material resting on their laps, had listened to almost forty-five minutes of reading, and "were beside [themselves] with wrath." From the view of a member of the audience, "downtown" must see them as incompetent, or why else would the sessions be so bad?

This view was echoed around the school. A kindergarten teacher, for example, stated that good in-service training provided "stimulation" and "rejuvenation" for teachers. Because she took her job seriously, she said, she wanted these sessions to stimulate her, to give her "new ideas." She then commented on the disastrous session on writing: "We obviously know how to read. What is it? They think we can't read? They don't respect us. Part of the reason for that is that people who go into administration are usually neither good teachers themselves nor very fond of teachers. And they run the show!" Another teacher agreed and added: "They have absolutely no idea what we think or do in the classroom. They're just so out of touch." That their top administrators did not seem to respect them added insult to injury.

Special-education teachers also felt devalued by the way their administration treated them. Teachers complained of a variety of issues, including the lack of feedback for hard work or innovative programming, as well as the high paperwork demands. After a teacher had spent substantial time preparing a "detailed" write-up on each child in her special class she was asked by the downtown special-education office to fill out a checklist on the same issues. The teacher described the checklist as very short and "not revealing anything at all about a child." She was convinced that her earlier painstaking descriptions would sit unread in a drawer. She interpreted this experience as an expression of the special-education office's lack of respect for teachers. If teachers' time and energy were valued, she said, they would not be asked to write redundant and sometimes competing evaluations of children. Having one's perceptions valued, she figures, emphasized her worth.

Parents

From these teachers' perspectives, the parents, whose respect they most wanted, often gave them none. The teachers felt both hostility and insecurity with this particular group. These parents, according to the teachers, did not respect their clinical or professional judgments about children as often as the teachers would have liked. When asked to identify which parents caused the trouble about which she had complained, a first-grade teachers said they were neither the "downtown" parents nor the "black" parents. They were the university parents. "You know the parents in this neighborhood are very social. They're wives of university professors and they're just so sure that their kids have to be bright and do well because they're bright and come from good familes." The teachers may have used the word *parent*, but the person they meant was *mother*.

Thus the women who taught at this elementary school had conflicts with a particular set of mothers, those with "professional" standing. More specifically, their major conflicts lay with mothers who did not work outside the home but who accrued professional status on several counts: they were professional because of their husband's occupation; they were professional mothers who spent considerable energy on their children's educational needs; and many of them were well-educated themselves, some even holding advanced degrees in education. These mothers interacted with teachers as part of their present occupational role just as teachers interacted with parents as part of their work role. As one mother, a single parent in transition from full-time parenting to full-time working, who chaired the Parents' Advisory Council put it:

> I think there are many women [in this community] who have a lot of ability, who are bright and talented who are not doing enough with their lives. And so their child's school becomes the focus. They get on the phone and they gossip about a teacher or an activity. They spend a lot of energy and a lot of thinking on this school. Some of it's worthwhile, but some isn't, because much of it doesn't get to the direct source.

Middle-class mothers who worked outside the home, however, were perceived to communicate with teachers as part of their private role. And they were generally perceived as less threatening.

What complaints and hostilities arose? Some of the younger teachers described parents' view of the ideal teacher: a person with no outside life who hands back corrected papers immediately, who is available for phone calls at all times, and who can meet in informal conferences on Sunday nights.[1]

Sometimes the behavior of parents made teachers feel like powerless objects. One behavior pattern was lack of consultation with teachers about children in their classrooms. A third-grade teacher had a little boy who was scared of math:

He'd get very upset if he didn't get it. I told him that I wept through almost every math class throughout elementary school and said that it wasn't a great favorite of mine either. I was trying to deal with his anxieties about math. Well, one day [a colleague] came to me and said, "He's not going to be in your class anymore." She said his mother had been down to talk with [the principal] and "the mother doesn't want him in your class."
Interviewer: Why?
Well, I never knew; that was part of the problem for me. The other teacher told me, "He's scared of you." I said to her, "I have to believe you, though I've been teaching for twenty years and this is the first child that I've heard of that was scared of me, but if he is, he is.' But why didn't the parent come and say, "Look, my child is having a problem with you." Instead, the parent goes to the principal. The principal doesn't come to me and tell me that the child is having a problem, nor did the principal say to his mother, "Did you talk to Kate Bridges?" So the decision is made and how do I hear about it? From other teachers—this happens a lot.

The teacher wanted to be consulted, wanted to feel that her view of the situation, of the child, had some merit.[2]

A first-grade teacher felt similarly demeaned. For several years parents had been allowed to visit classrooms each spring to see what teachers their child might encounter the next year. While this practice had just stopped, teachers still carried strong memories of its difficulty. They developed different strategies to gain control, but they did not always work. A couple had come into a first-grade teacher's classroom the previous spring while she was teaching. They sat near her desk. While she was doing some direct instruction with her class, she saw them rifle through different papers on her desk, open and glance through her lesson-plan book, and examine a pile of student dittoes. She said it was a "devastating" experience for her. She interpreted this experience to mean that "the teacher doesn't count but the parents do."

Parents' view of time was a frequent concern. A fifth-grade teacher criticized parents' spontaneous habit of dropping in on teachers after school to talk about their children. "One of the things that is really hard is that at the end of a long day, parents think that they can come in and talk to you for a long period of time about things." She often said to parents, "Well, how about if we make an appointment to talk about this?" Parents would often respond to her with, "Oh it will only take five minutes" and would then "stay for an hour." From the teachers' perspective, this parental behavior symbolized parents' lack of respect for teachers' work.

Other teachers expressed similar complaints. One teacher reported a discussion at a teachers' meeting:

> We had a meeting before Christmas where this came up again and again and again. The parent feels no need to stop at the office and say, "Would it be all right if I went down to the classroom?" Or to call the teacher the night before or send a note: "I would like to come." "Can I come in?" "When can I talk to you?" or whatever. They just feel they have complete open entrance!

Teachers wanted more control over the relationship. Parental disregard of time blocked that hope. The devaluation of teachers' time was seen as a sign of disrespect. A fourth-grade teacher objected to parents' privilege of visiting the classrooms during the day because it was too disruptive: "You can't visit a doctor or a lawyer anytime you want to, and my work is just as important as theirs." She saw the situation as a challenge to her professionalism.

Parental power was revealed not only by teachers' criticisms of parents' attitudes, but also by their dramatic reactions to parents' praise. In the midst of one lunchroom discussion about how pressured and difficult life was for these teachers because of parents, a teacher displayed a letter from the parent of a girl in her class. The teacher said that she was "thrilled" at the parents' comments, which included the message "As you know, we've had many ups and downs with Henrietta this year and having her in your class has just been a wonderful experience for us." The teacher added that she actually got quite a few letters like this. A sixth-grade teacher spoke at the beginning of a faculty council meeting about a "wonderful comment" that a mother had written on the most recent report card. She said that she wanted to "frame this comment" and asked the principal in all seriousness if she could cut it out of the report card. The principal said she would have it copied for her instead.

Looking at this issue at some distance, it becomes apparent that teachers must confront social norms which hold that teaching, particularly in the primary grades, is really only professional mothering. These social norms maintain that what stands between mothers like these and teachers is more technical education, perhaps, and a paycheck. The teachers' conflicts seemed most intense with mothers who emphasized high achievement for their own children and had ideas about how this achievement should be achieved. These mothers forced teachers to continually confront the fact that they did socially devalued women's work. Moreover, it was difficult for many teachers to put their fingers on exactly what did separate their work from that of the mothers. Since some mothers had master's degrees in education and spent time each week in the classroom running math or reading groups or tutoring individual children, the teachers sometimes felt particularly uneasy, even though they appreciated parental involvement. So teachers would say things like "I have the files so I know the real story." They turned to the trappings of professionalism to rescue themselves, to the window dressing of files, records, and labels.[3]

The Professional Antidote

These teachers regretted social devaluations of their occupation and wanted to appear in a different light. Professionalism seemed the answer. They were therefore attracted to a certain image of the professional. To them, the autonomous professional makes a socially recognized contribution. Special training is necessary, and the service that is provided is often not easily evaluated by the client to whom it is provided. This is the image of the professional that the teachers carried.

This image seemed more related to the idea than the reality of professional life. Teachers sometimes compared themselves to doctors, but their image of the doctor's professionalism seemed viewed through a time warp. As they saw it, doctors had absolute control over their clients, doctors always kept their patients waiting, and doctors' patients never complained to them about the doctors' behavior. In more recent years, however, the consumer movement has contributed to challenging the doctor's control. Patients will "shop around" for the doctor they like, they do challenge the doctor's decisions, and they request second opinions. Even earlier, doctors did not live up to the professional ideal. As critics of professionalism have suggested, that ideal has always been so far from the reality it pretends to describe that its usefulness is questionable:

> The symbol systematically ignores such facts as the failure of professions to monopolize their area of knowledge, the lack of homogeneity within professions, the frequent failure of clients to accept professional judgment, the chronic presence of unethical practitioners as an

integrated segment of the professional structure, and the organizational constraints on professional autonomy. A symbol which ignores so many important features of occupational life cannot provide an adequate guide for professional activity (Becker, 1970, p. 103).

Teachers' professional status is, of course, socially in question. Teachers have been called both the "proletarians of the professions" (Mills, 1951) and "semiprofessionals" (Etzioni, 1969). The sociological debate over the differentiation of occupations as compared to professions has had a long history (see, for example, Flexner, 1915; Cogan, 1953; Goode, 1957; and Wilensky, 1964.[4]

What these teachers meant by "professional" included their expertise and their specialized training, although the specialized training was debated. The kind of professionalism toward which these teachers gravitated was a traditional model which appeared to offer greater respect. Good teachers were professionals, but poor teachers were not. "There are teachers who are here for their paycheck only and who really don't put in a lot of extra time and really don't care. They're not professional."[5] The test of a professional was how well you taught the children. "Being able to know differences in kids and develop a plan for them to learn well and follow through on that plan is the test of whether or not you are a professional." The test of a professional was how well you taught the children. "Being able to know differences in kids and develop a plan for them to learn well and follow through on that plan is the test of whether or not you are a professional." If you were a professional, a teacher said, "then parents had to realize that you had to take responsibility for the decisions you made for the children."

Definitions emphasized both status and autonomy. "A professional is someone who's had some special training and contributes some service to the country. It's not like having a job like an assembly-line worker. It has to be more than a job. Professionals are not just concerned about pay, and many of them would work for low salaries because they have an intrinsic interest in their work." Here, service was emphasized. Autonomy was important as well. "Acting like a professional means that you look at the objective and then you decide yourself what content you're going to use to get there. You make these decisions." A student teacher said that she had learned what it meant to be a professional when she was in England:

In England, teachers have much higher standing as professionals because they make all the decisions about the curriculum. Here, the state makes the decisions about what the curriculum is going to be every year, rather than the headmistress in every school making these decisions. There, teachers really get to teach things they like. The things they don't like, they don't have to teach. In those ways, they end up being like a doctor—they get to make those kinds of decisions.

In her view, English teachers were held in more respect becuase they were allowed to make those decisions.

The traditional model distinguishes between professional and nonprofessional occupations in ways that attracted teachers. In this model, a nonprofessional occupation

has customers; a professional occupation has clients. A customer determines what services and/or commodities he wants, and he shops around until he finds them. His freedom of decision rests upon the premise that he has the capacity to appraise his own needs and to judge the potential of the service or of the commodity to satisfy them . . . . In a professional relationship, however, the professional dictates what is good or evil for the client, who has no choice but to accede to professional judgment. (Greenwood, 1957).

While the case for the inviolability of the professional appears dramatically overstated, it was just this authority which attracted the teachers. When teachers talked about parents visiting classrooms to observe them and to submit a preference to the principal for the following year, they described the practice as "shopping around for the teachers." Most teachers rejoiced when the practice ended. Teachers wanted the parents to act like old-fashioned clients rather than like customers, for the parents' behavior said to the teachers, "You are not a professional."

The author of a study of rural teachers suggested that teachers she studied kept separate the community stereotypes of teaching from their own contacts with members of the community in their teaching territory. They could do this, McPherson (1972) noted, because the teachers held similar stereotypes about themselves. At this school, however, teachers tended to associate social stereotypes about teaching with problems they had in their work, that is, with parents, curriculum controversies, the principal, and the district—in sum, with a host of intra- and extraschool concerns that they related to their low power as teachers. One teacher, however, suggested that teachers do not have built into their occupational image the expectation that they will have control over their working lives. In her words, teachers do not expect to feel that:

this is my school and what I think about, and the values I think are important, and the teaching approaches that I think are important, and the ways of relating to parents that I feel are important are going to be taken seriously...And that as a staff we will come to a decision about what this school means to us and what it will be like.

In her view, the teachers in her school needed to develop this sense as a group.

Unfortunately, the professional model many teachers at this school sought to dignify and enhance their social status formed a wedge that will actually stunt long-term development of a satisfying work setting. The search for this model does three harmful things. (1) It interferes with the construction of cooperative relationships with the lay community (parents, particularly mothers) so that parents and teachers become adversaries rather than partners. (2) It feeds the tensions which, for many teachers, arise out of the uneasy coexistence of love, concern for, and interest in their students on the one hand, and on the other, a dissatisfaction with certain working conditions of schools, particularly bureaucracy, and feelings of vulnerability and powerlessness. (3) It leaves unresolved the basic question of gender. The traditional professional model cannot question the social devaluation of women's work. It simply attempts to change the nature of the category.

Teachers analyze their vulnerability correctly. The role of the school has changed over the past one hundred and fifty years. Schools are now expected to teach much more than basic skills, and they have carried the weight of these expectations since the Progressive Era. Expectations of what teachers should do are high, but the corresponding authority to act to meet these expectations is not forthcoming. From what source, then, should their authority rise?

Conclusion: Democracy in the Workplace, Feminism in the Society

Whether or not it is within the scope of this chapter to offer suggestions to such complicated issues is unclear. Primarily, the research reported here supports the necessity of including gender as a variable in the consideration of educational concerns with teachers. But when gender has been a factor, it has always diminished rather than expanded our understanding of women who teach, because the model by which we analyze gender has not been generated from the lives of women. Future scholarship should carefully consider the ways in which gender issues, examined from feminist perspective, intersect with schools as social institutions.

Studying these issues from a feminist perspectives raises two other issues as well. The first is that those who work with children need to have the status of their work elevated. This can happen only when we come to value the domestic sphere and resist viewing work and family life as opposed to each other. Scholars have suggested that law and medicine were readily professionalized because the service element of those occupations was compatible with the idea of a "calling." The service element in work with children has never worked for women in this way, however, because the work that women do has been publicly disdained even while it has been required. Low monetary compensation in typically female occupations expresses the devaluation in the public sphere. The romanticization of the haven in the heartless world denotes the personal.

Schools must also change. Teachers can only gain more real power if they are allowed to participate in the authority of the school. One way to accomplish this goal would be to employ democratic procedures. Let teachers in a building elect their principal from a slate of candidates. While the specific way in which this could be done would need some attention, the general method would change the work environment of the school to one which increases teachers' responsibility as well as respect for their leadership.

Notes

1. While eating in the lunchroom one day, I witnessed a parent approach a teacher to talk about her son Scotty. The parent said: "Last year he got A's and B's. This year every time I ask someone on your team how he's doing, everybody says he's doing well, but he's not getting any A's at all. He's just getting B's" The teacher replied that when she spoke of Scotty doing well she was referring to his "adjustment." The parent said, "Yes, that's why I haven't been coming down on him because this is the first year I haven't had to drag him to school in the morning." The parent continued by repeating her need to talk with the teacher, whenever the teacher could manage. She (the parent) would drop everything, "*even if it was a Sunday night*" (Emphasis mine).

2. The teacher was also very critical of the principal's failure to mediate professionally.

3. For an interesting discussion of the ways in which the work of mothers with young children has been excluded from definitions of teaching, see Martin (1982).

4. While the debate has been long, it has also generally been fruitless. For critiques, see Hughes, 1971; and Roth, 1974.

5. This view is common in occupations striving for professional status. When the transition occurs, people in these occupations become self-conscious about many work-related issues. They become "dreadfully afraid that some of their number will not observe company manners and so will hurt the reputation of all . . ." (Hughes, 191, p. 311). Sloppy teachers did not observe company manners.

References

Becker, H.S. (1970). *Sociological Work*. Chicago: Aldine.

Biklen, S. (1985). "Can Elementary Schoolteaching Be a Career?: A Search for New Ways of Understanding Women's Work." *Issues in Education* 3, pp. 215–231.

Biklen, S., and C. Shakeshaft (1985). "The New Schoolarship on Women. In *Handbook for Achieving Sex Equity Through Education*. Baltimore Md.: Johns Hopkins University Press, pp. 44–52.

Bogdan, R., and S. Biklen (1982). *Qualitative Research for Education*. Boston: Allyn and Bacon.

Boston Women Teachers' Group (1980). *"A Study of the Effects of Teaching on Teachers."* paper presented at the American Educational Research Association annual meeting, Boston.

Cogan, M. (1953). "Toward a Definition of a Profession." *Harvard Educational Review* 23, pp. 33–50.

Coser, R.L., and G. Rokoff (1970). "Women in the Occupational World: Social Disruption and Conflict. *Social Problems* 18, pp. 535–554.

de Beauvoir, S. (1974). *The Second Sex*. New York: Vintage, 1974.

Dreeben, R. (1970). *The Nature of Teaching*. Glenview, Ill.: Scott, Foresman.

Epstein, C.F. (1976). "Sex Role Stereotyping, Occupations, and Social Exchange." *Women's Studies* 3, pp. 185–194.

Etzioni, A., ed. (1969). *The Semi-Professions and Their Organization*. New York: Free Press.

Feldberg, R.L., and E.R. Glenn (1979). "Male and Female: Job Versus Gender Models in the Sociology of Work." *Social Problems* 26, pp. 524–538. Reprinted in R. Kahn-Hut, A.K. Daniels, and R. Colvard (eds.), *Women and Work*. (New York: Oxford University Press), pp. 65–80.

Flexner, A. (1915). "Is Social Work a Profession?" *School and Society* 1, pp. 901–911.

Goode, W. (1957). "Community Within a Community: The Professions." *American Sociological Review* 22, pp. 194–200.

Grambs, J.D. (1957). "The Roles of the Teachers." In *The Teacher's Role in American Society*, ed. L. Stiles. Fourteenth Yearbook of the John Dewey Society, New York.

Grandjean, B., and H.H. Bernal (1979). "Sex and Centralization in a Semi-profession." *Sociology of Work and Occupations* 6, pp. 84–102.

Greenwood, E. (1957). "Attributes of a Profession." *Social Work* 2.

Hall, O. (1966). "The Social Structure of the Teaching Profession." In F.W. Lutz and J.J. Azzarelli. *Struggle for Power in Education*, ed. New York: Center for Applied Research in Education, pp. 35–48.

Hughes, E.C. (1971). *The Sociological Eye*. Chicago: Aldine.

—————— (1951). "Studying the Nurses' Work." *American Journal of Nursing* 51.

Kanter, R.M. (1975). "Women and the Structure of Organizations: Explorations in Theory and Behavior." In *Another Voice: Feminist Perspectives on Social Life and Social Science* ed. M. Millman and R.M. Kanter. Garden City, N.Y.: Anchor, pp. 34–74.

Laws, J.L. (1976). "Work Aspirations of Women: False Leads and New Starts." *SIGNS: Journal of Women in Culture and Society* 1, no. 3 (Part 2: Women and the Workplace), pp. 33–49.

Lortie, D. (1975). *Schoolteacher*, Chicago: University of Chicago Press.

Lightfoot Sara (1983). "The Lives of Teachers" in *Handbook of Teaching and Policy*, ed. Lee Shulman and Gary Sykes. N.Y. Longman.

Marrett, C.B. (1972). "Centralization in Female Organizations: Reassessing the Evidence." *Social Problems* 19, pp. 348–357.

Martin, J.R. (1982). "Excluding Women from the Educational Realm." *Harvard Educational Review* 52, pp. 133–148.

Mason, W., R.J. Dressel, and R.K. Bain (1959). "Sex Roles and the Career Orientations of Beginning Teachers." *Harvard Educational Review* 29, pp. 370–383.

McPherson, G. (1972). *Small Town Teachers*. Cambridge: Harvard University Press.

Miller, J. (1980). "Individual and Occupational Determinants of Job Satisfaction: A Focus on Gender Differences." *Sociology of Work and Occupations* 7, no. 3, pp. 366–377.

Miller, J., et al. (1979). Women and Work: The Psychological Effects of Occupational Conditions." *American Journal of Sociology* 85, pp. 66–94.

Mills, C.W. (1951). *White Collar*. New York: Oxford University Press.

Nelson, M. (1983). "From the One-Room Schoolhouse to the Graded School: Teaching in Vermont, 1910–1950." *Frontiers* 7, pp. 14–20.

Patrick, A., R. Griswold, and C. Roberson (1985). "Domestic Ideology and the Teaching Profession: A Case Study from Oklahoma, 1930–1983." *Issues in Education* 3, pp. 139–157.

Quantz, R. (1982). "Teachers as Women: An Ethnohistory of the 1930's." Paper presented at the annual meeting of the American Educational Research Association, New York, March.

Roth, J. (1974). "Professionalism: The Sociologist's Decoy." *Sociology of Work and Occupations* 1, pp. 6–23.

Saleh, S., and M. Lalljee (1969). "Sex and Job Orientation." *Personnel Psychology* 22, p. 465–471.

Sarason, S. (1982). *The Culture of School and the Problem of Change.* 2nd ed. Boston: Allyn and Bacon.

Schlechty, P., and V. Vance (1982). "Recruitment, Selection and Retention: The Shape of the Teaching Force." Paper presented at invitational conference, "Research on Teaching: Implications for Practice," Warrentown, Virginia, February.

Simpson, R.L., and I.H. Simpson (1969). "Women and Bureaucracy," In Etzioni, *The Semi-Professions* pp. 196–265.

Spenser, D. (1986). *Contemporary Women Teachers.* New York: Longman.

Stimpson, C. (1980). "The New Scholarship about Women: The State of the Art." *Annals of Scholarship* no. 2, pp. 2–14.

Tyack, David and Elizabeth Hansot. (1982). *Managers of Virtue.* N.Y. Basic Books.

Wilensky, H. (1964). "The Professionalization of Everyone." *American Journal of Sociology* 70, pp. 137–158.

Contributors

SARI KNOPP BIKLEN is Associate Professor in Cultural Foundations and Curriculum, Syracuse University, Syracuse, New York.

ILSE BREHMER is on the faculty at Bielefeld University, Bielefeld, West Germany.

JILL BYSTYDZIENSKI is an Associate Professor at Franklin College, Franklin, Illinois.

UTA ENDERS-DRAGASSER is on the staff at the Feminist Studies Research Institute, Frankfurt, West Germany.

MINEKE VAN ESSEN is a member of the faculty at the University of Groningen, Groningen, the Netherlands.

PENNY FENWICK is Deputy Secretary, Ministry of Women's Affairs, Wellington, New Zealand.

MARGARET GRIBSKOV is an faculty member at Evergreen State College, Olympia, Washington.

KIRSTEN MOELLER teaches at The Royal Danish School of Educational Studies, Copenhagen, Denmark.

CECILIA REYNOLDS is on the faculty at Brock University, St. Catherines, Ontario, Canada.

SHIRLEY SAMPSON is Senior Lecturer at Monash University, Melbourne, Australia.

PATRICIA A. SCHMUCK is Professor of Educational Administration, Lewis and Clark College, Portland, Oregon.

ANNA LIISA SYSIHARJU is Professor Emerita, University of Helsinki, Helsinki, Finland.

Index